In the last decade the thought of J. Gresham Machen has attracted the attention, and gained the appreciation, of even some Roman Catholic and main-line Protestant writers. Terry Chrisope's excellent study of Machen as a New Testament scholar adds another dimension to the understanding of this conservative theologian of the early 20th century who yet speaks into the post-modern culture of the 21st century. Making particular use of Machen's early significant book reviews, Professor Chrisope rightly emphasizes his opposition to a naturalistic historicism as the key to his rejection of theological liberalism and modernistic biblical criticism. Recognizing the role of presuppositions, yet arguing for the legitimacy of historical knowledge that includes the supernatural, Machen upheld principles that still serve well the Christian faith more than two generations after his death in 1937. Terry Chrisope has added to, and in some respects challenged, the recent conclusions of such able students of Machen as George Marsden, Bradley Longfield, and D. G. Hart.

William S. Barker
Professor of Church History
Westminster Theological Seminary
Philadelphia, Pennsylvania

D1474314

Toward a Sure Faith:
J. Gresham Machen
and the Dilemma of
Biblical Criticism, 1881-1915

Terry A. Chrisope

Mentor

© Terry A. Chrisope
ISBN 1 857 92 439 8

Published in 2000
by Christian Focus Publications
Geanies House, Fearn, Ross-shire, IV20 1TW, Great Britain
Cover design by Owen Daily

Contents

FOREWORD by David B. Calhoun 7

PREFACE 9

1. INTRODUCTION 11

PART ONE: THE HISTORICAL SETTING

2. THE RISE OF HISTORICAL CONSCIOUSNESS AND
ITS IMPACT ON BIBLICAL STUDY IN EUROPE AND
AMERICA 25

PART TWO: THE FORMATIVE YEARS, 1881-1906

3. MACHEN'S EARLY TRAINING AND THEOLOGICAL
EDUCATION, 1881-1905 57

4. MACHEN AT MARBURG AND GÖTTINGEN, 1905-1906 .. 77

PART THREE: THE DECISIVE YEARS, 1906–1915

5. MACHEN'S EARLY BOOK REVIEWS, 1907-1912 99

6. MACHEN'S PUBLIC EMERGENCE: THE MAJOR ESSAYS
OF 1912 115

7. MACHEN'S NEW TESTAMENT SURVEY,
ORDINATION, AND INSTALLATION, 1913-1915 137

PART FOUR : THE MATURE YEARS, 1915–1937

8. MACHEN'S LATER WORK AND ITS RELATIONSHIP
TO HIS EARLIER SCHOLARSHIP, 1915-1937 157

9. CONCLUSION 185

SELECTED BIBLIOGRAPHY 198

REFERENCES 207

PERSONS INDEX 234

SUBJECT INDEX 236

DEDICATED TO
THE WOMEN OF MY LIFE

Dorothy Lorraine Chrisope
1921-1993

Linda Carol Jones Chrisope
Lucile Jones
Catherine Nicole Chrisope
Sarah Anne Chrisope

FOREWORD

Church historians and other scholars are beginning to appreciate the significance of J. Gresham Machen, New Testament professor at Princeton Theological Seminary from 1906 until 1929, when he resigned to found Westminster Theological Seminary in Philadelphia. Machen is best known as a capable apologist for historic Christian orthodoxy, as evidenced by his masterful *Christianity and Liberalism*. His importance as a preacher has been recognized by the inclusion of one of his sermons in the newly published *American Sermons: The Pilgrims to Martin Luther King Jr.* His role as a churchman is seen in the continuing existence of the Orthodox Presbyterian Church and by his influence far beyond that small denomination. During the 1920s he became the spokesman for conservative people in all the major Protestant denominations. A Roman Catholic professor recently told me that if Machen had been a Catholic he would lead a movement for his canonization!

But Dr. Machen has not been adequately presented as a New Testament scholar. His two great books of New Testament scholarship, *The Virgin Birth of Christ* and *The Origin of Paul's Religion*, have been largely forgotten, and Machen's ability and convictions as a New Testament scholar have disappeared behind his active life as a critic of liberal religion and a defender of orthodoxy. His total commitment to this "mighty battle" and his early death at age fifty-five prevented Machen from making a greater mark on New Testament studies.

But make a mark he did, and Terry Chrisope presents a careful study of Machen's views concerning the Bible and the historical criticism to which the Bible was being subjected in the early twentieth century. A major question facing Machen – and still facing Christians today – is whether or not biblical authority can be maintained in the face of modern historical scholarship. Machen was no obscurantist. He knew the critical views firsthand and often felt the power and appeal of the liberal positions. His answers are the products of hard fought battles. With his rigorous methodology and his complete honesty, Machen in no way contributed to "the scandal of the evangelical mind." To follow Terry Chrisope as he follows Machen is not only a valuable exercise in historical study but a strengthening of one's faith in God's Word, which indeed shall "never pass away."

Although historical biblical criticism is the focus of this book, Dr. Chrisope skillfully weaves in much valuable information about Machen and his times. Especially important is his description of the conservative Christian movement in the 1920s and his reflections on the direction of American intellectual and religious culture. Chrisope's presentation of Machen's philosophy of history – as shaped by the Bible and by his Reformed theological heritage – provides an important understanding of how a Christian can "do" history, a topic much discussed and disputed by contemporary church historians.

David B. Calhoun
Covenant Theological Seminary
St. Louis, Missouri

PREFACE

The study which follows had its ultimate origin in an intellectual crisis of some duration, perhaps not unlike that experienced by J. Gresham Machen. That I did not possess the educational advantages and intellectual or technical equipment for resolving the crisis in precisely the same manner as Machen did is readily acknowledged. There were, however, three factors which, humanly speaking, led to at least a tentative resolution of the difficulty. One was the realization, early on in my studies, that presuppositions determine what kind of conclusions are possible. The second was an examination of the factual data from the standpoint of Christian supernaturalism, which proved itself quite capable of accounting for all the data. The third was the present study, which included two components: an examination of the intellectual milieu in which Machen operated, particularly the ascendancy of historicism with its concomitant naturalism in the study of the Bible during the modern era, coupled with the examination of Machen's own struggle and his writings which grew out of it. Machen's tutelage, through his writings, helped to confirm the author in a resolution of the difficulty similar to that which Machen himself reached, as described in the following pages. In this I consider myself in good company.

I trust that this public treatment of an intensely personal matter that I find seldom addressed in either academic or religious circles will be helpful to others who may be looking for some guidance along the way. For one person, at least, the consideration of Machen's example and his scholarly work has proven exceedingly beneficial, and I suspect that it may be the same for others as well.

The following study originated as a Ph.D. dissertation at Kansas State University, Manhattan, Kansas. Thanks are due my major professor, Robert D. Linder, for his mentoring in historical studies and for allowing me the freedom to pursue this project in my own fashion.

Appreciation is also extended to Pastor Steve Martin of Fayetteville, Georgia, and Professor Robert A. Peterson of Covenant Theological Seminary, St. Louis, Missouri, for their contributions, in different ways, toward getting this work published. Without the technical assistance of colleagues Ray Walden and Curtis McClain of Missouri Baptist College in computer-related matters, it is unlikely that the project would have reached this point. Professor David Calhoun of Covenant Theological Seminary, author of a magnificent two-volume history of old Princeton Seminary, graciously agreed to provide the Foreword to this volume, for which he is here thanked. Library work in the Machen Archives was facilitated by the assistance of Grace Mullen of Westminster Theological Seminary.

As J. Gresham Machen enjoyed a special relationship with his mother, so I wish to acknowledge the love, encouragement, and support of those women of my life who are named on the dedication page.

Terry A. Chrisope
Missouri Baptist College
St. Louis, Missouri

CHAPTER 1

INTRODUCTION

The following study deals with the early intellectual development of a Presbyterian biblical scholar, J. Gresham Machen (1881-1937). Machen taught New Testament at Princeton Theological Seminary from 1906 to 1929, authored several books on the New Testament and Christian theology, and became an influential figure in the so-called modernist-fundamentalist controversy of the 1920s in America. He was the founder in 1929 of Westminster Theological Seminary in Philadelphia, and after being forced out of the ministry of the Presbyterian Church in the USA (commonly known as the Northern Presbyterian Church), he established in 1936 a new Protestant denomination, now known as the Orthodox Presbyterian Church.

Most of the historical literature which deals with Machen treats him as a fundamentalist, drawing attention to his controversial activity in the Presbyterian Church and in wider circles during the 1920s and 1930s. The prevalence of such a portrayal of Machen is symptomatic of the fact that there is very little specialized literature on Machen himself – the only full-scale biography or other serious study that has been published since 1955 is D. G. Hart's 1994 study – and that the more general literature which does mention him does so almost exclusively within the context of the fundamentalist controversy. Such an approach is deficient in at least three ways.

First, it tends to stereotype Machen, applying to him the term fundamentalist (an identification which he himself generally rejected), with all the suggestion of narrowness and close-mindedness, obscurantism and anti-intellectualism, bigotry and rancor which that appellation carries. In short, it fails seriously to consider Machen on his own terms and in the context of broader intellectual currents.

Second, the common approach to Machen tends to pass lightly over the early period of his life, from 1881 to about 1915 (in 1915 Machen was installed on the faculty of Princeton Seminary, a particularly momentous milestone in his life; previous to 1915 he was only an Instructor, not a full faculty member). During those years his intellectual formation was being accomplished, and the events of that period strongly influenced the nature and direction of his later work; yet there has appeared no comprehensive treatment of Machen's writings or intellectual development during these years.

Third, this approach commonly gives scant attention to Machen's chosen field of professional labor, that of New Testament scholarship. Machen is more often mentioned as the author of *Christianity and Liberalism*, his major critique of theological liberalism, than as the New Testament scholar who produced penetrating studies of the virgin birth of Christ and of the relation of Paul to Jesus. It was in this arena that his early intellectual struggles took place, and it was his conclusions here that underlay his criticism of liberalism. This is therefore an aspect of his life that can hardly be ignored if a clear understanding of Machen is to be achieved.[1]

The historical context of Machen's early years included, among other things, the rise to dominance in American academic and intellectual circles of a mode of thinking, or set of assumptions, that may be called historicism or historical consciousness. Grant Wacker, a recent student of the subject, briefly defines historical consciousness as "the belief that culture is the product of its own history, that ideas, values, and institutions of every sort are wholly conditioned by the historical setting in which they exist." This outlook included "the assumption that knowledge of divine things, like knowledge of ordinary things, must be found squarely within the historical process or not at all." Historical consciousness or historicism tended to promote historical and cultural relativism along with a corresponding attitude of skepticism toward all exclusive claims to universal and absolute truth. The notions embodied in historical consciousness decisively shaped American intellectual culture in the twentieth century, and have exercised broad effects on various aspects of society, including religion. As applied to the New Testament, historicist teaching meant that the biblical documents and events must be explained as wholly the result of natural historical forces and processes, with the implication that no room was to be allowed for divine supernatural activity. Machen's early intellectual growth and religious experience were powerfully affected by his exposure to the effects of historical consciousness in biblical studies, and he cannot be adequately understood, either in his early development or in his mature work, apart from a consideration of this factor.[2]

Machen was a biblical scholar, and almost all his published work to 1915 was related to the world of New Testament scholarship. The questions of the interpretation of the Bible and the validity of its teaching were dominant issues in his own intellectual development as well as in the theological controversies in which he was involved in the 1920s. It is appropriate, therefore, to give particular attention, as this study will do, to the development of Machen's views regarding the Bible and the historical criticism to which the Bible was being subjected in his day. This delimitation will serve to focus the present study on an issue – historical biblical criticism – which was a central one for Machen and for early twentieth-century Christianity, and which has ramifications as well for American and Western culture considered more broadly.

The primary aim of this study is to tell the story of Machen's early intellectual pilgrimage, especially with regard to the development of his views concerning the Bible and historical scholarship, and to evaluate his development in light of the rise of historical consciousness. Its central thesis is that in his early years Machen developed and exhibited a profound conviction of the propriety and necessity of the historical study of the Bible, while at the same time he gradually became convinced that the New Testament and the events it relates were partially conditioned but not wholly determined by the historical environment in which they originated. Machen thus rejected the essential tenets of a consistent historical consciousness or historicism, and this stance put him and his interpretation of Christianity at odds with the prevailing tendency of his day.

Subsidiary aims are present as well. The exposition will attempt to point out the lines of continuity between Machen's early intellectual development and the work of his mature years. On the basis of such considerations, it will also seek to illuminate the nature of the conservative Christianity with which Machen was connected.

Why the Issue Is Important

The questions that confronted Machen in the early twentieth century continue to confront many thoughtful people at the beginning of the twenty-first century: Does historical scholarship pronounce a definitive judgment concerning the nature of the Bible and of Christianity? Can the historical method be separated from the anti-supernaturalistic orientation with which it is often associated? Is it possible to maintain one's intellectual integrity while adhering to traditional Christianity? Can biblical authority be maintained in the face of modern historical scholarship? Machen answered such questions for himself, and the answers he reached are largely those which the present writer has also accepted. This factor loomed large in this writer's attraction to Machen and in the motivation for this study. Machen's pilgrimage may be taken as illustrating one mode of dealing with the tension between the claims of historic supernaturalistic Christianity and the claims of modern "scientific" methods of inquiry. The questions are no less important now than they were in Machen's time, for the issues have not gone away, and furthermore, they are ultimate issues. If the teachings of historic Christianity portray the structure of reality in a way that is even approximately correct, then this fact has tremendous implications for twenty-first-century persons. But if first-century Christianity was merely the product of natural historical forces which were operative in that era and not the result of direct divine action in the external world, then that fact needs to be reckoned with as well. Whatever one's conclusion, the issues are momentous for several reasons.

In the first place, historical biblical scholarship (often known by the term biblical criticism, with no pejorative overtones intended) is important because it is a fact of life in Western culture since the eighteenth century. The modern critical approach to the Bible had its origin in the intellectual movement of the seventeenth and eighteenth centuries known as the Enlightenment and has become pervasive during the intervening span of years. This approach tends to treat the Bible as any other ancient literature, investigating its component documents as to their authorship, methods of composition, historical provenance, dating, audience, and related matters, typically with no special regard for the claims of the documents themselves or for any presumed authority of the Bible as a whole. Such a method, with the presuppositions commonly attending it, often results in conclusions at variance with the internal claims of the documents or with traditional Christian teaching and may result in a denial of the historicity of the events described in the documents. The widespread presence and influence of this approach to the Bible may be demonstrated by a perusal of any number of current textbooks or reference works or by attendance at a course which deals with the Bible in many universities or theological seminaries. Biblical criticism is simply a fact of modern life with which anyone desiring to deal with the Bible seriously must come to terms.

Indeed, events of recent years have dramatically increased the publicity given to questions of biblical criticism. The April 8, 1996 issue of *Time* magazine featured a cover story with the words, "The Search for Jesus." Inside, the heading of the article stated, "The iconoclastic and provocative Jesus Seminar argues that not much of the New Testament can be trusted. If so, what are Christians to believe?" The article surveyed recent radical theories concerning the reliability of the early Christian traditions about Jesus and presented responses from more conservative scholars and theologians. Other newsmagazines offered similar stories during Easter week of 1996. With such high visibility being given to questions of biblical criticism, it is difficult for thoughtful people to avoid the issue.[3]

Second, biblical criticism is an important issue because of the effects which it has had on the faith of many professing Christian believers. Although adequate documentation may be lacking, a primary effect of such criticism appears commonly to have been the weakening or destruction of the faith of professing Christians. Christianity has historically been a religion of authoritative proclamation, with the authority (at least for Protestants) residing in the Bible as the revelation of divinely-given truth communicated through human instruments in history. When the claimed human authorship, authenticity, truthfulness, or historicity of the biblical documents and the events they describe are thrown into doubt, this will provoke – and has provoked – a crisis of faith for many people who adhere to the scriptural record as the foundation of their faith. Regardless of how scholars and theologians may strive to reconcile the conclusions of modern criticism with the exercise of genuinely Christian faith, the fact remains that many ordinary Christians believe that the objective content of the faith – and hence their own personal faith – is threatened by such conclusions.

Third, biblical criticism is an important issue because of its broader cultural impact. There can be little doubt that the increasing prevalence of critical modes of looking at the Bible has resulted in a diminished confidence in the Bible, its message, and its authority throughout the culture of the United States and the Western world. Coincidentally, many observers have noted a broad cultural decline on several fronts – intellectual, educational, social, and moral. While such linkages are difficult to demonstrate, some would be prepared to argue that the decline of Western culture is closely connected with the diminished esteem in which the Bible is held. This diminished esteem is in turn, as already suggested, arguably related to the ascendancy of critical methods of handling the Bible itself. And again, even though some scholars will argue that post-Enlightenment methods of handling the Bible result in a greater understanding and appreciation of the Bible in its historical context, this argument is often lost on the ordinary layman. For such people, the Bible with its teachings and sanctions has lost binding authority because its authenticity and historicity have presumably been brought into serious doubt or altogether denied by the conclusions of many biblical scholars. This in turn has affected the way people view both themselves and others and the way they live out their lives.

Fourth, the issues raised by historical criticism of the Bible are significant because they reveal that not all biblical scholars begin with the same presuppositions or reach the same conclusions. J. Gresham Machen must be regarded as belonging to the front rank of New Testament scholars in his day (as demonstrated by the reception of his scholarly books), yet he reached conclusions that were sharply different from those of many of his contemporaries. Thus the impression (which is sometimes deliberately fostered) of a monolithic front in the field of biblical criticism is inaccurate. Furthermore, the intellectual starting point from which Machen began was different from that of many other scholars. Philosophical precommitments (including the naturalistic assumptions of historicism in the prevailing approach) led various scholars toward widely differing positions regarding the proper interpretation of the evidence, illustrating the fact that the presuppositions with which a scholar begins his research often play a large part in the conclusions he is allowed to reach. This is as fully the case today as it was in the first third of the twentieth century and must be given due weight in evaluating the work of current scholars, just as it will constitute a large element in recounting Machen's intellectual pilgrimage in the pages that follow.

Fifth, the issue of biblical criticism is important because of the inferior cultural position often assigned (at least since the beginning of the twentieth century) to those who question the presuppositions, methods, and conclusions of the discipline as it is commonly practiced. Such people, even if they possess the highest scholarly credentials, are often marginalized and written off as unworthy of consideration, frequently with the application to them of some pejorative term by those of the cultural elite who control the presumptively mainstream institutions. Thus Machen was (and still is) sometimes dismissed as a "fundamentalist," even though he consistently rejected the term as not providing an adequate description of his position. This marginalization is often, one suspects, a means of dismissing an uncomfortable intellectual position without having to deal with the issues which it raises.

In short, the issues involved in biblical criticism are important because they make a difference. It makes an enormous difference – for individuals, for society, and for the culture – whether the Bible is regarded as the written revelation of the living God or as the merely human record of the religious experience of ancient peoples. It cannot be denied that prior to the Enlightenment, and even prior to the twentieth century, the former was the commonly held view in Western culture, and that since the beginning of the twentieth century the latter view has come to prevail. The primary instrument for effecting this great change has been the dissemination of the results of a particular variety of biblical criticism. The issue, then, is not trivial, but one that is fundamental to the current direction and future course of Western civilization.

Why Machen Is Important

In confronting the issues involved in biblical criticism, J. Gresham Machen should be regarded as a significant figure. This is so for several reasons.

First, Machen experienced a severe crisis of personal faith with which many people will be able to identify. Early in his life, Machen felt compelled to wrestle both with the theological liberalism that was gaining ascendancy in major Protestant denominations and with the biblical criticism that typically accompanied such a theological stance. Thus he was forced to deal not only with technical critical questions (at which he came to excel) but also with broader questions such as, What constitutes the essence of Christianity?, and, Is Christianity as presented in the Bible really true? Machen himself, writing from the vantage point of a later time in his life and reflecting back on his earlier struggles, said that "all the usefulness of Christianity can never lead us to be Christians unless the Christian religion is true. But is it true or not? That is a serious question indeed." He went on to mention "the long and bitter experience that the raising of this question brought into my life." Machen's "long and bitter experience" in some respects will parallel that of many others who find their traditional views of the Bible challenged by alternative views held in either the church or the academy. Machen therefore may be seen as an example of a Christian reared in a theologically orthodox environment who suffers a potentially faith-shattering encounter with modern thought. It is likely that more than a few residents of the post-Enlightenment world can find a measure of identification with Machen's struggle.[4]

Second, Machen may be regarded as a significant figure because his Christian faith survived and was strengthened by his working through the intellectual crisis he faced. As the following pages will demonstrate, Machen was a person of intense intellectual honesty; he would not believe a historical claim which he was convinced was not historically true. His examination of the evidence for the historicity of the New Testament events, therefore, carries the greater weight because he was evidently prepared to reach opposite conclusions from those he did reach. That he did come down on the side of historic Christianity bears testimony not only to the survivability of such an intellectual crisis but also – for those who will receive it – to the power of the historical witness of the New Testament documents to convince one who has not ruled out their truthfulness beforehand on the basis of prior philosophical commitments. For Machen, as for many others, a faith tried and proven is stronger than a faith that is not tried at all. And, as he shows, such an outcome is eminently possible.

Third, Machen is important because he can provide a model for the historical treatment of the Bible. As will be argued in the pages that follow, Machen contended for a biblical criticism that was historical but not historicist. He claimed that the biblical history "should be studied by the best historical method which can be attained," and he devoted his scholarly efforts to achieving that end. He also recognized, however, that any method which rules out some potential conclusions before the investigation even begins is not a method designed to attain to truth but is rather an ideological program whose results have been predetermined by the philosophical presuppositions with which it begins. Thus Machen came to believe, through the anguish of his own personal struggle and at the culmination of that struggle, that the naturalistic philosophical assumptions inherent in the historicist approach to the Bible not only vitiated the conclusions of that approach but also disqualified it from being truly scientific. Machen's own method allowed for the full operation of historical forces and factors in the biblical events and in the production of the biblical documents while not ruling out the possibility of divine supernatural influences at the same time. Thus he took account of the genuinely historical elements in the biblical text while not falling into what he considered the errors of the naturalistic assumptions which underlay historicism.[5]

Fourth, Machen provides an example of a responsible evangelical approach to the matter of biblical authority. Throughout his intellectual struggle and in his scholarly writings, Machen never sought to cut off debate by appeal to some presumed authority of the Bible. Rather, he sought to demonstrate the historical tenability of the biblical documents and then left it to faith to receive the historicity of the events they relate along with the interpretation of those events offered in the documents. Machen indeed later defended and expounded a high view of biblical authority, including the plenary and verbal inspiration of the Bible. In his view the divine inspiration of the Bible secured the truthfulness of biblical claims not only in the realm of external history (which was open to historical investigation) but also in the realm of spiritual reality (which was not open to historical investigation). What the Bible taught in both spheres had to be received by faith; Machen never claimed that historical study could prove the truthfulness of the Bible. In the context of historical investigation, biblical authority was a point he argued toward rather than from, and which he utilized primarily in a negative way: one could not reject the historicity of the events the Bible relates and at the same time maintain biblical authority and historic Christianity. "Our salvation depends squarely upon history; the Bible contains that history, and unless that history is true the authority of the Bible is gone and we who have put our trust in the Bible are without hope." This approach demonstrates neither an obscurantist mindset nor a rationalistic understanding of biblical authority. Machen thus offers to Christian believers at the beginning of the twenty-first century a viable model of responsible handling of both history and the authority of the biblical text.[6]

Perspectives on Machen

It is difficult to describe established historiographical traditions regarding Machen, since he has been the subject of few specialized published works (though the number is increasing). George Marsden, who is a current authority on Machen, divides interpreters of Machen into two camps. On the one hand are those supporters who emphasize Machen's theological stance; on the other, detractors who regard the controversies in which he was involved as largely a product of his personality. Marsden considers both these interpretations to be reductionistic, and goes on to draw attention to two factors which he believes help to provide insight into Machen at a deeper level, namely his adherence to the philosophy of Common Sense Realism and his roots in the American South.[7] An alternative to Marsden's historiographical categories may be developed around the question of whether to regard Machen as a fundamentalist. Using this criterion, the literature on Machen falls into three categories.

One mode of treating Machen is to assume that he was a fundamentalist and to treat him as such either without discussion or without serious consideration of the question. This approach has most recently been taken by Roy A. Harrisville and Walter Sundberg and by Bradley Longfield in their treatments of Machen's life and work.[8]

A second approach is to categorize Machen as a fundamentalist, or even to argue for such an identification, while at the same time acknowledging that there were certain factors that distinguished him from the typical fundamentalists of the 1920s. The recent full-scale biography by D. G. Hart fits this pattern, as does the work of George Marsden on Machen and on fundamentalism, and the substantial biographical sketch by C. Allyn Russell.[9]

A third perspective is found in writers who emphasize those characteristics of Machen and his work that set him apart from fundamentalism and conclude that he was not a fundamentalist at all, but rather an "orthodox ally" of the fundamentalists, as one historian has put it. This was the position of Machen's first biographer and his former pupil and colleague, Ned B. Stonehouse. It is also seen in a recent history of the Orthodox Presbyterian Church co-authored by D. G. Hart and John Muether, and in a history of fundamentalism by an avowed fundamentalist, George W. Dollar. Such a perspective seems to be reflected as well in the two-volume history of Princeton Theological Seminary by David B. Calhoun and in a biographical sketch by W. Stanford Reid. This was in fact the position of Machen himself, who preferred not to be labeled by the term fundamentalist.[10]

The question of how Machen approached the Bible may well be relevant to the broader question of his relationship to the religious parties or movements of his day. Indeed, conclusions reached in this study will tend to support the third perspective mentioned above and will be used in an attempt to sharpen the definition of fundamentalism. Yet the primary concern here is with Machen's response to historicist modes of biblical criticism. It is therefore to the rise of historicism and its influence on biblical studies that attention must now turn.

PART ONE

THE HISTORICAL SETTING

CHAPTER 2

THE RISE OF HISTORICAL CONSCIOUSNESS AND ITS IMPACT ON BIBLICAL STUDY IN EUROPE AND AMERICA

Several recent historians of the late-nineteenth and early-twentieth centuries have concluded that underneath the views with which J. Gresham Machen had to deal was a revolution in Western thought, a revolution in the way people viewed history. Indeed, the outlook not only of Machen but of a much larger conservative religious movement of the 1910s and 1920s (commonly known as fundamentalism) can be defined in terms of hostility to the theories of historical development and historical knowledge that had come to predominate in progressive academic and religious circles and in the scholarly study of the Bible. Thus some historians argue (with a good deal of persuasiveness) that the so-called modernist-fundamentalist controversy was precipitated by a shift in historical outlook which occurred first in Europe, then in America, and had profound effects on Western culture as a whole. George M. Marsden, for example, claims that "totally opposed views of history lay at the heart of the conflict and misunderstanding between theological liberals and their fundamentalist opponents." A similar interpretation of the conflict has been put forth by Grant Wacker who argues that the real revolution in thought occurred in the first place not in changing views of the inspiration and authority of the Bible (although he believes this was the immediate issue) but in "a changed understanding of the nature of historical process." And Sydney E. Ahlstrom, in his *A Religious History of the American People*, has argued that "the burning question of the age" was to be found in the developmental and relativistic implications of historical scholarship. It was just those developmental and relativistic implications, as applied to the Bible, which led to Machen's own intellectual crisis, and against which his biblical scholarship must be understood. It is necessary, therefore, to give some attention to this apparently crucial shift in the Western intellectual outlook.[1]

The new historical perspective in Western thought has been called historicism, or historical consciousness. Its origins are traceable to Enlightenment ideas which were modified and brought to fruition by historians and philosophers in the eighteenth century and afterwards. The terms historical consciousness and historicism will be used in this study according to Wacker's carefully crafted definitions. Historical consciousness will thus denote "substantial or complete acceptance" of historicism. Historicism, in turn, will be understood as a "philosophical orientation" which incorporates "three closely related assumptions about the relation between history and knowledge." It is worth noting at the outset that historicism is at bottom a "philosophical orientation," that is, a set of assumptions based on other grounds than historical ones; it was not occasioned by any recent discovery of new historical data but by a shift in philosophical outlook. The assumptions which historicism incorporates may be denominated the explanatory, the epistemological, and the developmental assumptions.

The explanatory assumption is that "all cultural forms can be adequately explained by reference to the historical context in which they emerge." That is, all human activities and cultural phenomena are to be entirely understood as manifestations of the particular time and place in which they originate.

The epistemological assumption applies this principle to human cognition: "everything people know, including all they understand or think they understand about God's dealings with human beings, is forged in a particular historical setting and bears the unique imprint of that setting." The very act of cognition, then, is historically conditioned and time bound.

The developmental assumption supposes that "all creations of the human spirit are swept along in a process of ceaseless change, governed by functional laws of social development, but not by any sort of preordained destiny." This means that all intellectual and cultural forms are caught up in a process of continual development, that their nature is dynamic and changing rather than static and permanent.

As a consequence of these assumptions, when they are applied in an absolute and consistent way, historicism is generally hostile to the possibility of permanent truth or universally normative values. Some historicist thinkers have carried these ideas to the point of a complete historical or cultural relativism, often accompanied by skepticism regarding human knowledge and ethical norms. In practice, the moderate stance of seeing human experience as historically conditioned (which is difficult to deny) becomes the more extreme position of regarding all things as absolutely historically determined (which became the point at issue in biblical studies).[2]

The naturalistic and relativistic features of historicism are underlined by the definition offered by historian Michael Stanford. Stanford defines historicism in a broad sense when he says it is "the recognition that all social and cultural phenomena are historically determined." The significant terms here are "all," excluding nothing that falls within human experience; and "historically determined," that is, absolutely fixed or established by mundane historical factors (in contrast to "historically conditioned," which may be taken, in some contexts, as perhaps a less stringent affirmation). The necessary implication of historicism so defined is the exclusion of any factors that would be considered supernatural, those resulting from divine influence or activity in earthly history. Thus "it inevitably follows that no philosophy (or religion or science), however profound, can exceed the limitation of its age." Its relativistic implications are also evident. "As Wilhelm Dilthey put it: 'Every world-view is conditioned historically and therefore limited and relative.' Though not so intended by its founders, historicism leads to a position of relativism in knowledge and in ethics. . . ." Stanford's definition of historicism suggests that its naturalistic assumptions and relativistic implications are inherent in the outlook and are therefore inescapable features of this orientation.[3]

The ramifications of such an approach for historic Christianity are clearly serious. As stated by Mark Massa in his study of theologian Charles A. Briggs, "the epistemological relativism inherent" in the historicist position "appeared to affect most dramatically the belief system of Christianity." It did so "by dismissing the possibility of receiving or understanding any revelation from above or outside history." Since the Bible had traditionally been understood to claim to embody revelation from a transcendent God and to describe the activity of such a God in earthly history, it would seem that a conflict between historicism and historic Christianity was all but inevitable.[4]

The Rise and Advance of Historical Consciousness
Rushing up against the prevalent American Protestant view of the Bible, history, and truth – a Bible which was regarded as a revelation

from a transcendent God, a history into which such a God could act, and a truth which, when once established, is absolute, permanent, and universal – came a stream of European thought, a stream which swelled to a flood tide in the aftermath of Charles Darwin's publication of his views in *The Origin of Species* in 1859. The new mentality rejected the categories of the static, the eternal, the changeless, the universal, and defined human existence (and all other existence) in terms of growth, development, change, and process. It emphasized the temporal and the particular – in short, the historical. This new philosophy appealed to Americans – inhabitants of a new, dynamic and changing nation – although it gained momentum only slowly at first. But by the turn of the twentieth century it was becoming a potent force in American intellectual circles, and by 1930 it had become the dominant outlook among educated Americans.[5]

The development of modern historical consciousness is traceable to three major intellectual sources. First were the *philosophes* of the eighteenth-century Enlightenment. Thinkers such as David Hume (1711-1776), Montesquieu (1689-1755), and Voltaire (1694-1778), as well as others, gave serious attention to the nature of historical process, and they advanced three important concepts. They believed, first, that cultural forms are not necessarily universal but reflect the time and place in which they originate. They began to think in terms of cultures and civilizations, whose various features are part of a unitary whole. A second notion, not unique to them, was that the flow of history involves developmental change, that history is moving and is itself developing (Vico, the Italian philosopher, suggested the pattern of a spiral). The third idea suggested that history's development is directional – and the direction was generally thought to be that of progress, as defined by enlightened reason.[6]

A second source is to be found in the German romantic idealism of the eighteenth and nineteenth centuries. Differing in some ways from the Enlightenment emphases, the insights of this movement nevertheless helped to promote the development of historical thinking in the West. Johann Gottfried von Herder (1744-1803), a German preacher, teacher, and philosopher of history, argued that each people, culture or historical period has distinct characteristics which are the products of a particular time and place, and that each must be understood in the context of its own historical setting. Another aspect of Herder's thought was supported by the philosophy of Georg

Wilhelm Friedrich Hegel (1770-1831) who posited the absoluteness of developmental change in history, the continual emergence of the new from the old. Historian Leopold von Ranke (1795-1886) contributed the idea that there is an organic relatedness in history, an interconnection between various historical phenomena as well as between the past and the present. A true understanding of history will relate the particulars to the larger context of the organic whole.[7]

In the nineteenth century there arose a third component in the development of historical consciousness, Anglo-French positivism. Led by the thought of Auguste Comte (1798-1857), Karl Marx (1818-1883), Herbert Spencer (1820-1903), and Charles Darwin (1809-1882), this tradition, while possessing its distinctive emphases, offered a viewpoint which corresponded in many ways to the historicist impulse of the others. These thinkers argued for the radical historicity of all cultural forms, including the structures of human intellectual cognition, application, and ideology. They emphasized the nature of history as a ceaseless process of development. And they believed that the development is directional, being guided by an impulse which is inherent within the process of change itself.[8]

Several American social thinkers whose work gained prominence in the late nineteenth and early twentieth centuries were profoundly affected by this intellectual trend – and they in turn exercised their own broad influence on American thought and culture. Among this group may be included jurist Oliver Wendell Holmes, Jr. (1841-1935), philosopher John Dewey (1859-1952), economist Thorstein Veblen (1857-1929), historian James Harvey Robinson (1863-1936), and political scientist and historian Charles A. Beard (1874-1948). In a study of this generation, Morton G. White suggests that these men were united by their opposition to formalism, meaning the employment of formal logic and abstract reasoning in the social sciences in an ahistorical way. Two elements in the thought of all of them were historicism (which White defines as "the attempt to explain facts by reference to earlier facts"), a form of genetic (or historical) explanation; and cultural organicism ("the attempt to find explanations and relevant material in social sciences other than the one which is primarily under investigation"), a form of social or cultural explanation. The affinities with the European historical consciousness are clear: an emphasis on the process of historical development and on the organic unity of particular cultures. The proper understanding of law, ideas, economics, history, politics, and by implication, religion, is to be attained by reference to a continually unfolding historical process and the impact of the various elements of a culture upon one another.[9]

In the one-third-century following the Civil War, the progressive and dynamic nature of the world view offered by the new historical consciousness made it attractive to many Americans. Progressive idealism, heavily influenced by European thought, became the dominant perspective among philosophers and social thinkers. By 1900, many of the major social theorists of the nation were united by the convictions which characterized the historicist outlook: that "patterns of belief and value are created in the matrix of history"; that "history is a process of continuous development"; and that the process is guided by (supra-historical) laws toward a preordained destiny.[10]

It is doubtless coincidental, but not without interest, that Machen's public "coming out" from an earlier period of confusion and doubt occurred in the year 1912, just when a decisive turn in the nation's thinking was taking it in a direction the opposite of his. Only book reviews had come from Machen's pen since he began teaching at Princeton in 1906, but in 1912 there appeared over his name no fewer than four major articles which were to prove programmatic for his scholarly work in the years ahead. Three of these dealt with the virgin birth of Jesus and were published in successive issues of the *Princeton Theological Review*. The fourth, an essay on the historical connection between Jesus and Paul, was part of a special volume celebrating the centennial of Princeton Seminary. In these articles Machen argued strongly, on literary and historical grounds, for a supernatural element in the origination of the Christian movement, thus indicating how he had resolved an earlier perplexity on such questions.[11]

Machen's full emergence in 1912 as an advocate of the historical trustworthiness of a supernatural New Testament coincided with a crucial turning point in the American swing toward historicism. By 1912, says Morton White, the outline of the new ideology was in place; by 1914 some of its doctrines had become almost popular. Henry F. May locates in the years 1912 to 1917 a wide-ranging cultural revolution among the literary and artistic intelligentsia of America, in which many of the relativistic implications of the historical consciousness were adopted. In 1913 Charles A. Beard published *An Economic Interpretation of the Constitution*, in which he subjected this supposedly sacred American scripture to a historical examination, dredging up the economic forces allegedly involved in its production, and ending with a document in the full grip of history. In 1912 the University of Chicago Press published a volume by Louis Wallis embodying a course of lectures delivered at Ohio State University and several churches. In Wallis' book, significantly titled *Sociological Study of the Bible*, the Bible was assumed to be the decidedly unsupernatural product of the evolutionary development of Hebrew religion. Both the direction of contemporary intellectual currents and later scholarly opinion thus lend weight to the designation of the 1910s as that period when a decisive cultural transformation began in earnest in the United States, though it had been several decades in the making. Events viewed while they were occurring as well as from the vantage point of a later time appear to justify George Santayana's observation in 1913: "The present age is a critical one and interesting to live in. The civilization characteristic of Christendom has not yet disappeared, yet another civilization has begun to take its place."[12]

The horror of World War I was devastating not only to Europe but also to the concept of inevitable progress. By the 1920s, according to Wacker, most philosophers, historians, and social scientists had dropped the conviction that history is directional, guided toward a preordained destiny by laws inherent in the process of development but somehow transcending it. History, they concluded, has no goal; it only changes. And although some scholars stressed one aspect or another of the historicist position, yet increasingly, "a consistent and radical historicism, as evident in Max Weber and John Dewey, came to characterize the work of leading social thinkers." The result was the loss both of any objective basis for making value judgments and of any hope of a unified, synthetic knowledge of reality. Historical consciousness had, by about 1930, resolved itself into an "unflinching epistemological relativism," a belief in "the infinite plasticity of human nature," and the conviction that history is going nowhere.[13]

Certain factors in the American scene probably contributed to the widespread acceptance of the new viewpoint, as Wacker is undoubtedly correct in pointing out. The pressure of an unceasing tide of immigration, which reached its peak in the years 1905 to 1914, coming increasingly from southern and eastern Europe, helped to break down the apparent homogeneity which had characterized the United States in the nineteenth century. New ethnic strains, different cultural patterns, and non-Protestant religious traditions made it appear that particular cultural manifestations are indeed relative to time and place. The new immigration, as well as the continuing internal flow of Americans from the countryside to urban areas, hastened the process that was fragmenting life in the burgeoning cities. The urban social structure came to be dominated by the competing demands of various interests, as city-dwellers began to identify more with their own ethnic group, neighborhood, religion, or occupation than with any unifying loyalty. Finally, changing educational patterns affected the way Americans perceived the world. The growth of public education, the rise of the university system, and the development of graduate training patterned after the German model facilitated the exposure of Americans to the pluralistic nature of the world and brought new ideas into the mainstream of American thought. In the years surrounding the turn of the twentieth century, American society was becoming, in Robert Wiebe's term, "distended," stretched and diversified and factionalized, and this process no doubt helped to foster a mentality which was receptive to historical consciousness.[14]

Historical Consciousness and Biblical Study in Europe

When J. Gresham Machen elected to attend the University of Göttingen in the spring and summer of 1906, he chose a school with a rich heritage of historical scholarship. The university at Göttingen, founded in 1734, had acquired a distinguished faculty, and during the last third of the eighteenth century took the lead in developing the historical approach in various disciplines. It was here, suggests Herbert Butterfield, that modern historical scholarship had its origin in Germany. The Göttingen scholars and their students utilized a historical method in the study of classical philology, law, general history, church history, and the Bible. Their methodology included the adoption of a critical, analytical attitude toward sources, the use of cultural data and auxiliary disciplines to reconstruct broad historical contexts, and the principle that various phenomena are to be explained as products of their own time and place. When J. D. Michaelis (1717-1791) applied these principles to the Bible, the Mosaic law was capable of historical explanation without recourse to divine revelation, the Gospels were not without contradictions, and the unity of the New Testament canon as inspired scripture was opened to question. Johann Semler (1725-1791) used historical analysis in his study of the Bible, with similar results. According to New Testament scholar Werner G. Kümmel, the stimulus to historical scholarship which Semler provided merits him the title of "the founder of the historical study of the New Testament."[15] The Göttingen influence was extended through one of Semler's pupils, Johann Jakob Griesbach (1745-1812), a figure who, says F. F. Bruce, a leading twentieth-century biblical scholar, marks "the transition from the post-Reformation to the 'modern' age of New Testament study." Griesbach published a critical edition of the Greek New Testament (1774-75) and identified three main families of manuscripts according to text-types. He also engaged in literary criticism, attempting to determine the interrelationships between the "synoptic gospels," a term he coined.[16]

New Testament as well as Old Testament scholarship continued to develop along such lines for the next century and more. It is unnecessary for the purposes of this study to survey the whole development of biblical criticism prior to Machen's time. More relevant are the broader effects of the new historical mode of thinking on biblical and theological studies generally, and the major trends in New Testament interpretation – Machen's field – just prior to and during Machen's lifetime.[17]

Sydney Ahlstrom suggests five ways in which historical consciousness had an impact on theology during the nineteenth century, challenging traditional notions.

First, uniformitarian (naturalistic) principles of development were applied to all past events. The result was the exclusion of miracle and divine providence from the history of Israel, the life of Jesus, and the rise of early Christianity. The year 1835 saw the publication of three important books, one in each of these fields (by Wilhelm Vatke, David Friedrich Strauss, and Ferdinand Christian Baur), embodying this new perspective.

Second, the biblical literature began to be handled in the same manner as other ancient documents. Scholars such as Julius Wellhausen of Germany questioned the literary unity and traditional ascription of date and authorship of the Pentateuch and of other portions of the Old Testament, and of the New Testament as well, where the implications were more disturbing for some Christians.

Third, historical theology arose as an independent discipline, demonstrating that traditional Christian doctrines were themselves products of historical circumstances and internal development.

Fourth, the comparative study of religion raised questions about the influence of ancient pagan ideas on Israel's religion and on the theology of Paul. It also threw doubt on the claims of Christianity to exclusive truth and absolute superiority over other world religions, especially those of the east, such as Buddhism and Hinduism.

Fifth, "historicism" emerged as the culmination of these intellectual trends. The term historicism, in Ahlstrom's usage, means either the tendency toward relativism because of the absolute historicity of all things, or the tendency toward determinism, the belief that history proceeds according to a fixed pattern, whether that of Hegel and Marx, Henry Adams, or Herbert Spencer and William Graham Sumner.

The influence of all these tendencies is aptly summarized by Franklin Baumer when he says that the most important effect of biblical criticism was that "it taught people to think of religions as historical phenomena, appropriate to a particular time and place, but as outgrowing their original context, as ever changing in both form and content, their 'mythology' perhaps at last becoming outmoded."[18]

It was within this context of viewing all things in terms of historical flux, process, and development that there arose three important schools of New Testament interpretation. One of these schools antedated Machen and, though later thoroughly discredited, continued to wield great influence. The other two were contemporary with Machen, and occupied a prominent place in the battles he fought. The three may be denominated the Tübingen school, led by Ferdinand Christian Baur; the Ritschlian school, as represented by Adolf Harnack; and the history-of-religions school, of which Wilhelm Bousset was the most eminent spokesman.

Ferdinand Christian Baur (1792-1860) was appointed professor of church history and dogmatics at the University of Tübingen in 1826, and it was this university which gave its name to his distinctive and influential approach to New Testament interpretation. The central feature of Baur's reconstruction of early Christian history was his belief that there had occurred a severe and long-lasting dispute between the Petrine (Judaistic) and Pauline (Hellenistic) factions in the primitive church. This cleavage, which according to Baur continued well into the second century, was resolved in the emergence of the "catholic (institutionalized) church" in the mid-second century. The Hegelian scheme of thesis-antithesis-synthesis (Baur came under Hegel's influence from 1833 on) provided Baur with the framework for constructing a historical dialectic into which he fitted the various New Testament writings according to their tendency toward either Petrine, Pauline, or catholic Christianity. Baur's reconstruction led him to date several New Testament writings late in this process, toward the middle of the second century, well after the date traditionally assigned to them. It was left to the brilliant Cambridge scholar, Joseph Barber Lightfoot (1828-1889), to demonstrate that Baur's thesis was untenable because unhistorical. Lightfoot definitively established the early dates of the genuine epistles of Ignatius and of I Clement. These post-apostolic Christian writings exhibit a knowledge of many New Testament books and give no evidence of a continuing conflict between Jewish and Gentile Christianity. "It is not often," says Stephen Neill of Baur's hypothesis, "that a theory can be so completely overthrown." Yet, though the literary conclusions of the Tübingen school came to be rejected by most New Testament scholars, the historical picture constructed by Baur continued to exercise great influence, with the conflict simply pushed back to an earlier time.[19]

A second school of thought which manifested the strength of historical consciousness, perhaps as much a theological movement as a school of biblical interpretation but with a strong base in academic biblical studies, was Ritschlian or "liberal" Christianity. Its founder, Albrecht Ritschl (1822-1889), was originally a disciple of Baur, but he publicly broke with the Tübingen school in 1857. He taught New Testament as well as systematic theology at Bonn from 1846 to 1864, when he became professor of systematic theology at Göttingen. For Ritschl, who opposed all ecclesiastical dogma, the kingdom of God was the ethical community of love which God is establishing among men, and Jesus is the founder of that kingdom and the bearer of God's ethical lordship. Forgiveness is the restoration of man's filial relationship with God, not on the basis of any atoning value in Christ's death, but through the reproduction in the Christian community of Christ's unity with God and his attitude of trust and love toward God in the face of testing and death. In Ritschl's scheme, Jesus is not so much the object of faith as he is the archetypical believer; the Bible is not an inspired textbook of theology but a record of the early Christian interpretation of Jesus – and the Bible's pronouncements, though highly valued, may at times be set aside. This view of the Bible reflects a pragmatic strain that runs through Ritschl's thinking: he considered a doctrine to be true not because it was found in the Bible but because it proved itself experientially and practically in life.[20]

Ritschl's thought influenced many German scholars and theologians (including several whose lectures Machen heard, e.g., Wilhelm Herrmann, Emil Schürer, and Johannes Weiss), but the most illustrious of all was Adolf Harnack (1851-1930). Harnack was a multi-faceted scholar, an expert alike in patristics, the history of dogmatics, and the New Testament. He taught at Leipzig, Giessen, Marburg, and Berlin, and held prestigious scholarly posts outside the universities. On New Testament questions he was of a more critical bent than Ritschl, though his conclusions were sometimes sufficiently conservative to undermine current radical scholarship. In his classic statement of the liberal position, *What Is Christianity?* (1900), Harnack defended the general historical credibility of the synoptic gospels, but he contended that it was the historian's responsibility to distinguish in them the "kernel" and the "husk," that which was of permanent value as opposed to that which merely reflected the particularities of the historical situation in which Jesus and his disciples lived and taught. Like Ritschl, he rejected ecclesiastical dogma as a later Hellenistic accretion to the simple teaching of Jesus. That teaching revolved around three basic concepts: the kingdom of God (conceived as the present inner, spiritual experience of God's rule and power); the fatherhood of God and the infinite value of the human soul (both applied to all humans without distinction); and the higher righteousness and the command of love (an ethical ideal emphasizing disposition and intention, love and humility). For Harnack, the gospel could virtually (and legitimately) be reduced to general morality, an ethic of love. His approach resulted in the relativizing (that is, reinterpreting) of the major Christian doctrines, as he sought to find the kernel of truth amid the New Testament's and the church's husks of theology.[21]

The two aforementioned schools of interpretation, regardless of how they may have reflected historical consciousness and the growth of critical historical scholarship, perpetuated the tradition of viewing early Christianity in isolation from its broader environment. Christianity's connection with Judaism was obvious; it was a Ritschlian, Emil Schürer (1844-1910), who produced the definitive *History of the Jewish People in the Time of Jesus Christ* (1886-90). But the possible connections with the Hellenistic world were either ignored or denied until the advent of the so-called history of religions school (this is an awkward but commonly accepted translation of the

German *religionsgeschichtliche Schule*). The "father" of the school was Otto Pfleiderer (1839-1908), a student of Baur, who in 1887 suggested that Paul's understanding of the Christian sacraments was influenced by paganism and the mystery religions which were popular in the Hellenistic era. Pfleiderer aptly expressed in a single sentence the basic assumptions of the history of religions approach to the New Testament, making clear its debt to historicism. "Christianity as a historical phenomenon is to be investigated by the same methods as all other history, and . . . in particular, its origin is to be understood by being studied as the normal outcome of the manifold factors in the religious and ethical life of the time." In other words, Christianity was assumed to be the natural product of the environment in which it arose, and a historical explanation for its origin was to be sought in accordance with this principle.[22]

Wilhelm Heitmüller (1869-1926), under whom Machen studied at Göttingen in 1906, was another advocate of this method. Heitmüller advanced the view in 1903 that Paul's conceptions of baptism and the Lord's Supper were definitely derived from the surrounding pagan religious culture. Stephen Neill draws from Heitmüller's work four assumptions which fairly well define the outlook of the history of religions school:

(1) There was a radical difference between the teaching of Jesus and that of Paul.

(2) There was in Paul's theology a contradiction between faith and external religious observance of which Paul was only dimly aware.

(3) The cause of this contradiction was the entrance into Paul's theology of religious elements from the Hellenistic environment which were destructive of the idea of faith as simple trust in God, without sacramental or human mediation.

(4) In this distortion is to be found the origin of "catholicism," a reliance on external institutional ordinances to the detriment of the pure, simple gospel and to the horror of German Lutheran theologians.

The history of religions school was thus proposing that the New Testament be subjected to a radical historical criticism and that early Christianity can be properly understood only when it is seen as one among many similar religious phenomena in the Hellenistic world and the ancient Near East.[23]

Several other scholars were influential in promoting the views of this school. Among them was Richard Reitzenstein (1861-1931), a classical philologist who taught at several German universities. In 1910 and 1921 he published books in which he attempted to relate Pauline Christianity to the Hellenistic mystery religions and Iranian myths of a heavenly redeemer. Perhaps the foremost advocate of the history of religions approach in the early twentieth century was Wilhelm Bousset (1865-1920), whose lectures Machen heard at Göttingen, where Bousset taught for over twenty-five years. Bousset's most notable work was his 1913 volume entitled *Kyrios Christos* [Lord Christ], in which he argued that the primitive Gentile Christian communities, in their worship, transformed the essentially Jewish eschatological figure of the Son of Man into the figure of the Lord who is present with his church and with whom the worshippers experience immediate fellowship and unity through participation in the sacramental meal. The major influence upon this development, according to Bousset, was that of the Hellenistic mystery religions. The greatest popularizer of such views in the English-speaking world was the British scholar Kirsopp Lake (1872-1946), who came to the United States in 1914 to teach at Harvard, where he remained until 1937. By general agreement his best book was *The Earlier Epistles of Paul* (1911). Here, in attractive and dramatic fashion, Lake summarized for English-speaking readers the conclusions of the history of religions school in Germany, and made it necessary for English and American students of the New Testament to treat seriously the questions which that school had raised. The most influential representative of this school of interpretation, Rudolf Bultmann (1884-1976), exercised his greatest influence after Machen's death. During Machen's lifetime Bultmann was known for his work on form criticism of the synoptic gospels (the attempt to classify the various units of tradition according to their literary form) and for his initial attempts to interpret the New Testament in accord with the existentialism of the German philosopher Martin Heidegger. Needless to say, Bultmann's early New Testament scholarship was based on the assumptions of the history of religions approach.[24]

Indeed, Bultmann later produced one of the most straightforward statements of a consistent historicist position. In an article published two decades after Machen's death but expressing the principles to which Bultmann and the history of religions school adhered in the 1920s, Bultmann set forth his conception of the philosophical foundation of the "historical method":

The historical method includes the presupposition that history is a unity in the sense of a closed continuum of effects in which individual events are connected by the succession of cause and effect. . . . This closedness means that the continuum of historical happenings cannot be rent by the interference of supernatural, transcendent powers. . . .

Bultmann goes on to say that one may choose to believe that an event is an act of God, and that historical science cannot declare such faith an illusion. But historical science as such "cannot perceive such an act and reckon on the basis of it"; it must understand a historical event "in terms of that event's immanent historical causes." Clearly Bultmann's "historical method" allows no room for direct divine action in earthly history; such a possibility is defined out of existence on the strictly historical level and is relegated to the realm of "faith" – with a resulting dichotomy in human knowledge.[25]

There was another strain of the history of religions approach which claimed allegiance to the same method, but which arrived at radically different conclusions. This school has been given the name of "consistent eschatology," for it found the roots of Christianity in late Judaic apocalypticism. Johannes Weiss (1863-1914), one of Machen's teachers at Marburg, built on the work of earlier scholars and in 1892 put forward a "strictly futuristic, eschatological interpretation of Jesus' proclamation of the kingdom of God," in contrast to the present nature of the kingdom as expounded by the Ritschlian school. Richard Kabisch (1868-1914) performed the same service for Paul, discovering the essentially eschatological nature of Pauline theology in dependence on contemporary Jewish concepts. This mode of interpretation was epitomized by Albert Schweitzer (1875-1965), who in several works on both Jesus and Paul, most notably *The Quest of the Historical Jesus* (1906), explained early Christian thought in wholly futuristic and eschatological terms, grounded in Jewish apocalyptic thought. The consistently eschatological approach was not immediately widely received, but Schweitzer's influence eventually made it impossible to ignore the eschatological element in the gospels, and ultimately spelled the death of the "liberal" Jesus.[26]

The Historical Study of the Bible in America
The reception which historical biblical scholarship was afforded in the United States was conditioned by the prevailing American attitude toward the Bible. In the mid-nineteenth century, American Protestants

as a rule held to a high view of the Bible's authority. The position of Charles Hodge, though he was a theologian, may be taken to fairly represent the common Protestant view of the Bible during the third quarter of the nineteenth century. Summarizing the Protestant doctrine of scripture as found in the Lutheran, Reformed, Anglican, and Presbyterian confessions, Hodge wrote: "the Scriptures of the Old and New Testaments are the Word of God, written under the inspiration of the Holy Spirit, and are therefore infallible, and of divine authority in all things pertaining to faith and practice, and consequently free from all error whether of doctrine, fact, or precept." So as to leave no uncertainty regarding the precise implications of this statement, Hodge asserted a few pages later that inspiration "is not confined to moral and religious truths, but extends to the statements of facts, whether scientific, historical, or geographical. . . . It extends to everything which any sacred writer asserts to be true." The Bible, in this view, was considered to be infallible and without error in any matter which it touches. This was the understanding of biblical authority held not only by theologians such as Hodge, but by most Protestants. "The overwhelming majority of American Christians," Mark Noll writes, "shared beliefs in Scripture as the Word of God and in commonsensical methods for interpreting it." It was this understanding of the nature and authority of the Bible which was soon to be threatened by historical study and which led to stout resistance.[27]

Historical scholarship in the form of its specialized subdiscipline, biblical criticism, made its impact in America relatively late, as compared to Germany and Britain. Biblical criticism had become an important force in Germany in the 1830s and in Britain during the 1860s, but serious debate of the questions involved did not occur in the United States until the 1880s. British scholarship was especially influential in mediating the results of the new criticism to the United States. The Old Testament work of two men in particular, W. Robertson Smith (1846-1894) and Samuel R. Driver (1846-1914), served to disseminate the conclusions of European scholarship to a broad American audience. Smith's views were published in the ninth edition of the *Encyclopaedia Britannica* and elsewhere and earned him a spectacular heresy trial and subsequent dismissal from his professorship at Aberdeen in 1881. Driver's *Introduction to the Literature of the Old Testament* (1897) became the standard work for a generation.[28]

The chief share of credit for introducing Christians in the United States to biblical criticism belongs to the American Presbyterian scholar Charles A. Briggs (1841-1913). A professor at Union Seminary (then Presbyterian) in New York, Briggs had studied at the University of Berlin where he became convinced of the correctness of German critical views, especially regarding the Old Testament, and of their compatibility with historic Christian orthodoxy. He championed these views (with the help of two other scholars, Henry Preserved Smith and Samuel I. Curtiss) in a series of articles which appeared in the *Presbyterian Review* during the years 1881 to 1883. The conservative viewpoint was set forth in four articles in the same journal, written mostly by men connected with Princeton Seminary. At the same time, Briggs was working on a major book, *Biblical Study: Its Principles, Methods, and History*, published in 1883. This volume outlined the methods of biblical criticism and entered a plea for American involvement in the discipline. A few years later, Brigg's livelihood was threatened and his career affected as a result of views arising from his practice of biblical criticism. Upon being appointed to the newly-created chair of biblical theology at Union Seminary, Briggs in 1891 delivered an inaugural address on biblical authority which was immoderate in statement, hostile in tone, and offensive to many. Briggs listed six barriers to the operation of the divine authority of the Bible: superstition (in the form of bibliolatry); the doctrine of verbal inspiration; anxiety over the authenticity of biblical writings; the doctrine of the inerrancy of the Bible; the conception of miracles as violations of the laws of nature; and the conception of prophecy as minute prediction. He denied that Moses wrote the Pentateuch, that Isaiah was the author of half the book which bears his name, that Messianic prophecy had been or would be fulfilled, and called into question several traditional Protestant doctrines. The consequences of this address were manifold. Briggs's appointment was vetoed by the General Assembly of the Northern Presbyterian Church, as a result of which Union Seminary severed its connection with the denomination while retaining Briggs. The New York Presbytery tried and acquitted Briggs on charges of heresy, but on appeal the General Assembly convicted him of eight charges in 1893 and suspended him from the Presbyterian ministry. He entered the ministry of the Protestant Episcopal Church in 1898. Though the Presbyterian Church may have rid itself of Briggs, the controversy surrounding the case only served, as Lefferts Loetscher has pointed out, to "publicize and disseminate the new critical views within the church and far beyond."[29]

The Briggs case revealed the continuing strength of traditional views in the Northern Presbyterian Church; this body in 1892 and 1893 affirmed its adherence to the inerrancy of the Bible. But the case also demonstrated, through the New York Presbytery's acquittal of Briggs, the growing desire of many to accommodate the new views and to maintain harmony and efficiency in the church by means of a broad and inclusive policy. Tumult in Presbyterian circles over the acceptance of biblical criticism was further indicated by the ecclesiastical trial and conviction of Henry Preserved Smith (1847-1927) in 1892-1894 for his rejection of the doctrine of the inerrancy of the Bible, and by the voluntary resignation of Arthur C. McGiffert (1861-1933) from the Presbyterian ministry in 1900 under threat of prosecution because of his critical views on the New Testament.[30]

The Northern Presbyterian Church was not the only ecclesiastical body to feel the effects of the advent of biblical criticism in America. Conservatives among the Congregationalists, Methodists, and Baptists in the northern states, observes Norman Maring, "were unable to prevent the forces of Biblical criticism from breaching their defenses" – even though they tried. A wholesale turnover in the faculty of Andover Seminary in the 1880s led to that Congregational institution's adoption of the new critical views; and although one professor, E. C. Smyth, was tried and removed in 1885, he was reinstated in 1892. The Methodist bishops charged Hinckley G. Mitchell in 1895 with questioning the Mosaic authorship of the Pentateuch, and in 1905 he was removed from his professorship at Boston University. Baptists in the south were largely immune to the controversy, the only casualty being Crawford H. Toy, who was forced out of Southern Baptist Seminary in Louisville in 1879 because of his acceptance of the composite authorship of the Pentateuch and the evolutionary development of the Old Testament. Northern Baptists were generally more tolerant of divergent views, although in 1882 Ezra P. Gould was dismissed from Newton Theological Institution for his advocacy of critical theories.[31]

It was another Baptist, William Rainey Harper (1856-1906), an Old Testament scholar, who, as president of the new University of Chicago, championed a positive, constructive approach to biblical criticism. Harper placed his own view, which he called "rational interpretation," over against two "rationalistic" schools, one to the left of himself and one to the right. On the left was the naturalistic school, which built its position on the denial of the supernatural. On the right was the supernaturalistic school, which was just as rationalistic as the other, Harper claimed, because it based its scholarship on an *a priori* understanding of the nature of the Bible as divine revelation. Firmly convinced that both approaches were in error, Harper was sure that a moderate historical criticism would be salutary for both a proper understanding of the Bible and an intelligent faith. Under his leadership the University of Chicago was established as an influential force in critical biblical scholarship, though most of its scholars soon adopted a more radical approach.[32]

Not only was the academic world being touched by the results of biblical criticism, but popularizers were at work as well. Influential ministers such as Washington Gladden (1836-1918), the social gospeler, and Lyman Abbott (1835-1922), who occupied a famous Brooklyn pulpit, were concerned to disseminate the new views to the Christian public. Gladden's *Who Wrote the Bible? A Book for the People*, embodying critical conclusions, was published in 1891, and became his best-selling book. Abbott published his *Life and Literature of the Ancient Hebrews* in 1901, incorporating the work of England's Samuel R. Driver. Although the impact of such works was generally limited to the better-educated urban classes, it was nevertheless real.[33]

The conservative banner in the conflict was most ably carried by the circle of scholars connected with Princeton Theological Seminary. From Princeton issued a consistent stream of criticism which attacked the new views of the Bible and the liberal theology with which they were often associated. In journal articles, book reviews, and monographs, the Princetonians met the proponents of the common critical conclusions on the latter's ground, and argued as equals in scholarship. Leading the charge for Princeton, besides the earlier Hodges – Charles and his son Archibald Alexander (1823-1886) – were theologians Benjamin B. Warfield (1851-1921) and Francis L. Patton (1843-1932), Old Testament scholars John D. Davis (1854-1926) and Robert Dick Wilson (1856-1930), the New Testament scholar William Park Armstrong (1874-1944) and later, Machen himself, and biblical theologian Geerhardus Vos (1862-1949). William Hutchison, after describing several other institutions as weaker or less consistent centers of opposition to liberal methods and doctrine, comments that "the inspired obstinacy" of the Princeton scholars "shone in marked, self-conscious contrast with all such flickering lights." The difficulty that soon faced the Princetonians, however, was whether anyone in the liberal camp was even listening to their protests.[34]

Several students of the subject have concluded that the decades from 1890 to 1920 mark off a watershed period in American biblical studies. Although conservative strength appeared to be solid in 1900, this was illusory; the methods and assumptions of the new historical scholarship were quietly being felt in ever-broadening circles of influence, and led to a decisive decline of conservative power after 1900. In a recent study, Mark Noll attributes this decline largely to the changing academic environment in the United States at the turn of the century. With the rise of the modern university, dramatic changes had begun to take place – most significantly, the academic world was becoming professionalized. According to Noll,

> this professionalization involved at least the following commitments: (1) rigorous inquiry; (2) specialized study; (3) orientation to academic peers instead of the general community; (4) a German model of scholarship stressing scrupulous objectivity; (5) a commitment to science in organic, evolutionary terms instead of mechanical, static ones; and (6) an iconoclastic, progressive spirit.

Noll argues that conservative evangelical scholars, oriented toward the church, could handle rigorous inquiry and specialization; they had been engaged in both for decades. But they did not adapt well to other aspects of the changing situation. The reorientation away from students and church and toward academic peers began to remove the scholarly study of the Bible from the community of faith and to place it in the hands of an elite corps of academicians. The German seminar model, demanding detached objectivity, tended to isolate intellectual questions from the life and concerns of the larger community. And the assumption implicit in the doctrine of evolutionary development, that the later is always the more advanced, along with the anti-traditionalist spirit of the academy, seemed to answer questions by definition and hastily to disregard long-held views. As a result of this lack of sympathy with the new academic environment, evangelical scholarship seemed to be out of touch with current movements, and entered a period of disengagement from scholarly exchange with the contemporary academic community. Thus just at the time when biblical criticism was making its great thrust into American culture, evangelical scholars were in the process of withdrawing from the academic marketplace and limiting themselves to a narrow evangelical audience.[35]

Noll's insightful study documents this disengagement. Some of the evidence may be found in a comparison of authors who wrote for different types of journals. A series of scholarly journals issuing from Presbyterian circles during the half-century from 1880 to 1929 published much of the conservative Presbyterian scholarship of this era. Princeton Seminary professors were always active as editors and contributors, while the final journal in the succession was edited solely by the Princeton faculty and was known as the *Princeton Theological Review* (1903-1929). Although the journals were primarily Presbyterian in orientation, their pages included articles by writers from a diversity of traditions, including Baptists, Congregationalists, Lutherans, Anglicans, and some Europeans. Serious academic study of the Bible continued throughout the history of these journals, but the authors who appeared in their pages participated to a decreasing degree in the wider arena of professional biblical scholarship. "After the turn of the century," remarks Noll, ". . . writers who published in the Presbyterian reviews no longer published, as a general rule, in the professional journals." Before 1900, a small but significant percentage of contributors to these Presbyterian journals were also published in the *Journal of Biblical Literature*; after 1903, only two of 275 authors who wrote for the *Princeton Theological Review* contributed also to the *Journal of Biblical Literature*, with the last such article appearing in 1909. Warfield wrote several articles for the *Journal of Biblical Literature* in its early years; Machen contributed none – the bulk of his scholarly work appeared in the *Princeton Theological Review*. A great chasm was thus developing between conservative, church-oriented biblical scholarship and that produced by the professionalized academic world.[36]

Another indication of this gulf was the reception afforded the series of twelve small volumes called *The Fundamentals*. Financed by two wealthy Christian laymen, Lyman and Milton Stewart, and published during the years 1910 to 1915, these books were sent to Christian workers and students around the world. They consisted of essays, most of them quite competent, written by evangelical scholars and

ministers from America and abroad. Their purpose was to defend
traditional Protestant orthodoxy against the rising tide of liberal
theology and biblical criticism. About one-third of nearly one hundred
articles dealt with the Bible, reiterating conservative objections to the
assumptions, methods, and conclusions of the prevailing critical
orthodoxy. Despite the widespread dissemination of these books,
almost no notice was taken of them in academic centers. Noll
summarizes the response they elicited:

> In sharp contrast to the situation during the 1880s and 1890s, the academic
> world as a whole paid very little attention to the evangelical arguments
> in *The Fundamentals*. A nearly complete disengagement seems to have
> taken place. It is difficult to make a case on the absence of evidence, but
> a fairly broad survey of contemporary academic periodicals –
> conservative, modernist, academic, denominational – reveals almost total
> disregard for *The Fundamentals*.

Interpreting this lack of response as evidence of almost complete
"estrangement of evangelical scholars from the academic
marketplace," Noll concludes that conservative scholars were by this
time writing largely for the evangelical populace rather than for their
academic peers.[37]

While conservative evangelicals were responding to historicism
and its critical conclusions regarding the Bible with a policy of
repudiation and rejection, another segment of Protestantism was
finding ways to accommodate the new outlook. The theological and
religious movement that came to be known as liberalism was a result
of the effort to incorporate the insights of historicism into Christianity.
It was an expression of the attempt on the part of some Christians to
come to peaceable terms with the intellectual currents of the age.
Indeed, as Sydney Ahlstrom observes, historical modes of thought
"very nearly succeeded in determining both the strategies and the
content of liberal theology."[38]

Liberalism's debt to historical consciousness is evident in its
leading ideas. William R. Hutchison draws a distinction between
modernism, which he considers the central impulse of liberalism, and
the broader tradition of theological liberalism. The latter had its origins
in Unitarianism in the first half of the nineteenth century, building on
the foundations provided by the Arian, Arminian, and rationalist
movements of the eighteenth century. Liberal ideas spread in the

second half of the nineteenth century beyond the Unitarian movement to major Protestant denominations, especially the Congregational, Episcopal, Methodist, Baptist, Presbyterian, and Disciples churches in the northern portion of the country. The essence of the broader liberal tradition was found in the following cluster of notions: a conviction of the immanence of God both in nature and in human nature; a proneness to humanistic optimism; belief in and appeal to a universal religious sentiment; an emphasis on doing good works rather than on theological correctness; and the high value placed on the doctrine of the Incarnation as a symbol of God's presence in humanity. These liberal ideas could be held, Hutchison maintains, even in opposition to the prevailing currents of modern culture.[39]

Not so with the more intense expression of the movement, modernism. As its name indicates, modernism was characterized, in the first place, by the conscious desire to adapt religious ideas to modern culture, especially modern science and historical research. In the second place, modernism emphasized the immanence of God in, and the revelation of God through, human cultural development. Finally, modernists believed in the continuing progress of human society toward the kingdom of God, even though the goal may never be perfectly attained. The affinities of these ideas with historical consciousness are evident. In their stress on the fluid, developing nature of religious belief and on the virtual identification of divine revelation with cultural development and redemption with social progress, the leading concepts of modernism were thoroughly in accord with the new historical mode of thinking and constituted one of its most visible manifestations.[40]

Broadly considered, liberalism was a multiform rather than uniform phenomenon. A helpful analysis is offered by Ahlstrom, who suggests that liberals were divided over two basic issues: the nature of religion and the nature of revelation. With respect to the nature of religion, there were three varieties of liberals. The moralists, such as Walter Rauschenbusch (1861-1918), tended to identify religion with ethics. The experientialists were interested in analyzing religious experience and feeling; Newman Smyth (1843-1925) is an example. And the philosophers, among whom were Josiah Royce (1855-1916) and Henry Nelson Wieman (1884-1975), dwelt on metaphysics and the philosophy of religion. On the question of revelation, there was a rather sharp division between two schools of thought. The "Evangelical

Liberals" stayed close to the Bible, professed Jesus Christ as their standard, and used traditional theological terminology while adapting as much as necessary to changing times. The Baptists William Newton Clarke (1841-1912) and Rauschenbusch represented this approach. The "Modernist Liberals" were more radical, conformed more consistently to historical ways of thinking, and took modern thought rather than the Bible as their point of departure. The University of Chicago was important in developing this line of thinking, led by such men as Shailer Mathews (1863-1941) and Shirley Jackson Case (1872-1947). But the various forms which liberalism took should not be allowed to obscure the fact that liberals were united by a commitment to historical consciousness (in greater or lesser degrees) and to the biblical criticism which it had fostered. Because of this essential unity the term liberalism may legitimately be applied to the whole movement in a general way, including modernism – and will be so applied in this study – with appropriate distinctions made when necessary.[41]

Implications of the Traditional and Historicist Views for Biblical Study

A public exchange during the 1880s between the traditional camp in the Presbyterian Church and those within the same body who were more friendly toward the new criticism served to elucidate the implications of each view for biblical study. Two major protagonists in the exchange were Archibald A. Hodge and Charles A. Briggs, co-editors of the *Presbyterian Review*. From 1881 to 1883 this journal published a series of articles written by respected representatives of each camp (including Hodge and Briggs) in which the conservatives offered a wary assessment of the possibilities and contributions of biblical criticism, while Briggs and his party displayed a much more favorable attitude.

The most important statement of the conservative position, entitled simply "Inspiration," came from the pens of A. A. Hodge, then at the pinnacle of his career, and Benjamin B. Warfield, just at the threshold of his. Hodge produced the first portion of the essay, which included a section stating the traditional Protestant doctrine of inspiration as he understood it and dealing with questions connected with it. Since this essay is commonly considered to be a classic statement of the conservative evangelical stance, it is most interesting to find that

Hodge devoted a subdivision to the relation of the doctrine of inspiration to "the supposed results of modern criticism as to the dates, authors, sources and modes of composition" of the biblical books. Hodge proposed several guidelines which he regarded as setting "the limits within which the Church doctrine of inspiration is in equilibrium with the results of modern criticism." A consideration of these proposals is in order.[42]

In the first place, Hodge argued that naturalistic theories of the evolution of scripture were contrary to the received doctrine of inspiration, since that doctrine presupposed a supernatural revelation and supernatural guidance in the production of scripture. The supernatural cannot be reduced to the natural. In the second place, the authority of Jesus Christ as a witness to the character and contents of the Old Testament must be observed. Any view of the Old Testament which contradicts the pronouncements of Christ is unacceptable. Third, the authority of the New Testament is bound up with that of the divinely commissioned apostles – and their companions – who wrote it. Here the questions of inspiration, authorship, and canonicity merge: denial of apostolic origin constitutes a denial of inspiration and thus of a rightful place in the canon. Fourth, any conclusion of critical investigation which is inconsistent with the "absolute truthfulness of any affirmation" of the books authenticated by the foregoing criteria is inconsistent with the doctrine of inspiration. Let God be true and every contrary finding of criticism false. Thus did Hodge tightly bind up the practice of biblical criticism with the cords of biblical inspiration.[43]

In the pages which followed, Hodge showed just how tightly he intended to bind criticism, and almost paradoxically, how much room he was prepared to allow it. He made it clear that the "absolute truthfulness" of the affirmations of scripture included not only religious teaching, but also just those points of "history, natural history, ethnology, archaeology, geography, natural science and philosophy" which the critics were most likely to question. This stance, in combination with the demands of his position regarding the authenticity and authorship of the biblical documents, seemingly left very little room in which criticism could maneuver. On the other hand, however, he was quite willing to acknowledge the human and historical conditioning to which the scriptures were subject:

The information they convey is in the forms of human thought, and limited on all sides. They were not designed to teach philosophy, science or human history as such. They were not designed to furnish an infallible system of speculative theology. They are written in human languages, whose words, inflections, constructions and idioms bear everywhere indelible traces of human error. The record itself furnishes evidence that the writers were in large measure dependent for their knowledge upon sources and methods in themselves fallible, and that their personal knowledge and judgments were in many matters hesitating and defective, or even wrong.

Nevertheless, he claimed, "the historical faith of the Church has always been that all the affirmations of Scripture of all kinds, whether of spiritual doctrine or duty, or of physical or historical fact, or of psychological or philosophical principle, are without any error when the *ipsissima verba* of the original autographs are ascertained and interpreted in their natural and intended sense." Hodge proceeded to distinguish between, on the one hand, an exactness of statement and absolute literalness to which the Bible never pretends, and on the other hand, that accuracy which secures the correctness of its affirmations. For all its qualifications, however, Hodge's statement of the doctrine of inspiration was not calculated to give much comfort to the advocates of a thoroughgoing historical criticism. Rather it sharply circumscribed the rights of criticism and severely limited the sphere in which it could legitimately operate.[44]

The leader of the critical camp was Charles A. Briggs, who authored two of the four essays emanating from this side in the exchange appearing in the *Presbyterian Review*. Briggs amplified his views in his 1889 book, *Whither? A Theological Question for the Times*. While himself claiming to be orthodox in theology and faithful to the Presbyterian standards, Briggs accused some theologians (Hodge and Warfield were clearly in mind) of introducing innovative and false teaching with regard to scripture. This false teaching both went beyond the Westminster standards and went contrary to them. The extra-confessional formulations, in Briggs's view, included the doctrines of verbal inspiration, which practically denied the inspiration of any translation of the original, and inerrancy, which rested confidence in the inspiration of scripture on the ability to disprove alleged errors in the Bible. Both these formulations, he argued, had been overturned by biblical criticism. Those positions of the Princetonians which Briggs considered contra-confessional were again two in number. First, he accused the Hodge-Warfield camp of basing the authority of scripture on external evidence, including the testimony of the early church to the canon. This procedure encounters problems regarding the disputed books of the canon, and at any rate tends to ground faith on fallible human judgment. Second, Briggs claimed that his opponents were basing the canonicity of scripture on authenticity of authorship. But it cannot be proven that Christ and the apostles authenticated all the Old Testament books, nor that all the New Testament books were of apostolic origin or superintendence. To insist on this doctrine, Briggs charged, will require its adherents to reject historical criticism and its conclusions. The implications of the Hodge-Warfield position, with its prejudgment on questions of authorship and authenticity, seemed to Briggs to demand nothing less than the repudiation of biblical criticism and its findings. For one who had already rejected traditional theories of authorship of several Old Testament books, this was unacceptable and resulted in the campaign which he mounted against the Princeton position of which *Whither* was a part.[45]

As the two sides hardened into their respective positions, conflict became difficult to avoid. The irresistible force of historical criticism was meeting the immovable object of inspired scripture. Briggs and his allies believed the new criticism offered great and positive benefits for the understanding of the Bible. The Princeton theologians and those allied with them were certainly not afraid of critical scholarship, and attempted to meet it on its own ground. But they did not believe it contained the whole truth, they were apprehensive over its effects in the church, and they sharply restricted the range of its legitimate operation. In the short run – during the 1890s – and on the surface, the conservatives appeared victorious, but at a deeper level and over the succeeding two decades the forces of historical criticism came to prevail, both in the churches and in American culture.[46]

The Case of William Newton Clarke

A contemporary account of the passage from the old view of the Bible to the new is provided by a prominent liberal, the Baptist theologian William Newton Clarke. Published in 1909 near the end of his life, *Sixty Years with the Bible* chronicles Clarke's own pilgrimage from childhood to maturity. Clarke acknowledged the momentous nature of both the times in which he had lived and the change he had experienced: he was one who had "lived through the crisis of the Nineteenth Century" and "passed through the revolution to which my generation was born." His goal in writing was to convince his readers that "for reasons that are sound and by processes that are worthy one man has passed over from the old view of the Bible to the new."[47]

Clarke proceeded to relate, decade by decade, how his views had changed. Although he inherited from family and church the common reverence for the Bible which regarded its inspiration as rendering its authority absolute, its theological declarations normative, and its statements without error or contradiction, he gradually began to adopt the new viewpoint. As a child, in the 1850s, he was exposed to the view that the Bible contains unresolvable contradictions, and he later believed that during this period he was unconsciously accommodating his view of Genesis 1 to modern science. During the 1860s, as a seminary student, he came to reject the doctrine of verbal inspiration, identifying it with mechanical dictation. While serving in his first pastorate he encountered Herbert Spencer's concept of evolutionary development and was impressed by its massiveness and simplicity. He began to question the criterion of apostolic authorship as a test of inspiration, and was led as well to a realization of what it meant for the Bible to be a translated book, and "a genuinely historical book, having its rise and habitat in the human world, . . . and to be understood in the light of its historical origins, intentions, and development." The decade of the seventies saw Clarke reject the inerrancy of the Bible because he could not reconcile its apparently conflicting views of the return of Christ. He began to develop a theological method which was not dependent on the express statements of scripture but rather on its universal ethical principles and its revelation of the character of God as displayed in Christ. During the 1880s the progress of his views continued in the same vein. In a commentary on Mark which he authored, he acknowledged contradictions in the Gospels, but he held that they do not hinder the documents' witness to Christ. He was exposed to and adopted critical views of the Old Testament, and embraced the revised view of the nature of God and of the development of Old Testament religion which they allowed. At the opening of the last decade of the nineteenth century Clarke was made a professor of theology, which gave him opportunity to commit to writing his own theological system and to inculcate his beliefs and his method of handling the Bible in a rising generation of theological students. His method did not change as he entered the twentieth century, but he was rather confirmed in the direction he had chosen.[48]

At the end of his narrative, however, Clarke did address a problem which revealed that even he did not regard biblical criticism as being without difficulties for the Christian believer. The question was that of the authority of the Bible: how could it be maintained in the face of historical scholarship? Did not biblical criticism undermine even a general confidence in the religious teaching of the Bible, such as Clarke advocated, fully as much as it did the traditional doctrines of inspiration and infallibility? Clarke acknowledged that the chief danger regarding the Bible was that it would be studied merely in a critical manner, with neither regard for nor confidence in its religious value. In response, Clarke offered no objective grounds for confidence in the Bible; an appeal to common experience was the best he could do. While he allowed that there would always be open questions regarding the Bible, yet he maintained that "the question of its religious value is not an open question." Why? It is a fact "established by long human experience" that the Bible is "the book of divine religion," and "our guide to Jesus, to God, and to life divine." It seems that for Clarke, the Christian faith as well as its center of authority was becoming detached from the realm of objective history – where criticism could do its destructive work – and safely isolated in the realm of human experience. His approach sidestepped the questions posed by proponents of a more radical and more consistently historical criticism.[49]

Regardless of the problems inherent in his approach, Clarke exercised a broad influence. He taught at Colgate Seminary for nearly two decades, from 1890 to 1908. His *Outline of Christian Theology* (1898) was the first systematic presentation of liberalism in America; by 1914 it was in its twentieth printing. And his influence undoubtedly reflected what he declared to be true regarding his own experience of biblical criticism: "I saw plainly that the Bible would not come out of this crucible as it went in." But others, gazing into the same crucible, were coming to different conclusions. William Newton Clarke died in 1912, the year of J. Gresham Machen's public emergence.[50]

PART TWO

THE FORMATIVE YEARS, 1881–1906

CHAPTER 3

MACHEN'S EARLY TRAINING AND
THEOLOGICAL EDUCATION, 1881–1905

J. Gresham Machen's mature life was conditioned by a fierce intellectual and spiritual struggle which occupied the years of his early manhood. For an indefinite period beginning before his student days in Germany and continuing for some years after his return to teach at Princeton – roughly the first decade of the 1900s – young Machen was engaged in a personal battle over the validity of historic supernatural Christianity. In later years, after reaching firmer intellectual ground, he was far from reticent about this experience. He spoke of it repeatedly, believing that the story of his own pilgrimage might help others who were engaged in the same struggle. Thus in 1927 he told a London audience gathered under the auspices of the Bible League of Great Britain: "there was a time when I was greatly troubled in my faith by the defection of the modern world from Jesus of Nazareth as he is set forth in the Scriptures. But my faith is no longer so much troubled by the argument from modern authority...." In 1932 the motive of providing a helpful example to others led him to write an autobiographical sketch for the volume *Contemporary American Theology: Theological Autobiographies*. His experience, he believed, might show "how it is that a considerable number of persons have been led to resist the current of the age and to hold with mind and heart to that religion of supernatural redemption which has always hitherto been known as Christianity." Machen's early intellectual struggle thus loomed large in his own thinking, exercising such a decisive influence on his mature ideology and values that it warrants full and careful consideration.[1]

Family Life and Classical Training
Machen's upbringing certainly predisposed him toward an orthodox view of the Bible and of Christianity. His parents were both of Southern stock and Presbyterian heritage. Ned B. Stonehouse, Machen's biographer, aptly summarizes Machen's home life in the comment

that upon his birth in 1881 he "entered a home of devout Christian faith, of a high level of culture and social standing, and of a considerable degree of prosperity." His father, Arthur W. Machen (1827-1915), had his roots in the Washington, D.C. region of Virginia, and was the son of a clerk to the Secretary of the United States Senate. Arthur received his professional training at Harvard Law School, and after graduation, out of preference for Southern culture, settled in Baltimore in 1853 to establish a law practice. After a few lean years he achieved a measure of financial prosperity, and he continued as a member of the Maryland bar until his death in 1915. In 1870 Arthur met Mary Gresham (1849-1931) of Macon, Georgia, who was visiting in Baltimore at the time, and the two were married in 1873. Mary – who was universally known as Minnie – was the daughter of a prominent Macon attorney and churchman. She received her education in her home town at Wesleyan College, from which she graduated in 1865. While in Macon she taught Sunday School at the Presbyterian church, having fallen heir to her father's commitment to that ecclesiastical tradition. In Macon, Minnie was the close friend of both the sister and the wife of poet Sidney Lanier, and her contacts with Lanier himself were extensive after both of them had moved to Baltimore.[2]

As the contact with Lanier suggests, Arthur and Minnie Machen moved in the higher cultural, intellectual, and literary circles of Baltimore after they were settled there together in 1873. Minnie's aunt, Mrs. (Sarah) Edgeworth Bird, who also lived there, was a patron of the arts and of refined culture, and the Machens were incorporated into her social world. Besides Lanier, they counted among their intimate friends many who were associated with the newly-founded Johns Hopkins University (1876), including President Daniel Coit Gilman and classicist Professor Basil L. Gildersleeve.[3]

The Machens' church affiliation in Baltimore reflected their Southern sympathies. They were members of the Franklin Street Presbyterian Church, which was connected with the Presbyterian Church in the US, commonly known as the Southern Presbyterian Church. Besides participating in the regular worship services of the church, they were also active in various official capacities. Arthur was elected a trustee in 1880 and an elder in 1893, while Minnie served for several years as president of the Benevolent Society which gave support to the Presbyterian seminary in Richmond, Virginia.[4]

J. Gresham Machen spoke in appreciative terms of the influence of his parents on his own religious development. In 1932 he wrote concerning his father and mother: "from them I learned what Christianity is and how it differs from certain modern substitutes. I also learned that Christian conviction can go hand in hand with a broad outlook upon life and with the pursuit of learning." Machen characterized his father as "a profoundly Christian man" whose experience was quiet and deep, "not of the emotional or pietistical type," nor was it culturally backward. Arthur Machen, according to his son, exhibited none of the legalistic or ascetic mentality which marred some Christians' enjoyment of God's good gifts and the wonders of his world, leaving their minds impoverished. Rather, he was a man of broad experience who possessed a large and discriminating appetite for reading – he was familiar with Latin, Greek, English, and French literature – and an appreciation for beauty, especially as found in the fifteenth-century books which he loved to collect. Also characteristic was his faithfulness in Christian service, as reflected in his regular attendance at public worship and in the performance of his duties as an elder in the Franklin Street Presbyterian Church. In him were thus combined "true learning and true piety," a perhaps idealized portrait which nonetheless may reveal something of the values transmitted in the Machen home.[5]

By far the greater influence on Machen's early religious life was exercised by his mother. His description reveals her as a person of broad sympathies and wide reading, who possessed a great love for nature. It was at her knee that he gained such a thorough knowledge of the Bible that by age twelve, in his estimation, his familiarity with the scriptures surpassed that of the average theological student of a later generation. At a tender age also he had committed to memory the Westminster Shorter Catechism – its 107 questions and answers embodying the heart of seventeenth-century Puritan divinity – and could repeat it perfectly. Machen bore youthful testimony to the nature of the home training he received when, at age seven, he wrote to his mother in Macon, where she was attending to her own mother who was in failing health. He told her not only of his playtime activities, but also of the Bible reading he had accomplished, his recitation of the Catechism, and his father's reading to him from *Pilgrim's Progress*. Machen enjoyed an unusually close relationship with his mother for the duration of her life, and he credits her with helping him through his times of doubt, she herself having experienced similar intellectual struggles.[6]

Minnie Machen's literary and biblical interests found expression in her book published in 1903, *The Bible in Browning*. The volume displays an intimate acquaintance with the works of the English poet Robert Browning (1812-1889) and a thorough knowledge of the Bible. In an introductory essay of eighty pages she discussed the topic in a broad way, arguing that "many of Browning's poems cannot be thoroughly comprehended without an acquaintance with the Scriptures of the Old and New Testaments and their teachings on 'what man is to believe concerning God and what duty God requires of man'" (her citation here is from the Shorter Catechism). She argued further that Browning was a Christian believer. The bulk of the work consists of a series of extracts from Browning's "The Ring and the Book," representing biblical quotations, allusions, or references. Over 500 such references are arranged in scriptural order, with the corresponding biblical passages printed beneath Browning's words. Minnie Machen's book received favorable notice by Professor Gildersleeve in the *American Journal of Philology*.[7]

John Gresham Machen was born on 28 July 1881 in Baltimore. He enjoyed intimate and affectionate relationships with both his father and mother, as well as with his older brother, Arthur, Jr. (whom he called "Arly"), and younger brother, Tom. Like his parents, young Gresham was an avid reader, his tastes ranging from *Pilgrim's Progress* to a biography of Alexander the Great. During childhood his formal education was conducted at the University School for Boys, a private institution from which he graduated in 1898. The curriculum was strongly classical, requiring work in Latin by Machen's eleventh year of age and Greek by his fourteenth year. He consistently ranked at the top of his class. Other interests and activities which marked his boyhood and youth included music lessons, attending baseball games, playing tennis, bicycling, and family holidays in Virginia or Macon. The family often spent summers in the White Mountains of New Hampshire (where Gresham acquired a love for the mountains and for mountain-climbing) or in Seal Harbor, Maine.[8]

Machen enrolled in the three-year undergraduate program at Johns Hopkins University in the fall of 1898. He was awarded a scholarship on the basis of his scores on the entrance examinations, which placed him once again at the head of his class. At Hopkins he continued to pursue classical studies, taking further work in the Latin and Greek languages and literature, with considerable emphasis as well on rhetoric and English literature. Other subjects included French and German, comparative philology, economics, history, and philosophy. Machen led his class in academic honors and was elected to Phi Beta Kappa in April 1901.[9]

After experiencing the delights of a trip to Europe during the summer of 1901, the twenty-year-old Machen returned to Johns Hopkins in October in order to spend a year of graduate study under Professor Gildersleeve. Basil L. Gildersleeve (1831-1924) was the foremost classicist of his generation, having come to Johns Hopkins from the University of Virginia at the invitation of President Gilman. After his arrival at Hopkins, he had become the founding editor of the *American Journal of Philology*, a position which he occupied for forty years. Machen immensely valued the opportunity to work with a scholar of such distinction, and maintained personal contact with Gildersleeve until the latter's death in 1924. Adding to Gildersleeve's attraction for Machen was his character as a fellow-Southerner and his connection with the Franklin Street Presbyterian Church in Baltimore.[10]

Machen valued his time at Johns Hopkins for another reason, namely, the intellectual atmosphere. It was there, he said, that he "obtained contact with the rigidly scientific method" of historical study, and with the "contempt for mere clap-trap" which characterized the university at that time. And while contemplating the application of "modern scientific methods of research" to ancient documents, it occurred to him that there was a body of literature of vastly greater importance than even Homer or Plato to which he could give his attention. Thus he turned in 1902 to the study of the New Testament at Princeton Theological Seminary.[11]

Princeton Theological Seminary
Historically speaking, when J. Gresham Machen enrolled at Princeton Theological Seminary in the fall of 1902, he entered an anachronism. Princeton was the most visible and the most powerful institutional expression of a mode of thinking that was in decline everywhere in America. The rational and evangelical Calvinism of Princeton represented a Reformed perspective which seemed at one time to dominate American Christianity. But by 1900 this was no longer the

case. The Congregational remnants of Puritanism had largely slipped into Unitarianism and liberalism. The Episcopal Church had long been latitudinarian. Methodism had never been very strong on theology, and such theology as it possessed was anti-Calvinistic in emphasis. Presbyterians had to tolerate New School and Old School partisans (who were revivalistic and anti-revivalistic, respectively), with the New School being more open to accommodations in traditional doctrine and practice. Democratic and individualistic currents in nineteenth-century American life virtually swamped the Baptists and gave rise to such new religious expressions as the Christian Church-Disciples of Christ movement. By the mid-nineteenth century, as Winthrop Hudson has pointed out, evangelical Protestantism could be defined almost wholly in Methodist terms: an emphasis on free-will and Christian perfection was combined with a general de-emphasis of Christian doctrine and theological precision. Historical consciousness was also making itself felt, often mediated through theological liberalism and biblical criticism. This broadly-based defection from the traditional commitments of the Reformed position left Princeton standing virtually alone at the beginning of the twentieth century.[12]

Princeton indeed shared many elements of its outlook with nineteenth-century American culture and with other contemporary manifestations of evangelical Christianity. But the way in which it combined its distinctive emphases and gave forceful expression to the whole was unique in its day. Foremost among Princeton's distinctives was its commitment to Reformed confessionalism. For the Princetonians, Calvinism – as propounded by Calvin himself, the Westminster standards, and the seventeenth-century Reformed theologians – was the sum and substance of the Bible's teaching and of true religion itself. This attitude was most clearly exemplified by Benjamin B. Warfield, Machen's theology teacher, who wrote in 1904 that "Calvinism is just religion in its purity." Calvinism, he contended, is "that type of thought in which there comes to its rights the truly religious attitude of utter dependence on God and humble trust in his mercy alone for salvation."[13]

A second element of the Princeton theology, which has received much recent scholarly attention, was Princeton's commitment to a high view of the inspiration and authority of the Bible. Charles Hodge's position on scripture was simply a refinement of the position of

Princeton's first professor, Archibald Alexander. The process of refinement continued in the cooperative work of A. A. Hodge and B. B. Warfield, who jointly authored the definitive statement of the Princeton doctrine, their essay entitled "Inspiration," first published in 1881, and described above (pp. 48–51). The central affirmation of the Hodge-Warfield doctrine of Scripture was that God superintended the writing of the various parts of the Bible, without compromising the individuality of its several authors, so that the Bible in its original autographs constitutes the Word of God and is without error in all that it affirms. Warfield's work over the next thirty years brought this refining process to its culmination in a series of finely-wrought essays which spelled out the implications of the Princeton doctrine. In the Presbyterian ecclesiastical battles from the 1890s to the 1920s this theological position – often called concisely "the inerrancy of the Bible" – occupied a central role. Indeed, Machen's biographer claims (with particular reference to the Briggs heresy trial, but perhaps with broader application as well) that "to say that the issue was whether the Princeton view of the Bible or a lower view of its inspiration and authority was true and constituted the official doctrine of the Presbyterian Church would not be a serious oversimplification."[14]

A third component of the Princeton mentality was its adherence to the philosophy of Scottish Common Sense Realism. The Common Sense philosophy was a product of the Enlightenment in Scotland. Its originator and major proponent was Thomas Reid (1710-1796), who attempted by his philosophy to counter the skepticism of David Hume. Reid was followed by others of varying ability, including George Campbell (1719-1796), James Beattie (1735-1803), Alexander Gerard (1728-1795), Dugald Stewart (1753-1828), and William Hamilton (1788-1856). According to Reid, common sense was a function of reason, common to all mankind, which acknowledged certain first principles. These first principles were of two kinds, the necessary and the contingent. Necessary first principles are immutable and their contrary is impossible, and include "the axioms of grammar, of logic, of mathematics, of 'taste' (aesthetics), and of morals," and "the great metaphysical principles that Hume had called in question, viz. the existence of mind and of body as the subject of conscious thoughts and of material qualities respectively, the law of causality, and the legitimacy of inferring design and intelligence in the cause from marks of them in the effect." Contingent first principles are changeable and may have a beginning and end, and include "mental states given to us in consciousness, and the existence of objects of consciousness, the trustworthiness of memory, personal identity, the existence and nature of external reality as testified by the senses, the freedom of the will, the ability of our 'natural faculties' to distinguish truth from error, the possession of life and rationality by our fellowmen as manifested outwardly in their countenances, voices, and gestures, the propriety of paying a certain amount of deference to human testimony and to authority in opinion, and the instinctive belief in the uniformity of nature." Such first principles were considered to be built into the structure of the human mind.[15] This philosophy was brought to America by John Witherspoon and was spread through the writings of its Scottish expounders and their American adherents. From Archibald Alexander, Princeton Seminary's first professor in 1812, to Warfield, whose death in 1921 may be regarded as marking the passing of the old Princeton, the Princetonians relied on the intellectual foundation provided by this philosophy. Common Sense Realism gave to the Princeton theologians a basis for assuming a universal epistemology based on sense perceptions and intuitive knowledge common to all humans. It fostered confidence in empirical and inductive means of arriving at truth. It promoted a conviction of the necessity and validity of scientific investigation. It supported a conception of truth as an objective, unified, and universal entity, accessible and applicable to all men, all times, and all places. The Princetonians have come under heavy criticism from some quarters for their attachment to the Common Sense philosophy. Yet, as Noll observes, they never became mere tools of this philosophy, and the countervailing influence of Reformed theology always remained strong in their thinking, with the result that their thought taken as a whole contained many elements which were inconsistent with the Common Sense perspective.[16]

One of these elements constitutes a fourth component of Princeton's outlook, its emphasis on religious experience. Alongside its commitment to the rational approach to truth embodied in common sense realism was an equally fervent, if not as fully evident, commitment to the necessity of personal piety, vital religious experience, and the supernatural work of the Holy Spirit in the Christian's life. The Princeton theologians fell not one whit behind the most fervent revivalists in this respect, although the kinds of experience they encouraged may have differed rather widely. The real question regarding the Princetonians is not whether this element was present in their thought, but how it fit in with their other philosophical commitments.[17]

Machen's Princeton Years, 1902-1905

The decision to enter Princeton Seminary was not one that Machen reached easily. In the first place, the Southern Presbyterian Church, with which the Franklin Street congregation was affiliated, maintained its own seminary in Richmond, Virginia. Given his Southern sympathies and his mother's labors in behalf of this school, Machen might have been expected to be more naturally drawn to this institution. In the second place, although Machen may have been intellectually interested in biblical and theological studies, he was extremely unsure that he would enter the Christian ministry. So great was his uncertainty about his professional calling that he spent the summer of 1902 at the University of Chicago studying banking and international law, contemplating a career in the field of economics. That he did choose Princeton was probably due to several factors. These included the influence of his pastor at the Franklin Street Church, Harris E. Kirk, who encouraged him to go to Princeton; his discovery of the fact that he would not be required to come under care of the presbytery as a ministerial candidate, and therefore would have to make no commitment to enter the ministry; and the consideration that Princeton was indeed not connected with his own church body, and thus would involve perhaps less commitment to a ministerial career. But ranking above all these considerations, in Stonehouse's opinion, was the presence at Princeton of Francis L. Patton, the newly-installed president of the institution, a long-time friend of the Machen family and frequent guest in their home, and a man for whom Machen possessed the greatest respect and admiration.[18]

At the beginning of the twentieth century the faculty at Princeton was conscious of an unbroken continuity with the long tradition of the seminary, especially as found in the theology of Charles Hodge. The Princeton theologians were also aware of the new forms of opposition to its position and to evangelical Christianity in general. There was thus a new sense of urgency and militancy which charged the atmosphere at the institution. The faculty members who most influenced Machen, including Patton, reflected the realities of the new intellectual climate. Francis L. Patton occupied the newly created office of president of the seminary, a post he assumed in 1902 and held until his retirement in 1913. An 1865 graduate of the seminary, Patton had served in various pastorates and as professor of theology at the Presbyterian seminary in Chicago and had gained notoriety in the 1870s as the prosecutor in the heresy trial of Presbyterian minister David Swing. He was appointed to the Princeton faculty in 1881, occupying an endowed chair as Professor of the Relations of Philosophy and Science to the Christian Religion. In 1888 Patton was named President of Princeton College, which during his tenure became Princeton University and inaugurated a graduate program. In 1902 Patton took up the less arduous task of president of the seminary, though he continued to lecture at the university until his retirement. Having often lodged in the Machen home during preaching trips to Baltimore, Patton was well known to young Machen when they both came to Princeton in 1902. Machen later testified to Patton's helpfulness in his intellectual struggles: "Never did a doubter and a struggler have a better friend than I did in this wonderfully eloquent and brilliant man."[19]

A second influential figure for Machen at Princeton was the theologian Benjamin B. Warfield. Warfield was a graduate of Princeton College and Seminary, and had studied in Europe and taught New Testament at Western Seminary in Allegheny, Pennsylvania, before returning to Princeton as Professor of Didactic and Polemic Theology in 1887. Warfield's learning was massive and encyclopedic but unostentatious, and it took a few years for Machen to come to a full appreciation of Warfield's gifts and theological position. But such a growing appreciation allowed Warfield's influence to be more profound and more enduring than that of Patton. When Warfield died in 1921, by which time he had been Machen's colleague on the faculty for fifteen years, Machen wrote to his own mother that Warfield was "the greatest man I have known." Aspects of Warfield's thought which were reflected in Machen's intellectual development were the confidence that scientific inquiry would serve to vindicate evangelical Christianity and the Princeton view of the Bible, and the conviction that Calvinism was supremely the system of truth taught in the Bible and constituted that expression of Christianity which was most capable of reasoned defense.[20]

In Machen's field of New Testament, according to his own testimony, the presence of William Park Armstrong on the Princeton faculty was a great encouragement to him. Only a few years Machen's senior and a fellow Southerner, Armstrong took a special interest in Machen, guided him through times of intellectual turmoil, and eventually became his most intimate friend as well as colleague after Machen joined the New Testament Department. Armstrong had graduated from Princeton University and Seminary in the 1890s, spent two years in New Testament study in Germany, and joined G. T. Purves in the New Testament department in 1899. Machen regarded him as a scientific scholar of the highest caliber, an estimate which perhaps finds support in the fact of Armstrong's appointment as department head in 1900 upon Purves's resignation, and in his elevation to a full professorship in 1903 at the age of twenty-nine. Machen valued Armstrong's scholarship not only for its scientific method but also for its philosophical sophistication, since he possessed, in Machen's view, a fine grasp of the philosophical positions underlying the various schools of New Testament scholarship. In spite of their widely differing temperaments, Armstrong being reserved while Machen was aggressive, the two formed a close friendship which continued for the next three decades.[21]

Machen's three years as a student at Princeton could hardly have been more pleasing to him. He dined with the Benham Club, an eating club which provided much of the context for his social life, and he formed many lifetime friendships among its members. Machen's gregarious instincts were cultivated by the social atmosphere at Princeton, and during his student days he was already known by the nickname "Das," this being the definite article associated with the German word *Mädchen*. According to fellow Benhamite James B. Brown, whose later testimony is summarized by Stonehouse, Machen "was known among the students for his extraordinary love of walking and railroad trains and hearty good humor rather than for his scholarship." He continued to enjoy bicycling and tennis, and became a devoted fan of the Princeton University athletic teams, especially football, and sometimes journeyed to other cities to see the games.[22]

Machen pursued his play with vigor, and he approached his scholarly pursuits in the same way. Besides following the regular curriculum at the seminary, Machen attended selected series of lectures at Princeton University, including those on philosophy by A. T. Ormond and on American constitutional history by the new president of the university, Woodrow Wilson. The Wilsons were long-time friends of the Machen family, with ties in Southern culture, in Presbyterianism, and in academia – Woodrow was an 1886 Ph.D. from Johns Hopkins. Machen was an occasional guest in the Wilson home. But of course Machen's primary intellectual atmosphere was that provided by the seminary. His first year there seems to have been uneventful, and afterwards he spent the summer of 1903 at the University of Chicago poring over the Greek text of the classical poet Pindar under the guidance of Professor Paul Shorey (1857-1934), one of the foremost American classicists of the day. While at Chicago, he also engaged in work on the German language.[23]

Machen's second or middler year at Princeton was marked by three significant events which occurred near the end of the second term. First, pressure was put upon him by his pastor and by an uncle to present himself as a candidate for the ministry and come under care of the local presbytery, the meeting of which was scheduled for April 1904. Machen, with the support of his parents, resisted the pressure, unwilling to make the commitment for reasons not made clear in letters to his family. He did indicate, however, that he was not comfortable with his indecision. He wrote to his mother in early April, "it isn't mere trifling that leads me to shrink back, for I venture to say that it gives no one more pain than it gives me myself." In light of Machen's later statement that he had been facing intellectual doubts for "years" before he undertook studies in Germany, one wonders whether already in seminary his hesitation concerning entering the Christian ministry might have been occasioned by such considerations.[24]

Two other events in the spring of 1904, probably related to one another, give some indication of the impression Machen was making on the seminary faculty. First, he won the Middler Prize in New Testament Exegesis for 1903-04. This prize of $100 was awarded to Machen for the best paper on the exegesis of John 1:1-18. Machen's work on his paper occupied him for the two months from the beginning of February to the first of April, when the paper was due. Shortly afterward, President Patton approached him with the proposal that he consider preparing himself for a professorship in New Testament Greek at the seminary. In mentioning the paper to his family, Machen characteristically made light of its merits, and he failed to mention at all the proposition by Patton. These events do make clear, however, his strong interest and considerable abilities in the field of New Testament scholarship, and the recognition which those abilities were gaining from the Princeton faculty.[25]

The summer following Machen's second year at Princeton he spent in Germany, attempting to improve his command of the German language. He lived for a while in the small town of Sondershausen, where he was compelled to converse in German, and also in the university town of Göttingen, where he became familiar with German academic life and to which he later was to return as a student. He concluded the summer with a bicycle tour of Germany, amounting to several hundred miles, and then sailed for the United States early in September.[26]

During his third and final year as a student at Princeton, Machen entered the competition to win a fellowship in the field of New Testament. The fellowship, involving a financial subsidy for a year of graduate study, was to be awarded to the author of the best thesis on the assigned topic, "A Critical Discussion of the New Testament Account of the Virgin Birth of Jesus." Machen completed work on his thesis near the end of March 1905, and wrote to his mother, "My paper is finished after a fashion – such a wretched fashion that I am ashamed to hand the thing in." He wrote to her again on 2 April, indicating that he had turned in the paper the day before, and mentioned how much work, worry, and bother it had caused him. "If it were only a little less disgraceful," he claimed, "I should enjoy more the relief of having it off hand." The faculty, however, did not seem to share his deprecatory attitude, for within a few weeks he was writing to inform his mother that Professor Armstrong had told him that he was recommending Machen for the New Testament fellowship. The same letter mentioned that Machen was to receive the Bachelor of Divinity degree, a distinction not awarded to all graduates, since some merely received "ordinary diplomas"; the degree required extra work during the three-year curriculum, or an extra year's study, and usually accompanied the New Testament fellowship (thirty of the forty-nine men graduated in 1905 were awarded the higher recognition). Machen's paper was also granted the additional and unusual distinction of being published in the *Princeton Theological Review*, where it appeared in two parts, in October 1905 and January 1906.[27]

Machen's First Published Work: An Analysis

Machen's paper on the virgin birth is an impressive piece of work, especially for a scholar only twenty-three years of age. Running to a

total of some seventy-five pages in the *Review*, the two installments
of the essay subjected to a methodical analysis differing approaches
to the New Testament narratives of the birth of Jesus – with particular
attention being given to the question of the historicity of Jesus' alleged
virginal conception and birth. The first article took up the supposition
that the birth narratives in the first two chapters of Matthew and of
Luke were founded on historical events, and Machen attempted to
determine whether the peculiar features of the narratives can be
satisfactorily explained on this basis, and whether they are consistent
with the rest of the Gospel record and with the New Testament as a
whole. Machen concluded with a cautious affirmative: "the objections
against the trustworthiness of the accounts are not unanswerable." In
the second article, Machen dealt with the hypothesis that the birth
narratives had their origin in something other than factual events, and
he evaluated various attempts to explain the genesis of the ideas and
their incorporation into the Gospel accounts. These explanations fail,
he argued, because they cannot show that the crucial passages
incorporate interpolations or constitute later additions to the text.
Furthermore, theories which trace the origin of the idea of a virgin
birth to the Jewish mind or to pagan territory are not convincing – the
former on psychological grounds, the latter on literary. Most of the
scholarly literature which Machen cited was in the German language,
including both monographs and articles in theological journals.[28]

This essay, Machen's first published work, is significant in several
ways. It reveals Machen's early view of the Bible, displays his
presuppositions and modes of argumentation in handling critical
schools of thought, and provides a means for assessing his promise as
a young scholar – a means of which the Princeton faculty clearly
availed themselves. It is also noteworthy that the subject matter of
the essay, the virgin birth of Jesus, which was to constitute a major
focus of Machen's scholarly work for the rest of his career, was not a
topic of his own choosing but one assigned for the fellowship
competition. Because of these factors the essay is worthy of careful
consideration as Machen's initial public excursion into the field of
New Testament scholarship.

The methodological presuppositions on which Machen based his
work reflect an awareness that he was taking a generally conservative
stance. In a section which spelled out what he conceived as
"fairmindedness" with regard to the issue at hand, he offered two

objections to the assumptions commonly made by biblical scholars. First, he objected to the identification of an "apologetic" stance – one which defended the conservative position – with the "unscientific" or "dishonest." To characterize the conservative position in this way was to prejudge the issue apart from the evidence. Second, he objected to judging any issue taken out of organic connection with its broader context. Thus the birth narratives must be considered as portions of the first and third Gospels, which recent investigation had shown to be of very ancient origin and of "very considerable historical value." He thought it "as great an offense against scientific method to refuse to hold presuppositions founded upon proven fact as it is to insist upon holding presuppositions founded upon fancy." These comments also incidentally reveal Machen's conviction that historical scholarship is an endeavor to which "scientific" standards can and should be applied.[29]

The course of Machen's argument displays many traits which became characteristic of his later work. He gladly acknowledged whatever truth might be found in positions which were fundamentally different from his own. For the sake of argument, he often granted the premises of an opposing position, only to show that its conclusions were not necessitated by those premises. He also skillfully played off against one another the conflicting conclusions reached by different schools of critical opinion. Machen tended to be quite cautious in formulating historical judgments – he habitually spoke in terms of possibility, probability, likelihood, plausibility, and the like, thus acknowledging that absolute certainty is difficult to attain in historical scholarship. And he sought to show the logical motivations behind the positions taken by other scholars on matters of detail in the New Testament text, subtly demonstrating that their arguments were in fact necessitated by their conclusions or by the general position adopted rather than by the evidence itself.

This last point is related to the intriguing question of Machen's willingness to use presuppositional argumentation. In light of the alleged strength of Scottish common sense philosophy in Machen's intellectual heritage, it might be expected that he would argue entirely on the basis of the hard evidence rather than on the level of fundamental philosophical or theological commitments. Yet the latter mode of argument forms a prominent part of Machen's discussion. For example, in arguing against the objection that there was in Christianity

no adequate occasion for so miraculous an event as the virgin birth,
Machen countered in two ways. First, he distinguished between the
actual importance of an event and the human understanding of its
importance, the latter of which may itself be inadequate. Then he
offered the claim that there was indeed an adequate occasion for the
virgin birth, in the person of Jesus himself:

> If we admit that Christ was a supernatural person, we do not have to
> be able to explain the special reason for every one of His miracles in
> order to believe that the miracles really happened. The virgin birth,
> being connected with Christ, has an adequate occasion.

He concluded the paragraph with the statement, "Surely the
Incarnation, if it was real, was an event stupendous enough to give
rise to even the greatest of miracles." Such a line of argumentation
assumes the truthfulness of the traditional Christian view of Jesus,
and deals with ideological opponents on that basis, thus setting up
one conceptual system against another.[30]

Again, near the end of the second article, Machen argued in a
similar fashion:

> If Jesus was really divine, then we can say that probably there was
> something miraculous about his birth. Starting from that position, the
> most probable conclusion is that the canonical infancy narratives
> correctly inform us as to what that 'something' was.

This approach once more presupposes the orthodox theological
understanding of Jesus. And in his summary of the entire discussion,
Machen reached down to the level of basic philosophical assumptions
when he concluded – perhaps surprisingly – that "on the basis of a
narrowly historical and critical examination of this one account, we
can make no decision at all. The decision depends upon our point of
view with regard to the miraculous in general." Thus, he argued, for
someone who is predisposed against the miraculous, no amount of
evidence will be convincing; but for those who believe that Jesus
rose from the dead, "there is no reason to doubt that he was born of a
virgin." But ultimately, Machen contended as he closed his treatment,
the decision lay in a different realm, that of ethics. One's position
would be decisively conditioned by whether one acknowledged the
problem of human guilt – guilt which, by implication, was occasioned
by sin and which placed man in need of forgiveness and redemption

by supernatural means. It is striking that Machen, who received his theological grounding in the evidentialist atmosphere of Princeton, should argue thus. Such presuppositional argumentation may have been more common in the Princeton tradition than is usually recognized; at any rate, it is clear that Machen, having just completed three years of study at Princeton, was no stranger to it.[31]

Most significant for the present study is what this early essay reveals about Machen's view of the Bible. He did not appeal to any doctrine of inspiration or inerrancy in his treatment of historical and literary matters; he argued each question on its merits alone, on the basis of the evidence or lack thereof. Indeed, at one point he was willing to consider, at least for the sake of argument, the possibility of historical error in the text of Luke, namely, in Luke's mention of a census during the governorship of Quirinius (Luke 2:2). Even if mention of the census is considered the result of a "blunder," he claimed, "we need not necessarily give up the general trustworthiness of the account. It all depends on the nature of the blunder." Although he concluded that the question could not be resolved on the basis of the evidence available, apparently the presence of an error in the text of Luke's birth narrative would not, for Machen, have destroyed the general trustworthiness of the account as a whole.[32]

Also worthy of note is Machen's view of the accommodation of divine revelation to the ancient mind. In at least three instances in this essay he argued his case on the supposition of such an accommodation or on the lack of sophistication of those receiving divine revelation. Concerning the objection raised by some scholars that Mary's puzzlement over certain events or sayings following the birth of Jesus revealed her unawareness of the angelic announcement, Machen replied that while "a modern scientific mind might have had the whole thing reasoned out beforehand on the basis of the data already given [in Luke 1:30-38]," yet "the people of those days were not scientific," and therefore Mary's amazement or failure to understand was not unnatural. In another instance, some scholars had imagined that a serious difficulty was presented by the seemingly contradictory claims of the biblical text that, on the one hand, Jesus was the heir of the Davidic promises because he was the son of Joseph and, on the other, that Jesus was not begotten by Joseph. Machen seemed to think that the answer lay in the Jewish concern for putative genealogy rather than actual descent; thus the Davidic origin of Joseph,

Jesus' legal or adoptive father, would have been the question of vital interest, and since Jesus was the legal heir of Joseph, he was therefore a legitimate heir to the throne of David. In support of this line of reasoning, Machen remarked that "the promises were made not to modern persons, but to Jews, and the promise is fulfilled if the fulfillment corresponds to the expectations of those to whom the promise was made." For Machen, fulfillment of the biblical word was to be expected in terms defined not by the modern scientific mentality but by ancient Jewish understanding or custom. This interpretive approach is certainly far removed from a crass or "scholastic" literalism. Finally, in response to objections regarding the delivery of revelation through angelic appearances, Machen countered that in light of the simple, pious nature of the people to whom such revelations came, "the angels do not seem so unworthy of a God who adapts His revelations to the needs and capacities of His creatures." In light of such statements it may be questioned whether the notion of the accommodation of divine revelation to human limitations was so absent from the Princeton tradition as some have suggested.[33]

In another place, Machen made some comments which reveal his conception of the literary methods used by the biblical writers. He was discussing the apparent discrepancies or inconsistencies between the birth narratives of Matthew and Luke, and the possibility of combining them into a single harmonious account. Machen asked, "Are the narratives such as to preclude the view that each author used his sources faithfully in the main, though, here and there, in working up the narrative, he may have used terms of expression which he would not have used if he had known more?" This question involves several significant assumptions or arguments. First, it assumes that the biblical authors engaged in research and pursued their writing much as would be done in producing any historical narrative, using existing sources. Second, it assumes (indeed, Machen's previous sentence in this context states) that the writers had access to limited material and were "ignorant" of some aspects of their subject matter. Third, it argues that the terms of expression used by the biblical writers reflect their ignorance, yet not in a way that is inconsistent with the possibility of harmonizing their accounts. After posing this question Machen proceeded to outline a plausible scenario describing how the particular narratives of Matthew and Luke could have come into being.

He concluded with the modest suggestion that ". . . perhaps some of the difficulties may be due to our lack of knowledge." The line of reasoning that Machen pursued here suggests that whatever his view of biblical inspiration at this time in his life, it was not inconsistent with the full working of historical forces, with the personal idiosyncrasies or circumstances of the authors, and with common methods of literary production. His was a view of the Bible firmly planted in the realities of the historical context in which its writings originated. Yet at the same time, though he fully recognized the historical origination of the biblical documents, he was unwilling to accept the antisupernaturalistic assumptions which characterized the historicist outlook. This posed no problems while he was at Princeton Seminary, but it would likely be a different story at those German universities where he was soon to continue his studies.[34]

CHAPTER 4

MACHEN AT MARBURG AND GÖTTINGEN, 1905–1906

When Machen's career as a student at Princeton ended in May 1905, he was no closer to a decision regarding the Christian ministry than he had been three years earlier. He determined to use his fellowship to pursue a year of study in the field of New Testament in Germany, which, among the other benefits it would provide, also allowed him to postpone the difficult decision for several more months. Little did he suspect that the events of those months would render the decision more difficult than ever.[1]

It was in July 1905, a fortnight before his twenty-fourth birthday, that Machen departed on his third journey to Europe. He felt unworthy of so numerous opportunities for the kind of travel that many people could only long for, and he was determined to make the most of it. That meant not only studying hard, but also extending his first-hand acquaintance with the European countryside. Between the time of his arrival at Bremen late in July and his enrollment in the university at Marburg early in October, Machen engaged in an ambitious bicycle tour of Germany and Austria, with several stops along the way for one of his favorite pursuits, mountain-climbing. His letters home during this excursion are full of detailed descriptions of the towns and landscapes that he encountered, as well as of his climbing adventures. But, however fascinating may be such accounts of his travels, or the incidental details of his life, "the real story told by his letters," as Stonehouse correctly observes, "is that of his intellectual and spiritual reaction to the teaching in the university." It is fortunate for the student of Machen's life that he wrote frequently from Germany to his family, and that most of these letters have been preserved. Although his letters are not as full as one might prefer, they do allow for a general reconstruction of his intellectual pilgrimage during this period of his life. Indeed, as Stonehouse also notes, the letters written during his student days in Germany are more helpful than those from the periods before or after, for he had no other means of expressing himself to family or friends; that which might have been lost if expressed in conversation has been preserved because of the necessity to put it in writing.[2]

At Marburg
Machen spent the winter term, from October through March, at the University of Marburg. He was attracted to Marburg by the presence there of several New Testament scholars, among whom were Adolf Jülicher (1857-1938) and Johannes Weiss (1863-1914). Jülicher was the author of a major introduction to the New Testament and a monograph on the parables of Jesus. Although he rejected the supernatural and miraculous elements of the New Testament, he was judged by Machen to be "less radical" than other members of the same camp. Machen attended Jülicher's lectures on Paul's letter to the Galatians. Johannes Weiss's scholarship was undervalued by Machen while he was at Marburg, as he later acknowledged. He did not at the time "think him to be at all a scholar of the first rank"; this estimate Machen later revised, in light of Weiss's learned works on early Christianity and First Corinthians. Machen, in a letter to his brother, characterized Weiss as "anything but conservative," in contrast to his better-known father Bernhard Weiss, an eminent scholar of the previous generation for whom Machen had great esteem. Other New Testament scholars at Marburg were Rudolf Knopf, whose lectures on New Testament introduction Machen attended, and Walter Bauer (1877-1960), later a noted Greek lexicographer, who was lecturing on the Gospel of John during Machen's term there. Bauer, Machen noted, had a low opinion of the historical worth of John, and little appreciation for its religious greatness.[3]

By far the greatest impact produced on Machen by any of the Marburg professors was that of one who was not a New Testament scholar at all, but a professor of theology, Wilhelm Herrmann (1846-1922). Herrmann was an exponent – and a particularly eloquent one – of the Ritschlian or liberal theology, and in him Machen came into firsthand contact with a living and dynamic alternative to the evangelical Christianity in which he was reared. The other professors at Marburg dealt with details of exegesis and schemes of criticism, matters which Machen had shown himself, in his articles on the virgin birth, quite adept at handling. But Herrmann, starting with the liberal critical views of Jesus, dealt with man's relationship to God, and he did so in such a compelling way that it threw young Machen into a state of confusion and uncertainty which was not to be resolved for months – or even years – to come. "Herrmann," Stonehouse writes, "made Liberalism wonderfully attractive and heart-gripping. This he did not so much by the plausibility of intellectual argument as by the magnetic and overpowering force of his fervent religious spirit." In his mature years, Machen rejoiced that he had had the opportunity to hear Herrmann as perhaps the most brilliant representative of Ritschlian liberalism. At the time, however, it was no mere academic exercise that the youthful American Presbyterian was experiencing; rather, it was a profound and exciting yet disconcerting religious upheaval. And it turned his stay in Germany (as he recalled it in 1932) into "a time of struggle and of agony of soul."[4]

Something of Machen's mental and spiritual disturbance upon hearing Herrmann's lectures is communicated by the letters he wrote to his family from Marburg. On 24 October 1905 he wrote to his mother:

> The most important thing that has happened in my three days since Sunday was my first lecture from Prof. Herrmann. If my first impression is any guide, I should say that the first time that I heard Herrmann may almost be described as an epoch in my life. Such an overpowering personality I think I almost never before encountered – overpowering in the sincerity of religious devotion. Herrmann may be illogical and one-sided, but I tell you he is alive.

The terms that Machen used to describe his first encounter with Herrmann – epochal, overwhelming – indicate the depth of crisis that he was beginning to experience. He mentioned also that he was reading Herrmann's book *Der Verkehr des Christen mit Gott* (The Communion of the Christian with God). Just a few days later, on 28 October, a letter to his father confirmed the extraordinary disturbance that Herrmann had wrought in Machen's spiritual and intellectual moorings:

> I can't criticize him, as my chief feeling with reference to him is already one of the deepest reverence. Since I have been listening to him, my other studies have for a time lost interest to me; for Herrmann refuses to allow the student to look at religion from a distance as a thing to be *studied* merely. He speaks right to the heart; and I have been thrown all into confusion by what he says – so much deeper is his devotion to Christ

than anything I have known in myself during the past few years. I don't
know at all what to say as yet, for Herrmann's views are so revolutionary.

Machen then expressed his confidence in the genuineness of Herrmann's relationship to Christ, but immediately retreated into another
acknowledgment of confusion. "I don't know at all yet what to think."[5]
The relationship of Herrmann's theology to his view of the Bible
is the subject of some of Machen's later comments. Writing to his
brother Arthur on 2 November, Machen remarked that Herrmann had
given him "a new sympathy for the prevailing German religious
thought," and observed that "Herrmann affirms very little of that which
I have been accustomed to regard as essential to Christianity," yet
Machen had no doubt that Herrmann was a Christian. "It is inspiring,"
he wrote, "to see a man so completely centered in Christ, even though
some people might wonder how he reaches this result and still holds
the views that he does about the accounts of Christ in the New
Testament." Even in his confusion and in the first blush of enthusiasm
over a different way of viewing familiar things, Machen perceived an
inconsistency between Herrmann's critical views on the New
Testament and the theology which Herrmann espoused.[6]
On 10 December Machen again wrote to Arthur regarding
Herrmann:

> Herrmann is professor of Dogmatics, and represents the dominant
> Ritschlian school of whose principles I have very hazy notions. At any
> rate, Herrmann has shown me something of the *religious* power which
> lies back of this great movement, which is now making a fight even for
> the control of the Northern Presbyterian Church in America. In New
> England those who do not believe in the bodily Resurrection of Jesus
> are, generally speaking, religiously dead; in Germany, Herrmann has
> taught me that that is by no means the case.

In these comments Machen evidenced an awareness of the
theological camp which Herrmann represented, that it denied the
bodily resurrection of Jesus, and that this school of thought was even
then seeking dominance in the Northern Presbyterian Church in
America. The difference between liberalism in the two countries, in
Machen's view, was that the American liberal movement – at least in
New England – was religiously lifeless, while in Germany it possessed
great vigor. Machen went on in this letter to express the hope that

Herrmann did not possess the whole truth, but acknowledged that the German theologian had gotten hold of something that was neglected by the orthodox.[7]

The state of religious turmoil and intellectual confusion in which Machen found himself seems to have had two immediate practical effects. In the first place, it caused Machen to reconsider accepting the fellowship money which he had won. Machen wrote to Professor Armstrong from Vienna on 26 September, in advance of his arrival at Marburg and prior to any exposure to Herrmann, informing Armstrong that he had decided not to accept the monetary award connected with the New Testament fellowship. Armstrong's response of 11 October encouraged Machen to reconsider, and assured him that receiving the money carried no obligation beyond the undertaking of a year of additional study, which he had already begun. Machen wrote again on 29 October, after Herrmann's first lectures, reaffirming his decision not to receive the money. Armstrong's reply to this letter on 12 November sheds some light on the reasoning – or feelings – behind Machen's resolve. In the context of expressing confidence in Machen's character and work, Armstrong referred to the younger man's "trials," which had been "severe." He continued:

> Your suffering has been in that sphere where each of us stands face to face with God. It is in this sphere that relief will come. . . . I know your faith will give you the victory and with victory the joy and peace that comes from the quiet confidence in all God's providence and gracious leading of a child of His for whom Christ died.

It is apparent from these remarks that Machen had been cast into an acute crisis of faith, a crisis which led him to renounce the monetary award connected with the fellowship. He most likely did not want to incur any obligation – real or imagined – which acceptance of the money might impose, and wanted to maintain his intellectual independence. Machen evidently believed that in his intellectual turmoil it would be dishonorable to accept the award, that acceptance would obligate him for the future, and that it would hinder his intellectual freedom to follow where his convictions might lead.[8]

No doubt closely related to the refusal of the fellowship money was the second practical effect of Machen's intellectual and spiritual turmoil: his increasing determination not to enter the Christian ministry. Shortly after the beginning of 1906 he began writing to his family about the impossibility of his becoming a minister. Machen's first letter of the year has been lost, but both his brother Arthur's reply of 21 January and his mother's letter of the same date reveal that Machen had decisively rejected the possibility of entering the ministry. His determination seems to have been fed by his intellectual doubts and a sense of personal unworthiness. On 14 January Machen wrote to his father in emphatic terms: "Of course, the thing which makes all my pleasure in my work more or less a thing of the surface, is the practical *certainty* that I can never enter the ministry." He expressed his desire for a humble business position, but feared that it was too late for that.[9]

Machen continued to write to his family in a similar vein during the early months of 1906. His father, mother, and brother Arthur were supportive and encouraging, confident that he would make a worthy decision in the matter. But he could hardly be consoled. Even the prospect of teaching at Princeton Seminary afforded him little comfort, as his letter of 4 March to Arthur reveals:

> I am pretty certain that I shall never be able to put to practical use, in the way of a profession, anything that I may learn about the New Testament. Unfortunately taking a position at Princeton presupposes entering the ministry (instead of being something parallel with it), so that the two things are just about equally impossible for me.

He was clearly assuming that teaching at Princeton required his entrance into the ministry, and the impossibility of the latter precluded also the former.[10]

In March 1906, Professor Armstrong renewed the offer of a position at Princeton for the fall of that year. Machen replied that he was not prepared to accept the appointment, although Armstrong had assured him that ordination was not necessary. He did not mention the offer in letters to his family. Machen's brother Arthur, although not informed by Machen himself about the new overture from Armstrong, was nevertheless aware of it. Arthur sought to overcome his younger brother's reluctance by pointing out that teaching the New Testament is not the same kind of work as that of the preacher and possesses different qualifications. Machen replied: "In the field of N.T., there is no place for the weakling. Decisiveness, moral and intellectual, is absolutely required. Any other kind of work is not merely useless . . ., but is even perhaps harmful." Stonehouse regards Machen's response to the Princeton offer and his comments on teaching as remarkably revealing. For they show that Machen was not weakly grasping for a way out of his apparent impasse, and that he was profoundly aware that a dualism between the intellectual and spiritual was untenable. Teaching at the seminary could not be isolated from the larger issues of calling and the integrity of faith. Machen was evidently a young man for whom a sense of intellectual honesty would allow no path of expedient compromise.[11]

On to Göttingen

After some hesitation, Machen decided to spend the summer term of 1906 at Göttingen, in order to broaden his exposure to scholars in the New Testament field. At Göttingen he came into contact with Emil Schürer (1844-1910), the author of a massive work on *The History of the Jewish People in the Time of Jesus Christ*, who lectured on the exegesis of Matthew and conducted a seminar on the Pastoral Epistles. Other notable scholars at Göttingen were Wilhelm Heitmüller (1869-1926), whose lectures on the Gospel of John were considered by Machen to provide the best course he had; N. Bonwetsch, a lesser figure, who lectured on the Apostolic Age, and whom Machen called conservative but who in Machen's opinion represented the conservative position less capably than did Armstrong at Princeton; and Ferdinand Kattenbusch (1851-1935), who lectured on the history of Protestant theology since the Enlightenment. But the most significant impact on Machen at Göttingen was made by a prominent and brilliant representative of the history of religions school, Wilhelm Bousset (1865-1920). Bousset's course itself, on the exegesis of Galatians, Machen regarded as intended for beginners and too elementary to be of real importance. The true significance of Bousset was found in the approach to the New Testament which he advocated. Bousset, along with Heitmüller, had made Göttingen a center for the history of religions method.[12]

In a lengthy letter to his brother Arthur in June 1906 Machen sought to explain some of the fundamental tenets of the history of religions school. His explanation correctly reveals how heavily this school was indebted to historicist thinking:

The general aim is better to understand the Christian religion, by exhibiting it (in its beginnings, as well as in its later dogmatic form) in its relations to other religions, and by pointing out the influence which other religions have had upon its origin and later history. The idea is that only when we understand the New Testament in its historical relations, shall we be able fully to appreciate it.

Even Jesus, though he is not fully explainable, has a place in this endeavor:

> It is admitted that the personality of Jesus, like every great personality, introduces an element which it is useless to attempt to explain; but Jesus had a place in history, and the form of his teaching and work was conditioned by that place in the evolution of humanity.

Machen went on to observe that the new method sought its raw materials in the religious beliefs and practices of the masses, in contrast to the older approach which emphasized the literary and educated elite.[13]

Bousset's goal, Machen pointed out, was not limited to the world of scholarship; he wanted to popularize the results of recent investigation:

> One great aim of Bousset seems to be to bring the ideas of the modern theology before the *people*, that Christianity may be freed from the load of dead form, and that thus the gospel of Jesus may once more ring out with its old power. The *form* even of the preaching of Jesus was conditioned by an antiquated view of the world; the real essence of it is eternal truth – that is the principle proclaimed by Bousset and his associates among the 'liberal' theologians of Germany.

Then Machen delivered his own assessment of Bousset's efforts:

> The aim is a noble one, but it may well be doubted whether it is being attained. What Bousset has left after he has stripped off the form is certainly well worth keeping; but whether it is the Christian faith that has been found to overcome the world is very doubtful.

Machen thus intimated what later became the central argument in his case against liberalism: that liberalism is something which is so different from historic Christianity that it must be regarded as a different religion altogether. In concluding his remarks on Bousset,

Machen referred to his place in contemporary German life and compared him to other scholars:

> His fight against orthodoxy in the Church has made Bousset a very prominent man in German public life, and he is certainly also brilliant as an investigator; but he lacks the caution of men like Schürer or Jülicher.

Machen was later to repeat his assessment of Bousset as "brilliant," and the German scholar's reconstruction of early Christianity became one of Machen's principal targets in his 1921 book, *The Origin of Paul's Religion.*[14]

For the present, however, it was likely that Bousset's views provided as much challenge to Machen's faith as to his critical acumen. In the evangelical tradition, especially as emanating from Princeton, faith was considered to be grounded in factual events of history, namely, the incarnation, death, and resurrection of Jesus Christ, and when those facts are called into question then faith is in danger of losing its foundation. Thus, for Machen, Bousset's "fight against orthodoxy in the Church" was a matter of no mere academic interest. At stake were the nature of Christianity, the direction of the church, and most urgently, Machen's own personal faith. That Machen viewed the situation in such radical terms is disclosed by an event which transpired during his stay at Göttingen. Machen had arranged a conference in July between himself and Professor Heitmüller to discuss the religious stance of a student society of which Machen was a member. The conversation turned from personal and social matters to broader questions of theology and religion, in particular the religious significance of the difference between the new liberal theology and orthodox theology. Machen, in the midst of his own struggle, significantly took the position, against Heitmüller, that the difference "affected the very essence of Christianity." Machen was unsuccessful in convincing Heitmüller, but he was evidently becoming convinced himself that Christianity according to liberalism and Christianity according to the traditional faith were two different things. And for Machen, wherever the truth lay, it could not be with both camps at the same time: traditional Christianity could be true, or the modern theology could be true, but they could not both be true.[15]

In his effort to determine where the truth did lie, Machen was unwilling to cut any corners. Only a full and fair hearing of all positions would suffice. Thus he wrote to his mother in July 1906, from Göttingen, ". . . I do not believe in combatting religious errors by any outward means such as trying to prevent the propagation of such ideas." He continued with an expression of doubt which Stonehouse regards as a "mood of the moment" rather than a settled conviction: "Nor am I by any means certain where the truth lies – probably it is something that none of us at present sees" – though he did not like to think that Bousset and Heitmüller had gotten hold of it. Machen had become persuaded that the best way to deal with the historical criticism of the Bible was to confront it full in the face. To his father he had written in February: "as for the present Biblical criticism, I am fully convinced that if it is to be overcome, it will be overcome not by those who look at it in a hostile way, as if from a distance, but by those who have learned to appreciate it." This remark indicates Machen's basically conservative stance, which regarded the new criticism as something to be overcome; but he maintained that it had to be overcome from the inside, as it were, with due appreciation for its accomplishments, rather than denounced from the outside. He wrote in the same letter, "if there is one thing that I have learned here in Germany, it is to accept the aid of men of all kinds of opinions, even with regard to the most serious affairs of life, without being repelled by differences between some of their opinions and my own." Machen thus declared himself open to truth from whatever source it might come, including scholars whose fundamental viewpoint differed sharply from his own.[16]

According to Machen, refusal to isolate oneself from contemporary currents of thought was an attitude which was inculcated back at Princeton itself. Machen explained in a letter to his brother Arthur that he had not gone to Erlangen to hear the renowned conservative scholar Theodor Zahn because Professor Armstrong had advised against it. Erlangen, Armstrong said, was a one-man faculty, Zahn being the only illustrious scholar there. It would be erroneous, Machen told his brother, to think that the Princeton faculty would recommend a school simply because it was conservative. Contrary to the practice of some conservative institutions, Princeton "does not hide from itself the real state of affairs in Biblical study at the present day, and makes an honest effort to come to an understanding with the ruling tendency." In accord with the scholarly conservatism of Princeton, and his own manifest intellectual integrity, Machen had given a hearing to the outstanding liberal scholars of his day – men such as Herrmann, Jülicher, Schürer, and Bousset – and he had read their books. His openness had left his faith shaken, but not overthrown. But the troubling of his faith left his prospects for the future all the more uncertain.[17]

The Decision to Teach at Princeton

In May, Armstrong renewed his invitation for Machen to come to Princeton in the fall of 1906. An offer was also extended to Machen in June by Ethelbert D. Warfield, President of Lafayette College in Pennsylvania, who wanted Machen to teach Greek and German at that institution. Machen promptly refused the Lafayette offer, both because an immediate reply was requested and because he wanted to keep open his option at Princeton, if he could see his way clear to go there – a possibility concerning which he still had grave doubts. The cause of Machen's uncertainty is revealed by a letter which Armstrong sent him in July. Armstrong assured the younger man that he would not have to be "licensed, ordained, or even come under care of a presbytery. . . . And in regard to your theological opinions you do not have to make any pledge." Armstrong emphasized that Machen would not be expected to have reached final decisions on all theological matters before teaching at Princeton; rather, in his teaching he would be expected only to "stand on the broad principles of the Reformed Theology and in particular on the authority of the Scriptures in religious matters. . . ." If Machen were ever to reach conclusions that made it impossible to uphold the seminary's position, he need only say so and depart peaceably. It appears from Armstrong's letter that Machen's intellectual struggles over theological questions and his consequent unwillingness to take steps to enter the ministry lay at the root of his hesitation to accept the teaching position at Princeton. It was such considerations that Armstrong was attempting mightily, yet patiently and tactfully, to overcome.[18]

The decision to teach at Princeton was reached only after Machen had returned to the United States in August 1906 and met with Armstrong early in September. Even shortly before this meeting the issue was still in doubt. Apparently Machen had in mind to occupy the Princeton post for only one year, after which he would return to Germany for further study in the classics, with the expectation of later teaching in that field. He was not planning to enter the ministry.[19]

At just this time a controversy occurred between Machen and his mother over his plan to return to Germany after a year at Princeton. Their relationship, normally a warm, intimate, and trusting one, suffered a distinct chill for several days until the difficulty was cleared up. The exchange of letters between them – and between Machen and his father – provides, however, the clearest possible indication of Machen's intellectual character, and is worthy of extended attention. Unfortunately, the full correspondence surrounding the matter has not been preserved. Stonehouse has included in his account of the affair lengthy excerpts from several of the important letters that have survived, making the documents readily accessible to the casual reader, although he has slighted perhaps the most revealing letter of the entire exchange, one written by Machen to his father. Briefly put, it seems that Minnie Machen had expressed opposition to her son's plan of returning to Germany after his year at Princeton. The ostensible reason was her reluctance to have Gresham so far separated from her once again, but in his letter of 9 September 1906 Machen – now in Princeton – pressed her for the "real reason." He wrote again two days later, attempting to explain his position and to gain her approval of his plan, not mere acquiescence in it. In this letter he expressed the hope that the year of quiet study at Princeton would afford him the opportunity "to attain moral, religious and intellectual clearness of vision." He went on to describe his hopes for the future: "My ambition is to be a student of the classics – who from the vantage point of a broader philological knowledge than he would under other conditions have, and *in perfect freedom*, tries to contribute something to our knowledge of the New Testament." He concluded the letter with a postscript indicating that he was to be appointed to the rank of Instructor, for one year, and that he was *not* (double underlining) a minister "or anything more than a mere layman." The new element here, amidst the familiar strains of Machen's interest in the New Testament, his intellectual turmoil, and disclaimers regarding the ministry, is his urgent insistence upon absolute intellectual freedom, almost as if he believed that this was being put in jeopardy by his mother's attitude.[20]

Machen's apprehensions were confirmed by his mother's reply, which he understood to express her fears that he might lose his Christian faith if he were to return to Germany for further study. His response of 14 September 1906, written from Princeton, is labelled by Stonehouse an "impassioned outburst." It was, indeed, an outburst of a most remarkable kind. The letter, which runs to several pages in the original manuscript (and three pages of tightly-packed print in the Stonehouse volume), constituted a plea for intellectual liberty and for his mother's understanding. The essence of Machen's argument was that he must have absolute freedom to investigate both the traditional and the modern views of the New Testament if he was going to attain to any certainty in the matter. "The only way in which the thinker can hold to the old belief is by piercing below the surface and thus finding that on the merits of the question the old view has the facts on its side." His mother's position (as he understood it) was counter-productive, he argued, for in suggesting that he not proceed with a full and fair investigation, it implied that the traditional view of the New Testament could not hold up under close scrutiny, and this tended to push him toward the opposite camp. He was, however, sufficiently acquainted with the question on its own merits to avoid being swayed by such extrinsic considerations as his mother's attitude. But he could allow no abridgement of his intellectual freedom, for that would compromise his intellectual integrity – an intolerable situation. New Testament scholarship, he wrote, is

> primarily historical work, which requires absolute honesty. . . . Don't you see, that however right your action is from your point of view – however loyal and admirable even – if I should follow you I should be guilty of simple old-fashioned intellectual dishonesty?

He did not object to his mother's trying to influence him, but he did object to the argument which he perceived her to be using.[21]

Whether Machen correctly understood his mother's objections to his proposed studies in Germany may never be known – her letter which provoked the controversy has been lost. And her reply on 17 September disclaimed any intention of stifling his intellectual freedom: "my whole life has been a protest against the very position which you suppose me to take. . . . I do not and never have looked at free probing for truth as anything to be afraid of." She attributed the whole affair to his inability to understand her expressions of motherly concern and solicitude that he continue in the faith.[22]

Regardless of whether Machen had properly understood his mother, the brief controversy presented him with the opportunity – and, he believed, the necessity – of explaining his own position more fully than he had done before. As openly as Machen expressed himself to his mother, however, he wrote to his father with even more forthrightness. On 14 September 1906, besides writing to his mother, Machen responded to a letter from his father which had described Minnie Machen's state of mind. Because this letter affords a remarkable revelation of Machen's intellectual character and discloses the depth of his struggle and emotional distress, it is here reproduced in full:

Princeton, N.J.
Sept. 14, 1906

Dear Father,
Of course, I am distressed at what you say about Mother's state of feelings. I thought she was a strong Christian, with whom I could discuss religious matters freely. Instead of that I find that she has not faith enough in the truth of her religion to be willing to open the way to free investigation. To save my life I can't remain in such a position. I can't continue to hold for true something that I know I should find to be false if I honestly investigated the other side. If I thought three or four more years in Germany might place me on the other side of the question, I should consider it my duty to start on those three or four years at once, before taking up such a work as the work here. This is nothing more or less than honesty, any other course of action is simply dishonesty, which is a far greater sin than unbelief.

Mother's mistake is the old, old mistake of the orthodox, which shows how uncertain they often are of their position. She has of course discouraged me beyond measure as I take up my work here, and if I felt that my life here was a seclusion from the influences that would be brought to bear on me in Germany, I should have to give it up. To investigate only one side of the question because to investigate the other side is dangerous, simply shows that you really believe the other side to be true. It is dangerous only if it is true.

The discouragement consists in the fact that anybody whom I love so much looks on me in that disgraceful light, as a child who has to be hindered from seeing things clearly. Really Mother's efforts to keep me from going to Germany have more than anything else tended to make me see that I am not in the right place here. If she has that impression of me, perhaps others will have it as well.

Your letter came, therefore, as a fearful blow. But I thank you for your personal willingness to let me have my own way, though I *had* hoped for a better understanding of my position.

Yours affectionately
J. Gresham Machen

P.S. Of course you made no mistake in letting me know what Mother's real objection is. I suspected it anyhow, and certainty is far better than the miserable feeling that something was being kept from me.

P.S.S. There is just *one* way for me to attain a strong Christian faith – namely by patient, *absolutely* free investigation of all contending views in a large-minded, reverent way. Just so far as Mother tries to hinder me from that, does she prevent me from emerging from the uncertainties of doubt. She could not possibly have chosen a way better suited to attain to the opposite end to that which she desires, than her present course of action. Her present actions are making the path terribly hard for me, as they tend to obscure my clearness of visi[o]n. Absolute clearness is what I must have. If you and Mother do not see that, then my confidences in you are simply at an end. I must from now on go forward on my own path.

This setback is particularly hard at the time when I had made my first great advance toward a real Christian faith. Your talk about "unsettling" influences, etc, as I cannot but feel, is of a piece with Mother's great mistake. We must simply investigate the influences as they are, with perfect fairness, and only after we have pronounced on the truth upon which the[y] claim to be based, can we approve them as injurious. A man who consciously spares himself from any purely intellectual influences is a man that is simply afraid of the truth.[23]

Machen's writing style in this letter occasionally betrays the state of emotional turmoil in which he wrote it. This fact in itself speaks of his fierce determination to maintain his intellectual independence and integrity, as well as of his consternation over his parents' assumed attitude. Furthermore, Machen's insistence on the necessity of free investigation as the only way to advance beyond doubt suggests that he was still in the throes of considerable uncertainty as he took up his work at Princeton. Apparently his questions were not yet wholly resolved, and his struggles did not cease just because he was about to begin teaching at the most prestigious conservative theological institution in the land.

This episode provides a fitting conclusion to the early period of Machen's life and dealings with the Bible. The incident discloses a young scholar battered by intellectual doubts and hindered by spiritual uncertainties, yet ferociously jealous of his right to pursue the truth for himself. But it also shows a young man who is at the same time, however haltingly, set to teach the New Testament and the Christian faith in the tradition of his fathers.

Summary Observations

Considerable attention has been given here to the early years of Machen's life. This is appropriate, for during these formative years – although his intellectual and spiritual formation was anything but complete by the time of his twenty-fifth birthday – Machen developed several traits of aptitude, character, and conviction which served to influence the direction of his work during his years of maturity.

It is beyond question that Machen was reared in an environment of conservative Protestantism, and that he generally accepted this stance as his own. It is perhaps open to question, however, how much genuine spiritual experience his religious culture encouraged, given Machen's confession of experiential shallowness when confronted with Herrmann's religious devotion in Germany. In an essay full of insight, Charles G. Dennison, official historian of the Orthodox Presbyterian Church (the denomination Machen founded at the end of his life), has characterized the Presbyterianism of Machen's youth as possessed of a broad cultural vision, as revering the *idea* of the church, as less Calvinist than Presbyterian, and as possessing more the aura of respectability than of profound holiness. The Baltimore Presbyterianism of the Machen household likely provided its middle son with the proper cultural associations, a genuine reverence for the Bible along with a solid knowledge of its contents, and a foundation of doctrinal correctness, while perhaps at the same time unwittingly grooming him for the kind of upheaval which he experienced in Germany and for which Herrmann was the catalyst.[24]

It is also beyond dispute that Machen early showed great promise as a New Testament scholar. His training in the classics, begun in his early teens and continuing through his graduate degree at Johns Hopkins, provided what was arguably the best possible preparation for New Testament studies. His work at Princeton, a stronghold of open and informed yet conservative scholarship, was such as to impress even its distinguished faculty and to warrant publication in the seminary's journal. There Machen was encouraged in one of the attributes of genuine scholarship, the willingness to consider positions contrary to one's own. And while in Germany, Machen was exposed first-hand to the best of European New Testament scholarship and became well-acquainted with the positions occupied by various schools of thought. Before finishing his work in Germany, his scholarly potential was given further formal acknowledgment by the Princeton faculty in the form of earnest solicitations for him to teach there.[25]

It was while in Germany that Machen experienced the most traumatic event of his early life, an intellectual struggle over the truthfulness of Christianity as presented in the New Testament and in the orthodox Protestant tradition. His intellectual interest in such questions was perhaps evident earlier in his decision to attend Princeton Seminary while refusing seriously to entertain the idea of entering the ministry. From Germany he expressed himself openly to his family – without being as specific as one might wish – regarding his doubts and confusion. There need not be any question that this intellectual and religious turmoil was precipitated by his exposure to biblical criticism and liberal theology, in advance of his arrival in Germany as well as afterwards, and was probably related to questions concerning the historical validity of the New Testament accounts of Jesus and of the origin of Christianity. This intellectual upheaval may with good reason be regarded as the crucial formative event of Machen's life, for from it flow his mature convictions with regard to the Bible and its historical study, the nature of Christianity, theological liberalism and its relationship to the church, and questions of intellectual and ecclesiastical integrity.[26]

The seeds of his later thinking are apparent, for example, in Machen's attitude toward theological liberalism. Although he was powerfully affected by Herrmann's Ritschlian theology, he was at the same time growing in the conviction that there existed a sharp disjunction between the new theology and traditional orthodox Christianity. This opinion was voiced in his comments regarding the nature of Bousset's re-formed Christian faith, and in his conversation with Heitmüller concerning the religious implications of the modern theology. Machen adhered to this view of liberal theology for the remainder of his life, and it formed the heart of his argument against liberalism in the Presbyterian Church during the 1920s.

Also characteristic of Machen's whole life was his early insistence upon intellectual integrity. The dispute with his mother in September 1906 revealed Machen's resolute determination to confront rather than avoid the intellectual and historical difficulties connected with the Christian faith, especially those raised by biblical criticism. Something of this outlook is reflected in his autobiographical account of 1932. "Obviously it is impossible," he wrote, "to hold on with the heart to something that one has rejected with the head, and all the usefulness of Christianity can never lead us to be Christians unless the Christian religion is true." He then referred to "the long and bitter experience that the raising of this question brought into my life." But his struggle was long and bitter only because he insisted on facing the problems openly and fully. His struggle, though difficult, bore other kinds of fruit later in his life, after the doubts had been resolved. Stonehouse speaks of Machen's compassion and patience toward those who were undergoing intellectual struggles similar to his own; he knew how anguishing such an experience could be.[27]

Along with intellectual integrity, Machen during this period manifested extreme scrupulousness in matters of practical honesty. His refusal of the New Testament fellowship money was stimulated not by any terms or stipulations connected with the award itself, but by his own sense of integrity. He believed that it would be dishonorable for him to accept the money while in a state of intellectual uncertainty. Further, his refusal to offer himself as a candidate for the ministry is almost certainly to be understood in connection with his intellectual and religious turmoil. Machen was evidently possessed of the conviction that one who is in an unsettled state regarding the truthfulness of Christianity has no place in the Christian ministry. This explains his hesitation regarding the ministry upon entering Princeton in 1902, when his doubts had apparently already begun, and his seemingly final decision in the early months of 1906 while in Germany. An appreciation of this aspect of Machen's personality goes far toward explaining his position of later years. He held that it was essentially dishonest for men who rejected the factual truthfulness of Christianity to seek for, or to continue in, the status of ordained minister in the Presbyterian Church. Machen attained his own official standing only after a long and painful ordeal – he was not ordained until 1914 – and he was filled with indignation at those who formally subscribed to the Bible as the Word of God and to the Westminster Standards while rejecting the theological substance which they contained.[28]

Finally, it can at least be said that Machen was beginning to recognize that the difference between the traditional and the common critical views of the Bible lay in their differing philosophies of history. Machen's description of the tenets of the history of religions school of New Testament criticism suggests as much. He was becoming aware that this approach to the Bible sought to explain first-century Christianity as wholly the product of its historical environment. Even though some adherents of such an approach might attempt to preserve certain religious values from the Bible, at its most consistent level it excluded the possibility of genuine divine influence on the events of the external world – that is, on human history – and in this it differed sharply from the evangelical Presbyterianism of Machen's youth. It was precisely this question that would continue to occupy the center of his attention and prolong his intellectual turmoil for the next several years.

PART THREE

THE DECISIVE YEARS,
1906–1915

CHAPTER 5

MACHEN'S EARLY BOOK REVIEWS, 1907–1912

The years 1906 to 1915 mark a natural epoch in Machen's life. The period begins with Machen's appointment as Instructor at Princeton Seminary and concludes with his installation as Assistant Professor in May 1915. The former position did not involve membership on the regular faculty; the latter did, thus bestowing voting rights and requiring ordination. Much more important than this academic transition, however, was the inward transition that Machen experienced during this span of years. His tenure at Princeton had begun under a cloud of intellectual doubt, as his letters in the fall of 1906 testify. But by the time of his nomination to the Princeton faculty in the spring of 1914, he had emerged from the storm of doubt to enjoy the cloudless skies of intellectual clarity and spiritual assurance and had seen fit to present himself as a candidate for the Presbyterian ministry.

There was a close connection between Machen's ordination and his intellectual struggle. In Machen's view, intellectual clarity and commitment were requisites to serious consideration of the ministry. The high office of minister of the gospel was no place for one who entertained doubts about the truthfulness of the gospel message itself. Accordingly, Machen delayed his ordination – indeed, gave little thought to it for several years – until he had resolved to his own satisfaction the historical questions regarding Christian origins which had troubled him since his early twenties. As Stonehouse observes in picturesque language, the "volcanic eruptions" of doubt "subsided fairly soon" after Machen came to Princeton, but "the rumblings continued for a number of years." Stonehouse continues, "It was not until the fall of 1913 that he attained to such assurance and calm that he could undertake the first step looking toward ordination, that of being taken under care of presbytery, and could confidently and joyfully look forward to ordination."[1]

The interval between Machen's arrival at Princeton in 1906 and his installation on the regular faculty in 1915 offers several sources –

primarily in his published writings – for observing his intellectual pilgrimage, or perhaps more accurately, for beholding the destination to which his pilgrimage brought him. The one source which offers the most potential for assessing the actual process of Machen's growth is his book reviews. From 1907 until 1928 Machen was a regular reviewer for the *Princeton Theological Review*, and his book reviews offer a significant if limited disclosure of his own positions during the years 1907 to 1912. Also important was the publication in 1912 of four major essays which made known the results of his own research on two questions: the virgin birth of Jesus and the relation of Paul to Jesus. These essays were momentous not only for revealing his early conclusions on these questions but also for marking off the subject matter of his scholarly work for the next two decades. The year 1912 further witnessed the delivery of a more popular address on "Christianity and Culture." Moreover, in 1914 Machen was engaged by the Presbyterian Board of Christian Education to write a year-long series of Bible lessons covering the entire New Testament. This work, when completed, amounted to a virtual "introduction" to the New Testament, and set forth Machen's conclusions on a multitude of critical, historical, and theological issues. Finally, this period culminated with Machen's licensure, ordination, and installation on the Princeton faculty in 1914 and 1915, events which were as full of symbolic meaning as they were fraught with practical significance.

Back at Princeton
Upon Machen's return to Princeton in September 1906, the young scholar was immediately plunged into the academic world as viewed from the other side of the desk – as an instructor. His responsibilities that first semester included teaching beginning and elementary Greek as well as exegesis courses in the Gospel of John and Galatians. According to Stonehouse, Machen's teaching load over the years varied little from this program, though it was brightened with opportunities to conduct upper-level elective courses. The work load was initially heavy for Machen, and his letters to his parents find him complaining often of being swamped with work, of having too little opportunity for reading in topics of special interest to him, and of his meager teaching ability.[2]

During the 1906-1907 academic year Machen was still uncertain about his future, and his uncertainty may well have been due to his still unsettled intellectual state. Shortly after the beginning of 1907, he referred to what he feared were "insurmountable obstacles" ahead of him, and on 3 March of that year he described Dr. Patton as "a mighty good friend to me in a time of difficulty and perplexity." But apart from such possible allusions, Machen made no specific mention of his intellectual difficulties in the surviving letters to his family throughout the whole of the academic year. He was now, of course, as Stonehouse points out, in frequent personal contact with members of his family, and matters of faith and theology could be discussed without resort to letters. Furthermore, Machen was in almost daily contact with Armstrong, his mentor, friend, and now colleague at Princeton. The value of this latter relationship for Machen was expressed in the same letter that mentioned the insurmountable obstacles confronting him. "My association with Army," he wrote, "is perhaps my greatest delight." One may fairly conclude, then, that a good deal transpired in Machen's intellectual journey that left no permanent record apart from his later declaration in print of the conclusions he had reached.[3]

Early Book Reviews
From 1907 until 1912, Machen's published writings consisted almost entirely of book reviews. (His other publications included a three-part series of articles in German, published in *Der Schwarzburgbund* in 1906 and 1907, describing American universities, and the translation from German of an essay by August Lang.) Machen's book reviews were all published in the *Princeton Theological Review* and, except for the years 1907 and 1912 when only one review appeared, they were evenly distributed chronologically: four reviews were published in 1908, five in 1909, four in 1910, and three in 1911.

The first review to appear over J. Gresham Machen's name dealt with a title in the field of his expertise, *The Birth and Infancy of Jesus Christ According to the Gospel Narratives* by Louis Matthews Sweet. Machen rendered a generally favorable judgment on Sweet's work, noting that the author had begun his study with a skeptical bias regarding the birth narratives but eventually became convinced of their historicity. Sweet's handling of Luke 1:5–2:52 came in for some criticism, Machen contending that Sweet had ignored important arguments respecting this passage. The most telling of Machen's comments, however, was directed not against Sweet's volume but against Sweet's opponents. Machen voiced the opinion that the objections to the birth narratives lay more in the fields of philosophy and theology than in that of literary criticism. He thus took the argument to the level of fundamental presuppositions, and drew attention to the conditioning effect of a scholar's philosophical or theological commitments on his technical judgments. This kind of criticism, far from being something new for Machen, was simply the continuation of a line of reasoning – a variety of presuppositional argumentation – first used in his virgin birth articles.[4]

Of Machen's four reviews published in 1908, two consisted of very brief comments on elementary titles intended for use in German schools, both of them works on Romans. The other reviews dealt with substantial volumes. Machen declared his appreciation for Konrad Meyer's treatment of the purpose of the Gospel of John. Meyer had concluded that the author of the Gospel "claims to make report as an eye-witness of the life and death of Jesus Christ, for the furtherance of faith." Such a conclusion, in Machen's view, was "thoroughly sane and reasonable," and Meyer's method exhibited independent thinking. The method and conclusion of the book also clearly possessed for Machen the additional advantage of giving adequate attention to the self-testimony of the Johannine literature regarding the Gospel's purpose.[5]

The subject of the second major review of 1908 was James Orr's *The Virgin Birth of Christ*. Orr, a Scottish theologian, was a strong supporter of orthodox doctrine from the standpoint of his "modified Calvinism" and out of his profound knowledge of European philosophy and theology. The present volume consisted of a series of lectures in which Orr sought to give popular expression to his own scholarly conclusions on the question at hand. He argued that the virgin birth was a fact and that it was an important element of Christian doctrine. Orr covered much of the same ground that Machen had in his own treatment of the subject, with similar results. The only criticisms which Machen offered involved disagreement over the arrangement of material and over the degree to which Orr had popularized his presentation; otherwise, Machen received the book warmly. He singled out for special commendation the last two lectures, which Machen considered the best in the book. They made evident the bearing which the question of the harmony of the Virgin Birth with other Christian doctrine has even upon the question of fact. The real believer in the Incarnation must be favorably disposed towards the historical evidence for the Virgin Birth. And this logical necessity has been evident from the history of criticism; for as Dr. Orr insists in his first lecture, those who have denied the Virgin Birth have with scarcely any exceptions also denied the doctrine of the Incarnation.

In agreeing with Orr's point, Machen enunciated the principle that one's prior theological bias will influence one's attitude toward the historical evidence; he thus once again acknowledged the power of presuppositions.[6]

Clearly Machen was willing, by this time, to give open support to a conservative position in matters of biblical criticism and Christian theology. This willingness continued during 1909. Of the five reviews authored by Machen during this year, one in particular contained remarks which demonstrate the nature of the convictions he was coming to hold. Machen was sharply critical of a volume by George Holley Gilbert entitled *Interpretation of the Bible: A Short History*. Machen's criticism rested on four grounds. First, Gilbert favored an untheological interpretation of the Bible, as evidenced by his strictures against Theodore of Mopsuestia and Martin Luther for giving undue attention to theological passages. This gave occasion for Machen to comment on the baneful influence on the church of two tendencies, the attempt to separate the teaching of Jesus from the rest of the revelation given in the New Testament, and the attempt to derive an artificially undogmatic Jesus from the Gospel accounts. Second, Gilbert favored those interpretations which broke with the first three centuries of the church's tradition; Machen wondered whether agreement with the early church was always a sign of poor interpretation. Third, Gilbert favored interpretations which abandoned the traditional doctrine of inspiration. Here Machen questioned whether the old view had been as injurious, either to exegesis or to the propagation of Christianity, as Gilbert supposed. "The authoritative Bible has been and is to-day the very foundation of popular Christianity ... the Christianity that does without it has never exhibited the power to become anything more than a religion of the few." He further took Gilbert to task for sentimentalizing the humanization of the Bible, as if it were somehow an advance in the appreciation of the divine character of the Bible to consider it now a merely human book. Fourth, Machen maintained that Gilbert had not displayed sufficient sensitivity to the Bible's religious message and significance. "Without the religious sense and the consciousness of one's own personal need," he argued, "all the historical and grammatical study in the world will never penetrate beyond the shell," and on the other hand the possession of such a religious sense will impart abiding value to interpretations which are defective from the viewpoint of modern scholarship.[7]

Machen closed his review with a critique of Gilbert's final chapter, on the scientific era of biblical scholarship. He labelled the chapter "disappointing" because of its nature as a general survey and its "overflowing enthusiasm" for the presumed accomplishments of the nineteenth century. Gilbert acknowledged that the changes newly wrought in the dominant conceptions of the Bible and in its interpretation could hardly have been imagined at the close of the eighteenth century, and would have been considered injurious to the cause of true religion if they had been conceived. Machen appealed to history and experience when he claimed:

> the new conceptions of the Bible have as yet given rise to no religious movement that can, for a moment, be compared with the great movements of the past. . . . The new view of the Bible may produce a greater and stronger Christianity in the future; it has not done so as yet.

While Machen appreciated the genuine contributions of modern scientific scholarship to historical exegesis, he doubted that newer conceptions of the Bible marked any advance over the older views. All told, Machen's criticisms of the Gilbert volume constitute a calm but forthright affirmation – his strongest affirmation yet – of the Bible's religious content and significance, of the validity of the traditional doctrine of inspiration, of the traditions (and presumably the supernaturalism) of the early church, and of the necessity of a theological understanding of the Bible.[8]

The other reviews of 1909 were of lesser significance for the expression of Machen's views. He dismissed with a single paragraph a brief German commentary on Romans; and he offered some technical, stylistic, and organizational criticisms of A. T. Robertson's *A Short Grammar of the Greek New Testament*. Two other volumes merited more extended treatment. George Milligan's commentary on the Thessalonian epistles earned Machen's endorsement because of its use of newly discovered ancient Greek papyrus inscriptions to illuminate the everyday Hellenistic language of the New Testament world. Machen was happy to welcome this new aid to the understanding of the New Testament text generally, and he commended Milligan's commentary as a useful contribution on the Thessalonian correspondence in particular.

The final review of 1909 was Machen's sharply critical response to Paul W. Schmiedel's volume on *The Johannine Writings*. Schmiedel, a professor of theology at Zurich, rejected attempts to harmonize the Fourth Gospel with the Synoptics, and declared the former to be without value as a historical narrative. In his five-page review, Machen disputed Schmiedel's arguments in some detail, drawing attention to areas of weakness. He attempted to show that it is not impossible to harmonize John with the Synoptics, either chronologically or conceptually; both agree in presenting a Jesus who is at once more than human and yet not less than human. He also offered some countervailing considerations to Schmiedel's positions on questions of the authorship, date, and provenance of the Johannine literature, supporting, for example, the identity of authorship of the Gospel and the First Epistle. In closing, Machen charged Schmiedel with a lack of logical perspective which led to confusion in determining the real issues, and with a lack of deep understanding of the Fourth Gospel.[9]

These reviews only serve to confirm the impression left by Machen's comments on the Gilbert volume: that he was by 1909 coming down firmly on the side of a traditional Protestant view of the Bible and its inspiration (one cannot yet say the Princetonian view), an orthodox Christology, and a conservative assessment of the origin and historical value of the New Testament documents. This conclusion accords well with other developments in Machen's life at this juncture. Since his appointment to the Princeton instructorship in 1906, Machen had been reappointed on an annual basis in the spring of each year, in 1907 and again in 1908. Yet on both these occasions he expressed some doubt about remaining at Princeton – it seems he wanted to get on with his life and a permanent career. But in the letters he wrote in 1909 and the succeeding years, Stonehouse observes, he never again expressed such hesitation. Stonehouse concludes, on the basis of this and other observations – acknowledging the danger of argument from silence – that "by the spring of 1909 he had identified himself so closely with the work at Princeton that he could not be thinking seriously of another field" – although Stonehouse hastens to add that Machen was still far from resolving the question of his call to the Christian ministry.[10]

An indication that Machen had by 1909 committed himself to Princeton and to its broader purposes was the stance he adopted in the face of a "rebellion" by Princeton Seminary students. In the spring of 1909 some students at Princeton petitioned the seminary's board of directors for changes in the curriculum and in the mode of instruction at the institution. The students wanted more courses of a practical nature, and, it appears, less rigorous courses academically. The attack was aimed against three members of the faculty in particular: Professor John D. Davis of the Old Testament Department, President Patton, and Armstrong. Machen sided with the faculty in the dispute, not only out of his personal regard for Patton and Armstrong, but also out of a genuine desire to maintain high academic standards and the solid biblical and theological substance of the curriculum.[11]

In another sphere of labor, that of preaching, Machen was far from active, but a subtle change occurred in 1909 which may reflect a deepening of his intellectual clarity or religious commitment or both. Stonehouse notes that prior to his ordination Machen preached only seldom. In the spring of 1908 he fulfilled for the first time his obligation in the regular rotation of faculty speakers at the seminary chapel, and it became an annual event for him. He did not at first relish the opportunity, though apparently he preached quite effectively. Stonehouse comments, however, that beginning in August 1909 (after Machen's second chapel sermon) he would "on very rare occasions" accept preaching opportunities when no one else was available. This change in attitude was less than momentous but still significant, and may indicate that a step toward a decisive commitment had been taken.[12]

The year 1910 saw the production of four book reviews by Machen. Three of these dealt with works of New Testament criticism, the fourth a commentary on Romans. The Epistle to the Galatians was an area of Machen's special interest and expertise; he regularly taught an exegesis course on this portion of the New Testament. It is not surprising, therefore, that he was assigned a German volume on

Galatians by Alphons Steinman, a Roman Catholic scholar who taught at Breslau. The entire volume was devoted to a discussion of the recipients of the epistle, a matter of warm dispute at the time. Steinman defended the view Machen himself favored, the so-called North Galatian theory, which held that Galatians was addressed to churches in the northern rather than the southern portion of the Roman province of Galatia. Machen found Steinman's presentation of the evidence convincing, and in commending the book he deplored the indifference which Protestant scholars often showed toward the work of Roman Catholics.

A title by Robert Scott of Bombay received a decidedly less favorable response from Machen. *The Pauline Epistles: A Critical Study* provided an instance, Machen claimed, of criticism having become "astonishingly uncritical." Scott had segmented the various letters of the Pauline corpus in the most remarkable fashion, assigning authorship of these fragments to Paul and to various of his companions, all on the basis of internal criteria alone. Entirely lacking was the substantial evidence and argumentation necessary to establish such a revolutionary undertaking, and in places, according to Machen, the book "reads almost like a burlesque on criticism." Nevertheless, Machen found some praiseworthy observations in the volume, most of which could be used against the prevailing trends in New Testament criticism. The single sentence which constituted the final paragraph closed the review with dry humor: "The most that can be said for the accenting of Greek words throughout the book is that it is sometimes correct."[13]

A third title dealt with the testimony of the second-century church father Irenaeus to the authorship of the Fourth Gospel. The study by Frank Grant Lewis was, in Machen's view, essentially a vindication of the trustworthiness of Irenaeus as a witness to the Johannine origin of the Fourth Gospel, a tradition which had been passed to Irenaeus by his teacher Polycarp. Lewis refused to acknowledge Johannine authorship, however, explaining the Gospel as a collection of booklets written probably by a disciple of John and collected near the middle of the second century. Machen offered several objections to such a theory, not the least of which was the Irenaeus testimony itself, which Machen considered consistent with authorship by the Apostle John in the first century and which much of Lewis' study served to vindicate. Machen thus utilized Lewis' arguments against him, a device he was

often to use, and underscored his own preference for Johannine
authorship, considering it consistent both with ancient tradition and
modern scholarship.[14]

Machen's attempt to maintain an evangelical balance between piety
and historical scholarship was revealed in his fourth review of 1910.
The book under review was a commentary in German on the Epistle
to the Romans by a Lutheran scholar, George Stockhardt of Concordia
Seminary in St. Louis. Stockhardt disavowed the purely historical
interest which characterized much contemporary scholarship,
intending to deal as well with the "eternal, divine thoughts" of the
epistle. In principle, Machen agreed with Stockhardt's approach: "The
protest is a just and timely one; the grammatico-historical method of
exegesis is sometimes falsely regarded as involving aloofness of the
interpreter from his subject-matter or an emphasis upon the mere
environment of the book to be interpreted at the expense of its inner
teaching." While Machen appears certainly to have been an advocate
of grammatico-historical exegesis, here he distinguished what he
considered the proper use of that method from an assumed objectivity
or mere contextual study. In practice, however, he believed that
Stockhardt had gone too far in the other direction, in two respects.
First, the author, although well-read in the older works, showed only
limited acquaintance with recent scholarship on Romans, an omission
which constituted a defect, in Machen's eyes. Second, Stockhardt
had neglected to deal with some of the vexing historical and textual
problems which Romans presents to the interpreter, an oversight
Machen considered inappropriate in a volume of over six hundred
pages. While Machen therefore appreciated the doctrinal and
devotional thrust of the commentary, he found it defective in its
handling of the literary, historical, textual, and linguistic aspects of
the epistle; as a result, he could give it only a limited commendation.
It appears that Machen could not readily accommodate himself to an
evangelical scholarship that, although theologically orthodox, was
weak in its application of historical criticism.[15]

Another volume on Galatians provided the occasion for Machen's
longest review of 1911. A commentary on the Galatian epistle by
Benjamin W. Bacon, a professor of New Testament at Yale, was the
first in a succession of titles by this author to be subjected to negative
reviews by Machen. Three features of the review are relevant to the
present study. First, Machen criticized Bacon for his reconstruction

of the history of the apostolic age, a reconstruction based on Bacon's comparison of Galatians with Acts, much to the discredit of the latter. Bacon's approach was similar to that of the Tübingen school of the mid-nineteenth century in that it sought to portray a deep and persistent rift between Paul and the leaders of Jewish Christianity in Jerusalem. Machen wondered whether Bacon had not "substituted the comfortable simplicity of fiction for the baffling complexity of fact" in his reworking of apostolic history. There is a method, Machen suggested, for harmonizing Galatians with Acts, and when it is properly used, any apparent contradictions disappear. Second, Machen took exception to Bacon's attribution of the "moral influence" theory of the atonement to Paul. This theory contends that the exhibition of God's love in the death of Christ moves men to repentance and moral improvement, but that no objective atonement was accomplished in Christ's death. Machen was not surprised that Bacon held this view, but he found it remarkable that Bacon should attribute it to Paul – especially in light of Galatians 3:13 ("Christ redeemed us from the curse of the law, having become a curse for us"). Third, Machen took note of the popular nature of the book. Bacon's commentary belonged to a series entitled "The Bible for Home and School," and was specifically directed toward the general reader, such as Sunday School teachers. This development – the aiming of largely negative critical conclusions at a general audience – should, thought Machen, "help to dispel the astonishing indifference of the American branch of the Church toward historical questions." Bacon's book afforded evidence, if any were necessary, that "the popularization of the naturalistic view of Christianity is inevitable"; and when such views of the New Testament are transmitted through Sunday School teachers to young people, they "will produce a Christianity very different from the religion that has formerly been designated by that name." "New Testament criticism," he concluded, "is a very practical thing."[16]

The concerns and convictions that Machen voiced here were becoming characteristic of his essential position. He was convinced that the historical difficulties presented by the New Testament are capable of reasonable and scholarly explanation when the documents are correctly understood. Furthermore, he stoutly maintained that Christianity was at its center a religion of supernatural redemption and that any contrary interpretation misconstrued its essential character. In addition, he was exceedingly anxious for the future of the church (or "the Church," as he put it, meaning Christianity at large), fearing that the expanding influence of naturalistic biblical criticism and liberal theology would alter the historic identity of Christianity, to its own spiritual impoverishment and weakness. Back of this anxiety was his evident frustration that the church was not vigorously addressing the intellectual challenges it faced, but met them rather with "astonishing indifference." In light of Machen's strong advocacy of positions such as these, from which he did not deviate in succeeding years, it seems warranted to conclude that by 1911 the mature Machen was beginning to appear.

Other reviews written in 1911 were not without significance as well. Machen's treatment of George Milligan's *Selections from the Greek Papyri* demonstrated that he was not temperamentally hostile to new developments in New Testament research. Milligan's volume consisted of fifty-five selections taken from the numerous newly-discovered papyrus fragments which preserved in their texts the everyday Greek language used in the ancient Roman world. Machen welcomed the collection, for it showed the affinity between the language of the New Testament and the popular Greek of the era, and it illuminated the everyday life of common or "real" people as opposed to the artificial characters found in literature. The final review of 1911 dealt with a book by a Roman Catholic scholar, Alfred Durand, defending the historicity of the virgin birth of Jesus. Machen offered several minor criticisms of the volume, but in general expressed his approval, as well as his appreciation of the fact that "scholars of the Roman Church have rallied to the support of supernatural Christianity." Such a statement revealed a freedom from narrowly parochial attitudes and a willingness to make common cause with scholars from other communions who would lend their support to the historic faith.[17]

In retrospect, it is not surprising that Machen took the firm stand that he did in 1911. By that time he would have been well advanced in his work on the four major articles he published in 1912, the first of which appeared in the January number of the *Princeton Theological Review*. These articles marked the public emergence of Machen from his years of doubt and confusion, and they decisively declared his positions on crucial questions of New Testament scholarship. Those positions were not reached suddenly, but were the culmination of years of study and reflection. It is certainly to be expected that indications of the destination toward which Machen was moving in his intellectual pilgrimage would be seen before he finally arrived. Machen's book reviews through 1911 give an increasingly clear glimpse of that destination.

Machen's sole review of 1912 underscored his high regard for historical scholarship and, perhaps corresponding to this, disclosed a preference for a historical over an experiential method in Christian apologetics. The subject of the review was the volume *Christ and His Critics* by F. R. Montgomery Hitchcock, a British writer who had authored several popular titles. Besides commending the author for his views on the trustworthiness of the New Testament and the supernatural origin of Christianity, Machen offered two criticisms of Hitchcock's position. In the first place, despite the title of the book, Machen complained, "Mr. Hitchcock apparently has little regard for historical criticism." Machen pointed out serious flaws in Hitchcock's argument, flaws which revealed that the author had little acquaintance with recent criticism. This was to be expected, however, for in the second place, Hitchcock exalted "the argument from Christian experience at the expense of other kinds of evidence." Hitchcock gave priority to the subjective experience of faith in Christ over the argument from the authenticity of the Gospels as the ground for believing the orthodox view of the person of Jesus. Such a position clearly involved for Machen an inadequate appreciation of historical evidence. Furthermore, the author had failed to define the relationship between the two kinds of evidence for the truthfulness of Christianity, the historical and the experiential. Machen was puzzled by a passage in the book which seemed to suggest that the fate of Christianity was independent of that of the New Testament at the hands of modern criticism. Such an idea was preposterous to Machen, for it surrendered the historical grounding of the Christian faith. In spite of these theoretical problems, Machen regarded the book as an expression of genuine religious experience, and as a demonstration that "real Christian experience is possible only if Jesus be regarded as a supernatural person." Machen closed by acknowledging that the argument from Christian experience was a potent one – but not the only one – for the historicity of the New Testament.[18]

These comments reflect a concern which Machen was to maintain for the rest of his life. Perhaps as a result of his own experience in wrestling with critical questions, he was vitally concerned that the factual historicity of the New Testament receive due acknowledgment on the basis of the historical evidence. Though he readily acknowledged the validity of the argument from Christian experience, yet historical scholarship provided for him the first line of defense of the documents and events of the New Testament; these were, after all, historical documents reporting purportedly historical events. In Machen's own struggle, it was the historicity of the supernatural origin and nature of Christianity which had hung in doubt. And he had settled the question for himself by means of his own thorough, painstaking (but hardly dispassionate) investigation of the available historical data and conflicting historiographical viewpoints. It was not unnatural for him, as a consequence, to give preeminence to the historical argument for the validity of Christianity. While he was willing to acknowledge the strength of the argument from Christian experience, this apologetic could not serve for Machen as more than a confirmation of the argument from historical evidence.

Machen's Progress to 1912

A survey of Machen's book reviews from 1907 to 1912 by no means fills all the gaps or answers all the questions about his intellectual progress during this decisive period of his life. At no point did Machen inform the reader of the whole scope of his own theological beliefs, nor could he readily do so, given the nature and limitations of the format in which he was writing. Furthermore, as a reviewer for the staunchly conservative *Princeton Theological Review*, he would have been expected to adhere more or less closely to the Princeton position on controversial questions; and, in fact, he showed little interest in departing from the party line. It is, however, possible to detect a measure of progress in the stance that Machen adopted and the positions he was willing to affirm: the latter portion of this period seems to display a distinct advance over the earlier in these respects.

With regard to the earlier portion of the period, the years 1907 and 1908, three observations are pertinent. First, Machen commonly confined his remarks to technical and critical matters. When he did discuss theology, it was generally the question of the Incarnation and its mode that concerned him; this was, of course, the central issue with which he was struggling. This particular theological emphasis is partially explained by the fact that two of the five books he reviewed during these years dealt with the virgin birth. It should also be remembered, however, that it was undoubtedly his continuing interest and growing expertise with respect to this question, coupled with his willingness to review books on the topic, that encouraged the assigning of such volumes to him.

Second, while Machen was certainly willing to align himself with conservative views on theological and critical questions, it is worthy of note that he displayed no developed doctrine of scripture during these years. Although five reviews admittedly provide only slender evidence, and the argument from silence is not without its dangers, yet it may be observed that Machen never mentioned the inspiration of the Bible, nor did he ever appeal to it in argumentation, but always based his case on historical evidence. He appears to have been concerned more with the factual historicity of the New Testament than with the theological implications of its nature as Holy Scripture. It can scarcely be doubted that for him, the latter meant nothing apart from the former; the inspiration of the New Testament could hardly be considered if the essential truthfulness of its documents regarding Jesus and the gospel was shown to be doubtful in historical terms.

Third, Machen continued to give prominence to a type of presuppositional argument. In his earlier article on the virgin birth he had allowed for theological bias as a factor which conditioned scholarly evaluations of the evidence, and this consideration surfaced again in his reviews of the Sweet and Orr volumes on the same topic. He was not unaware that a scholar's judgment is affected by his prior philosophical or theological commitments; indeed, he refused to separate this factor from the main question. Machen repeatedly affirmed that one's position with respect to the possibility of supernatural events in general, and the Incarnation in particular, will exercise perhaps a decisive influence on one's verdict regarding the historicity of the virgin birth.

In the reviews which Machen wrote during the latter portion of this period, from 1909 to 1912, several changes are evident. A difference is observable in the tone he adopted: Machen's reviews became less tenuous, more confident. Although he still commented on technical matters and critical questions, he entered more readily into discussion of controversial theological questions besides that of the Incarnation, as in his critiques of the Gilbert and Bacon volumes. His criticisms became more pungent, as particularly seen in his comments on the Scott title. Machen in these years showed a growing

concern for the spiritual well-being of the church at large as the effects
of critical views and liberal theology made themselves felt more
widely, especially at the popular level. For the first time he made
reference to the traditional doctrine of inspiration, and utilized it as a
basis for criticizing an author's stance (though not as the basis of
appeal for determining a historical question). And he came down
strongly in favor of a historical apologetic without repudiating his
previous use of presuppositional argument. These two approaches
may have been closely related in Machen's thinking, for although he
believed that the intellectual case for supernatural redemptive
Christianity rested on historical evidence, yet he also acknowledged
that one's presuppositional bias could result in a rejection or
misinterpretation of that evidence.

The conclusion that there was a definite shift in Machen's posture,
observable in his reviews beginning in 1909, is consonant with
Stonehouse's suggestion that by the spring of that year Machen had
come to identify closely with Princeton Seminary and its work. It
also accords with other changes that were occurring in his life, such
as his gradually expanding preaching ministry. It is possible, then, or
perhaps even likely, that back of these visible changes Machen had
reached a decisive settlement of that troublesome historical and
intellectual question that became so spiritually and emotionally
disturbing as well. It is probable that by 1909 Machen had definitively
resolved for himself the question of the supernatural origin of
Christianity, deciding in favor of the historicity of the New Testament
accounts. The essays that Machen published in 1912, dealing with
just such matters, lend support to this thesis, for the allowance of
adequate preparation time for their production would require a starting
point at least several months before the end of 1911. Indeed, Machen
had indicated in August 1910 that he was working on the topic of the
virgin birth, but that progress was slow and "it is difficult to say how
long it will be before my magnum opus will appear." It was fully
twenty years before *The Virgin Birth of Christ* was published in 1930,
but the first installments of that volume appeared in the *Princeton
Theological Review* in 1912. Attention now turns to the essays of that
year.[19]

CHAPTER 6

MACHEN'S PUBLIC EMERGENCE: THE MAJOR ESSAYS OF 1912

The year 1912 was a momentous one for both American culture and J. Gresham Machen. By 1912, as Morton White and Henry F. May have argued, the ideology of historicism was in place in America and was beginning to make itself felt in several circles of literary and artistic intelligentsia. While America was thus poised to enter an era of unprecedented bewilderment, confusion, and doubt, Machen had largely resolved his own intellectual and spiritual difficulties and now emerged as a scholarly proponent of supernatural redemptive Christianity. American culture and J. Gresham Machen crossed paths in 1912, but they were headed in different directions, Machen toward certitude and the confidence it brings, the culture toward historical relativism and the resultant epistemological skepticism. That the dominant culture later rejected Machen should not be surprising; given the divergence of their movement, it could hardly have been otherwise.

Machen's direction in 1912 was heralded by four scholarly essays which he published in that year. These essays may be taken to mark his public emergence as a scholar, for they set forth the results of several years of study and outlined the future course of his scholarly work. Three of the essays dealt with the virgin birth and appeared in the *Princeton Theological Review*. The fourth was a study of the historical connection between Jesus and Paul, and constituted Machen's contribution to a commemorative volume celebrating Princeton's centennial. These two topics formed the subjects of Machen's later works of New Testament criticism: *The Origin of Paul's Religion* (1921) and *The Virgin Birth of Christ* (1930). The 1912 articles served, therefore, to lay out the program of Machen's scholarly labors for the next two decades; they also indicate that his major monographs were the fruit of years – even decades – of serious consideration of the problems involved.[1]

Machen's Articles on the Virgin Birth

Because of their similarity of subject matter, the first two of Machen's articles on the virgin birth may be considered together. "The Hymns of the First Chapter of Luke" appeared in the January number of the *Princeton Theological Review* for 1912, "The Origin of the First Two Chapters of Luke" in April. Combined, the two articles run to more than one hundred pages, constituting a not inconsiderable debut for the re-emergent young scholar – Machen now being thirty years old. Both articles dealt with the question of the possible sources behind the first two chapters of Luke's Gospel, containing the birth narratives of Jesus and John the Baptist. The common method for explaining the Hebraistic style of Luke 1:5-2:52, in contrast to the pure Greek style of the prologue (Luke 1:1-4), had been to assume that Luke was using a source for the birth narratives, and that he left essentially unaltered the Hebraistic flavor of the original. Machen was particularly concerned to refute the theory of Adolf Harnack that these chapters were composed by Luke himself, who adopted for them an Old Testament style in conscious imitation of the Septuagint, the Greek translation of the Hebrew scriptures.[2]

The first essay was devoted to a consideration of the song of Mary the mother of Jesus in Luke 1:46-55 (the "Magnificat") and the song of Zacharias the father of John the Baptist in Luke 1:68-79 (the "Benedictus"). Harnack contended that although Luke may have utilized oral tradition in the production of the narrative as a whole, he had no such source when composing the hymns of Mary and Zacharias, but pieced them together himself from phrases garnered from the Septuagint. When the Septuagint words and phrases are removed from the Magnificat and Benedictus, Harnack claimed, the remaining portion of the hymns bears the clear impress of Luke's style, thus demonstrating Lucan authorship. This Machen denied.[3]

Machen found it unnecessary to treat in detail Harnack's argument with respect to the Magnificat. That piece of work had already been done by the German scholar Friedrich Spitta, and Machen considered Spitta's criticism to constitute a complete refutation of Harnack. Machen now proposed to subject the Benedictus to the same kind of examination, following a method similar to that of Spitta. He wrote:

The words and phrases which Harnack, Zimmermann and other investigators regard as Lucan characteristics should be examined as to their occurrence in the Septuagint. If it be discovered that the supposed Lucan characteristics are also characteristic of the Septuagint, the argument for Lucan authorship will be decidedly weakened. . . . If this Septuagint element be subtracted, are there enough Lucan peculiarities left to prove anything more than Lucan editorship?

For some ten pages following, Machen took up, one by one, the words, phrases, and grammatical constructions of the Benedictus which were alleged by Harnack and others to be marks of Luke's authorship. He found many of these to be used in the Septuagint, and others which admitted of a different explanation than authorship by Luke: "The Lucan expressions are found to be also Old Testament expressions, which would occur naturally to any Jewish Christian." As a result, the residue of truly Lucan linguistic characteristics was greatly reduced; that residue would not be inconsistent with the hypothesis of Luke's translation of the hymns from an Aramaic original.[4]

The structure of the hymns was next given consideration, Machen arguing persuasively against Harnack that they were Hebraistic rather than Greek in poetic structure. Machen then pressed his own case based on the content of the hymns, contending that their non-Christian (or more precisely, pre-Christian) character made it extremely unlikely that they were composed by a Christian, Jewish or Gentile, or were inserted into the narrative by a Christian author if they were not authentic. After examining various proposals regarding the authorship of the hymns, Machen concluded that the hypothesis which best accounts for all the facts is that the Magnificat was derived from an Aramaic song of Mary; that it circulated separately from the birth narratives themselves; and that it was inserted by Luke in its present position in the narrative after having been translated, perhaps by Luke himself. A similar case could be made for the Benedictus.[5]

This essay was momentous not only because it first announced Machen's presence on the scene as an evangelical scholar to be reckoned with, but also because it constituted in substance the first chapter to be written for his magnum opus of 1930, *The Virgin Birth of Christ*. Chapter IV of his book was to bear the same title as this article, and although the detailed argument from the Septuagint was omitted from the chapter, the discussion was brought up to date with the consideration of scholarly opinion on the subject through the 1920s.[6]

Additional material for the book was provided by the second article in this series. Elements of "The Origin of the First Two Chapters of Luke" found their way into several of the early chapters of *The Virgin Birth of Christ*. Its primary contribution, however, was unique to this essay. Machen performed for the rest of Luke 1:5-2:52 the kind of labor which in the earlier article he had bestowed on the Benedictus and which Spitta had done for the Magnificat. In a piece of work which must have been tedious and demanding, he again considered, by comparison with Septuagint usage, those Greek words, phrases, and grammatical constructions which were alleged by Harnack and others to be Lucan characteristics. In many cases, Machen found evidence to support Harnack's contention, or at least to lend weight to it. In many other instances, however, Machen found that Harnack's case was weakened by the occurrence of the words or phrases with sufficient frequency in the Septuagint to cast doubt upon their distinctiveness as peculiarities of Lucan style. For some forty pages Machen laid out the results of such painstaking linguistic investigation, moving verse by verse through Luke 1 and 2. He then turned to the interpretation of the phenomena he had uncovered. In contrast to Harnack's hypothesis that Luke was the outright author of chapters one and two, Machen saw at least three other possibilities. It was possible that both Luke (in the rest of the Gospel and in Acts) and his source for the birth narratives had been influenced by the Septuagint. Or Luke could have been dependent on a source for the early chapters of Acts (which exhibit the greatest linguistic affinity with Luke 1:5-2:52) which was similar in character to his source for the birth narrative, both sources originating in the Jewish Christian community. Or, finally, Luke himself could have been influenced by his source for Luke 1 and 2, so that his own style elsewhere reflected the "simple grandeur and poetic dignity" which the source possessed in common with the Greek Old Testament. When all the linguistic evidence was considered, Machen concluded that it pointed clearly to the narrative's Jewish Christian origin and just as distinctly to Luke's work as editor.[7]

Machen then turned to a consideration of the content of this section. He contended that its acquaintance with Palestinian conditions and Jewish customs, its accurate reflection of the Jewish religious ideal, and its intimate familiarity with Palestinian persons argued strongly for the Palestinian and Jewish Christian origin of the birth narrative. How then did the narrative originate? Machen regarded Harnack's

contention that Luke composed it without the use of written sources
as possible, but unproven; at any rate, such an origin would support
an early date for the writing of Luke-Acts, because of the authentically
Palestinian character of the birth narrative. Also possible were the
hypotheses that Luke translated an Aramaic written source, or that he
utilized a Greek written source. Such matters could not be decided
with certainty. Two facts, however, had been established. "In the first
place, the birth narrative formed an original part of the Third Gospel,
and in the second place, it is genuinely primitive and Palestinian."
These conclusions, he claimed, were "independent of the disputed
questions" and constituted "the really important facts." Machen closed
the article with a defense of the unity of the written source behind the
narrative (if there was one) against attempts to divide it into distinct
elements.[8]

Several aspects of these two essays are worthy of note. First, it
may be observed that Machen was arguing for the historical integrity
of the birth narrative and for the historicity of the events therein
described. In what amounts to an interesting twist for conservative
criticism, he was arguing against the Lucan authorship of the passage,
but in behalf of a more authentically historical account than even Luke
himself could have provided. In claiming that the narrative originated
within a primitive Jewish Christian setting, Machen was insisting that
there had been preserved an authentic tradition that derived from the
real flesh-and-blood history of supernatural events. This stance was
consonant with his conviction that historic redemptive Christianity
was grounded in genuinely historical events. Whether or not all these
events could be historically investigated was another question –
although Machen certainly seemed to think the utmost effort should
be made – yet for him it was inconceivable that Christianity could be
true at the same time that the alleged events that lay at its foundation
were false or legendary. It was perhaps the primary conclusion of his
long intellectual struggle that Christianity was founded upon true and
truly historical (even if supernatural) events. But underlying that
struggle was the assumption that gave birth to it: that Christianity
could not be spiritually true and historically false. From the beginning
of his struggle, Machen seemed unwilling to tolerate any dichotomy
between the historical truthfulness of Christianity and its alleged
religious value; when he concluded that Christian teaching was true,
that meant historically true. His personal inquiry had led him to wrestle

with this central question, and when he had arrived at a satisfactory answer for himself, he then devoted his scholarly abilities to the elucidation of that answer for the benefit of others – as in these essays.

Furthermore, Machen was convinced that his position could be supported by reasonable argument. His whole endeavor in producing these articles was predicated on the assumption that rational argumentation based on the available historical evidence could lead to the not unreasonable conclusion that the events narrated in the first two chapters of Luke were true – that is, they actually occurred in essentially the way described. It may be warranted to conclude that, even at this early point in Machen's career, faith was in his view not an irrational leap contrary to all evidence, but was rather a conviction which was fully in accord with the evidence, rightly interpreted.

But this did not mean that Machen ignored the possibility that the evidence could be misinterpreted. He allowed once again for the influence of presuppositions. Machen argued throughout these articles that if the events described in the birth narratives actually occurred, then the events themselves account for the observable phenomena of the documents. Yet he recognized that the contrary assumption – that the events did not occur – could lead to different conclusions regarding the documents. In his argument regarding the Magnificat, for example, he acknowledged that the common assumption that Mary and the other characters in the narrative were legendary figures would bias an investigator against Machen's argument that the Magnificat actually derived from an Aramaic hymn of Mary. Thus while he considered the evidence to be powerful, and certainly adequate for a rational conviction, yet he did not regard it as necessarily compelling for someone else. He acknowledged that an antisupernaturalistic bias could lead to an antisupernaturalistic conclusion.[9]

Machen's scholarship in these articles was of a high order. He maintained a commendable level of objectivity in making detailed critical judgments, not allowing his overall position to predetermine his decisions, and he carefully weighed the alternatives. Although he defended the historicity of the supernatural events narrated in Luke 1 and 2, he also displayed a remarkably open attitude toward the historical genesis of the written account. Completely absent was any stereotyped or doctrinaire view of the manner of composition of the biblical documents. He considered Luke to have been an investigator, a historian who interviewed his subjects, made use of written sources, utilized whatever artistic and intellectual abilities were at his command, and who was himself subject to historical influences. Nor did the questions of textual criticism pose any problem for Machen. In the first essay on Luke he engaged in an extended discussion of the correct Greek text of Acts 3:21, deciding for a reading which differs somewhat from the text underlying the King James translation. This particular textual decision tended to undercut Machen's exegetical position, for one of the variant readings would have lent more support to his argument. Such objectivity is also to be seen in the long section of the second article in which he evaluated the allegedly Lucan linguistic characteristics of Luke 1 and 2 against the occurrence of these characteristics in the rest of the New Testament and in the Septuagint. He judiciously weighed the evidence, often disputing the conclusions of Harnack, but often conceding that Harnack's point was well taken.[10]

In short, Machen studied the Bible historically. His classical training had given him great familiarity with the historical context in which the New Testament originated, and he acknowledged that to a large degree the New Testament was conditioned by that context, both in form and in content. But he was unwilling to concede that its content – that is, the events it portrays and the message it contains – was wholly an expression of that historical context. Herein lies the difference between Machen and biblical scholars who had accepted historicist assumptions, such men as Arthur C. McGiffert, Gerald Birney Smith, and Shirley Jackson Case. Herein also lies the explanation for the great gulf which opened up between evangelical biblical study and the scholarship of the professionalized academic community and the liberal element in the churches. In accord with his own hard-won convictions, Machen was willing to allow for historical events that could be explained only by postulating direct divine involvement in earthly affairs. For Machen the virginal conception and birth of Jesus truly constituted the means by which God sent his Son into the world as a man in order to accomplish redemption for fallen humanity. Machen's refusal to accept the premises of historicism made it unnecessary for him to accept its conclusions, a posture which insured that he would soon stand outside the mainstream of American biblical scholarship – if he was not indeed outside it already.[11]

The Virgin Birth Tradition in the Second Century

The third of Machen's major essays of 1912 appeared in the October number of the *Princeton Theological Review*. This essay was of a different character from the others in that it did not involve direct study of the biblical text but rather examined the evidence for Christian belief in the virgin birth of Jesus during the second century of the Christian era. While the essay did not treat the biblical documents themselves, the labor required was much the same as that demanded in New Testament exegesis: establishing ancient historical contexts, determining the dates of documents and persons, ascertaining the content and meaning of Greek and Latin texts, and making judgments with respect to complex historical questions. In all this Machen showed himself nearly as much a master of the second century as he was of the first. This essay, modified by the elimination of some detailed argumentation and by the incorporation of references to more recent literature, eventually became Chapter I of *The Virgin Birth of Christ*.[12]

The purpose of the essay was to demonstrate the strength and early date of Christian belief in the virgin birth in the second century. Machen sought to accomplish this by first noting the prevalence of the belief in the time of Irenaeus (ca. 175-195), and then tracing the tradition backward toward the beginning of the century. He examined the evidence offered by the Apostles' Creed and the old Roman confession on which it was based, and by the church fathers Clement of Alexandria, Justin Martyr, Aristides, and Ignatius. He concluded that by A.D. 110 belief in the virgin birth as a fundamental fact of the life of Jesus was firmly rooted in the Christian community.[13]

Machen then turned to denials of the virgin birth in the second century, which he divided into three categories. The denials of the virgin birth by pagan opponents of Christianity possessed little value, he argued, for historical investigation as a means of religious argumentation was unknown in antiquity; therefore Christianity's pagan opponents would not have possessed reliable historical tradition concerning the birth of Jesus. Denials of the virgin birth by Jewish opponents of Christianity, such as those advanced by Trypho and those mentioned by Celsus, consisted mainly of objections to the virgin birth but embodied no positive historical tradition to the contrary. Denials of the virgin birth by professing Christians included, in the first place, those of Marcion, Carpocrates, and Cerinthus, all of whom were Gnostics and not orthodox Christians at all, and whose rejection of the virgin birth was demanded by their philosophical presuppositions. The virgin birth simply did not fit into their system of beliefs. Also among professing Christians who denied the virgin birth, in the second place, were certain Jewish Christians, some of whom were labelled "Ebionites" by Christian writers. Machen discussed the sometimes confusing references to various Jewish sects in Justin Martyr, Origen, Epiphanius, and Jerome, and included a lengthy discussion of the so-called "Gospel According to the Hebrews." A careful examination persuaded him that Jewish Christian denials of the virgin birth were prompted by prior philosophical commitments (to Gnosticism or Pharisaic Judaism) and thus carried little weight as evidence against the virgin birth. Such denials were again based on no independent historical tradition as to the earthly origin of Jesus, and at any rate were outweighed by the Jewish Christian affirmation of the virgin birth.[14]

The essay closed with a treatment of the recent work (1911) by Alfred Schmidtke on the Jewish Christian gospels. Machen concluded that Schmidtke's historical reconstruction, while quite innovative, did not overturn his own argument. Machen's argument came in two propositions at the end of the essay:

1. A firm and well-formulated belief in the virgin birth extends back to the early years of the second century.

2. The denials of the virgin birth which appeared after the beginning of the second century were based upon philosophical or dogmatic prepossession more probably than upon genuine historical tradition.[15]

The cautious way in which Machen stated his primary conclusions bespeaks the exercise of a careful and balanced judgment in his scholarly work. He gives the appearance of attempting not to overstate his case, and he certainly seemed to be aware that historical conclusions are at best only probable conclusions.

Another indication of carefulness and thoroughness is found in his discussion of a disputed reading in the Greek text of Justin Martyr's *Dialogue*. Following Harnack's example, he had personally examined the primary manuscript of the *Dialogue* in the Bibliotheque Nationale at Paris, and determined that the long-accepted reading of the disputed passage was clearly in error. He attributed the mistaken reading, which had given rise to much confusion and needless argument and speculation, to a careless blunder on the part of Stephanus (Robert Estienne), the first publisher of the printed text in the sixteenth century, a blunder which had been copied by editors ever since.[16]

Perhaps the primary significance of this essay, apart from its central thesis, is what it reveals about Machen's conception of the historical study of the Bible. He pursued the study of the New Testament in its full historical context, which meant that the Christianity of the first century could not properly be investigated apart from that of the second. Thus he went to the second-century evidence – the creeds and the church fathers – to determine what was commonly believed about the virgin birth. This investigation was undertaken in light of contemporary scholarship and included a good deal of interaction with the leading scholars in the field, who were mostly German.

Machen's conclusions in "The Virgin Birth in the Second Century" also laid the groundwork for a type of argument which he was often to employ, that which rests on the need for historical explanation of particular phenomena. In this case the phenomenon was the firm and well-formulated Christian belief in the virgin birth in the early second century, a belief rejected only by aberrant forms of Christianity. What accounts for this belief? Machen did not pursue the question to its ultimate conclusion at this point, but in light of his other current writing on the virgin birth as well as his later work, it is clear what he considered a historically adequate answer to be. The virgin birth was a fundamental element of Christian belief in the second century only because it was part of the original basic teaching of Christianity in the first century; and the adequate explanation for the latter fact is that it was a true account of how the Son of God entered the world. Such a line of argumentation shows both Machen's adoption of the historical method and his alienation from some of its commonly-held presuppositions. On the one hand, he observed the phenomena of the second century and sought a historical explanation for them in terms of previous events and processes, namely, first-century Christian beliefs about the virgin birth. On the other hand, when historical argument led back to the possibility of an actual virginal conception and birth at the beginning of the earthly life of Jesus, he did not rule out such a possibility *a priori*, as a consistent historicism would have required, but was willing to accept the event as a genuine supernatural occurrence if the evidence demanded it. Machen's Christian philosophical presuppositions allowed him to reach conclusions which differed from those of most practitioners of the historical method; yet he strongly insisted that as a New Testament scholar he was a historian, and he seemed to have little doubt about the validity of his use of the historical method. Indeed, he pushed the demand for historical explanation against his scholarly opponents, seeking not only a plausible but a demonstrably correct historical account for the evident phenomena.[17]

Jesus and Paul

Machen's three 1912 essays on the virgin birth dealt only in a limited way, and indirectly, with the supernatural element in Christianity. Those essays were chiefly occupied with technical questions involving Greek words and literary dependence and theological formulations, questions which when resolved at Machen's hand left room for just the possibility of divine activity in earthly affairs. The question of the supernatural origin of Christianity was not skirted – it was always indirectly in view and was the main target toward which Machen was headed – but it was not the immediate question under investigation, however much it might have been suggested by Machen's conclusions. The case was otherwise with the final essay of this year. The issue of the supernatural origin of Christianity was immediately broached and constantly addressed in Machen's treatment of the relationship between Paul and Jesus.[18]

Indeed, "Jesus and Paul" addressed much larger issues than Machen's other essays. Perhaps the momentous nature of the occasion for which it was produced encouraged him to plumb the depths and soar to the heights of both religious feeling and historical argument. That occasion was the celebration in 1912 of the one-hundredth anniversary of the founding of Princeton Theological Seminary. Besides holding a week-long centennial observance in the spring of that year – attended by President William Howard Taft, Chief Justice Edward D. White, Scottish and Irish Presbyterian church officials, and other dignitaries – the seminary also issued a commemorative volume, *Biblical and Theological Studies*, consisting of essays written by the seminary faculty. Machen's prior reflection on the meaning of the anniversary, in combination with his recent scholarly work, may have sharpened his appreciation of the distinctive emphases of Princeton's theological stance. In describing the week's events to his family, he commented on how frequently during the proceedings Princeton's Calvinism was mentioned but lamented the fact that few speakers dealt with the burning issue of the day:

. . . comparatively few of the speakers – whether friend or foe –
seemed to recognize clearly the real thing for which Princeton is
fighting, namely *supernatural* Christianity. Dr. Patton was almost
alone in isolating the big issue clearly from all the others and putting
it squarely in the foreground. What opportunities the speakers missed!
How few big men there are in the Church and in the world!

Although Stonehouse warns against reading too much into this remark,
it seems justified to conclude that Machen at this time believed that
the issue which most needed to be addressed was the supernaturalness
of Christianity (he later came to believe that Calvinism was the most
consistent vantage point from which to address this issue). Machen's
comment also suggests that he was convinced that there was a specific
need for men who indeed would address the question. Recognizing
the need, would he himself be willing to step forward and fill the
gap? The evidence offered by "Jesus and Paul" suggests that he was
attempting to do just that.[19]

The essay is also significant because of its relationship to Machen's
later work. Nearly a decade later he published his first full-scale book,
The Origin of Paul's Religion (1921), which was an elaboration of
the arguments he employed in "Jesus and Paul." In the book, of course,
he could enter into much more detailed discussion of the evidence,
treat some topics left untouched in the essay, and make full and specific
reference to the literature on the subject. But the essay contained, in
seed form, the essential ideas and arguments found in the book. This
fact serves as another indication that by 1912 Machen had reached a
decisive juncture in his intellectual life, and also that his mature
scholarship as found in his major books was the fruit of long reflection
on the questions he addressed.

The central argument of "Jesus and Paul" is that Paul was truly a
disciple of Jesus only if Jesus was a supernatural person and that such
a conclusion concerning Jesus is the only adequate way to account
for the available data. After arguing for the importance of the question
of the relationship between Paul and Jesus – it is "absolutely
fundamental," for Paul has always been received in the church as
only a witness to Jesus – Machen used the conclusions reached by
Wilhelm Wrede as his starting point. In his 1905 book *Paulus*, Wrede
had brought into the open what was already implicit in the liberal
reconstruction of Jesus: that Paul was no disciple of the "liberal" Jesus.

If the liberal Jesus were the true Jesus, then Paul was not his disciple, for Paul's theology portrayed Jesus not as a religious teacher but as a supernatural redeemer. Machen disputed the liberal solution to this problem, which attempted to separate Paul's theology (derived from non-Christian sources) from Paul's religion (the imitation of Christ) in order to save the latter. All such attempts had resulted in failure, Machen declared: Paul's piety cannot be cut off from his theology. The true solution to the question of Paul's relationship to Jesus is to be found by examining Paul's religion and theology together within the context of the early church. Starting the investigation with Paul is an appropriate method, both because Paul is more readily known from the sources than is Jesus, and because in a situation where the question of dependence is in dispute, it is significant that Paul came after Jesus.[20]

One of the central issues, Machen claimed, was whether the original apostles of Jesus regarded Paul as an innovator, either with respect to his teaching on Christian freedom from the law or with respect to his view of the person of Christ. Machen argued that they did not, and that Paul was regarded both by his contemporaries and by himself as a true disciple of Jesus. In so arguing, Machen countered three opposing viewpoints. First, he consciously consigned to oblivion F. C. Baur's thesis of a sharp disjunction between Palestinian and Pauline Christianity concerning Christian freedom from the law, and he noted Ritschl's and Harnack's opposition to that thesis as well. Second, Machen registered his disagreement with the "modern radicalism" which saw Paul's view of Christ as essentially different from the Palestinian view. Nowhere in the New Testament, he said, is there a trace of conflict between Paul and the Palestinian Christians over the doctrine of the person of Christ – everywhere they are in perfect agreement. Third, Machen disposed of the objections that Paul himself insisted on the independence of his gospel from tradition and that Paul neither knew nor cared much about the earthly life of Jesus. To the first of these Machen replied that what Paul received at his conversion was proof of the resurrection of Jesus and a new interpretation of the facts about Jesus; Paul received the facts themselves from other sources. To the second objection Machen responded that Paul actually said more about the earthly Jesus than is sometimes claimed, and that he knew more than he said.[21]

This representation of Paul as a true disciple of Jesus is not overturned, Machen argued, by an examination of the Gospels. It

cannot be proved that the Gospel portrayal of Jesus, either in John or
in the synoptics, is dependent on the Pauline conception of Christ.
There is a marked difference of expression between Paul and the
Gospel of John. And if the synoptic Gospels reflect the Pauline
conception of Christ, then there remains "not a single document which
preserves a pre-Pauline conception of Christ" – a remarkable if not
impossible situation, considering the absence of any sign of struggle
between an original primitive conception of Christ and the supposedly
later Pauline conception. Therefore "the transition from the human
Jesus to the divine Christ," if there was such a transition, "must be
placed . . . not between the primitive church and Paul, but between
Jesus and the primitive church." Machen argued that such a rapid
deification of a human being, among his own contemporaries and
representing serious conviction, would constitute an apotheosis
unparalleled in human history – as the most naturalistic of New
Testament scholars will admit (H. J. Holtzman, for example) – and
still lacks adequate explanation. It would appear, suggested Machen,
that the alleged starting point of this process is faulty, and that there
never existed a purely human Jesus. Such a Jesus would have to be
reconstructed from the documents by critical scholarship, a feat which
has never been accomplished. Believing that Jesus' disciples made a
leap from knowing him as a mere man to worshipping him as the
God-man requires more credulity than simply believing the
straightforward supernaturalism of the Gospel accounts.[22]

The harmony between Paul and Jesus further appears in Paul's
reflection of just those elements of Jesus' teaching considered by
modern critical scholarship to be most characteristic of Jesus: the
Fatherhood of God, and love as the fulfillment of the law. Paul also
exhibited great appreciation for the character of Jesus, but it is not in
this, nor in the mere imitation of Jesus, that the heart of Paulinism is
to be found. Not at all, declared Machen.

> The essence of Paul's religious life is not imitation of a dead prophet.
> It is communion with a living Lord. . . . The centre and core of
> Paulinism is not imitation of the earthly Jesus, but communion with
> the risen Christ. It was that which Paul himself regarded as the very
> foundation of his own life.

But, Machen argued, if communion with Christ was at the center of
Paulinism, "then quite the most fundamental thing about Christ is

that he is alive. It is sheer folly to say that this Pauline Christ-religion can be reproduced by one who supposes that Christ is dead." This explains Paul's seemingly disproportionate emphasis on the death and resurrection of Christ: it was by means of his death and resurrection that Christ accomplished forgiveness of sin and enabled the Christian believer to enjoy fellowship with a holy God. In the very nature of things, this truth could not be taught as clearly by Jesus before his death and resurrection as it was by Paul afterward. But the fact remains that for Paul as well as for the primitive church, Jesus was the founder of Christianity not because of what he taught, but by virtue of what he did. And what he did had cosmic significance only because he was a supernatural person, "a divine being, come to earth for the salvation of men." Thus, Machen concluded forcefully, "If Jesus was not a supernatural person, then not only Paulinism but also the whole of Christianity is founded not upon the lofty teaching of an inspired prophet, but upon a colossal error."[23]

So sharply did Machen discern the issues and lay them out that no middle ground remained when he finished. The alternatives were simple. Either Jesus was a supernatural person, Paul was his disciple, and historic Christianity is true; or Jesus was not a supernatural person, Paul was not truly his disciple, and historic Christianity is false. In an almost evangelistic appeal, Machen closed his essay with the recognition that accepting the former alternative would be difficult for many modern people. To acknowledge a supernatural Jesus required the overcoming of "our most deep-seated convictions"; but, he said, "unless we fulfil that condition, we can never share in the religious experience of Paul." At the root of the problem was the matter of one's approach to history. Machen wrote:

In exalting the methods of scientific history, we involve ourselves hopelessly in historical difficulty. In the relation between Jesus and Paul, we discover a problem, which, through the very processes of mind by which the uniformity of nature has been established, forces us to transcend that doctrine – which pushes us relentlessly off the safe ground of the phenomenal world toward the abyss of supernaturalism – which forces us, despite the resistance of the modern mind, to make the great venture of faith, and found our lives no longer upon what can be procured by human effort or understood as a phase of evolution, but upon him who has linked us with the unseen world, and brought us into communion with the eternal God.[24]

Clearly, Machen acknowledged that the historical question of the origin of Christianity could not be resolved by purely historical means. Mere scholarship is inadequate to grasp the supernatural. Scholarship can perhaps point the way because it leads to an insoluble historical problem; but the solution to that problem can be grasped only by "the great venture of faith." A worthy foundation for human life is to be found not in what can be "procured by human effort" (rationalistic scholarship?) or "understood as a phase of evolution" (a naturalistic conception of Christianity?) but in that supernatural person, Jesus Christ, who has become man's link to the unseen world and who has made possible man's fellowship with God. This passage is particularly significant because it appears to set Machen's conception of Christianity over against the historical consciousness that was coming to prevail in American intellectual circles even as he wrote. In this essay, which as Stonehouse suggests, constituted something of a confession of faith for Machen, the young scholar recognized in Christianity something which transcended the capacity of scientific historical scholarship to grasp. Even though he utilized with considerable skill the devices of historical argumentation to establish his case, Machen was driving toward a dilemma which he acknowledged historical scholarship powerless to resolve. The act of personally appropriating the supernatural reality of Jesus was one which did not contradict the best critical argumentation (he has just spent thirty closely reasoned pages making his historical case) but it did move far beyond mere critical acumen; it is an act of faith, not of scholarship. With this declaration, Machen disclosed his essential principles and made a decisive break with the assumptions underlying historicism.

The other contributions of "Jesus and Paul" to an understanding of Machen may also be noted. Among them is the sharpness with which he drew the distinction between supernatural and nonsupernatural versions of Christianity (although the latter, in his view, was an impossibility). Machen had decided in earlier years, while still wrestling with his doubt and confusion, that the difference between the new theology and the old affected the very essence of Christianity. When he finally resolved the issue for himself, and in this essay above all the others of 1912 declared himself, he was not inclined to leave any intellectual middle ground. Indeed, he could see none. The historic interpretation of Christianity as a supernatural religion of redemption – the historic faith of the church – was either true or it was not. In either case the implication was clear. If it be true, it should continue as the faith of the church; if untrue, it was unworthy of anyone's adherence and should be honestly given up. This conviction had a greater effect on Machen's attitude toward ecclesiastical antagonists than toward scholarly opponents. On the one hand, he discussed critical options, from the most conservative to the most radical, with reasoned calmness, and treated critical scholars in the same way, often showing appreciation for their learning and brilliance. On the other hand, as his interest and involvement in church affairs increased, he manifested a distinct unwillingness to consider liberal churchmen as anything other than dishonest traitors who were denying the faith they professed. The difference in attitude may be accounted for by the different realms in which the two classes of opponent operated: scholarship was the sphere of intellectual exchange, while the church was the divinely-ordained agency for the proclamation of the truth of the gospel. Tolerance in the former sphere was necessary and commendable. In the latter it had definite limits, and Machen's limit was reached when ministers, teachers, and officials of the church undermined the faith he had struggled so long to secure for himself and which they had pledged themselves to uphold.[25]

Also to be seen in this essay, perhaps more so than in any of Machen's writings so far, is his use of the argument of historical explanation. Typical is his statement summarizing the thesis he was advancing: "If Jesus was simply a human teacher, then Paulinism defies explanation." His central argument was a historical one, and in Machen's hands it showed both the strength and limits of the historical method. The power of Machen's argument lay in his insistence that the phenomenon of Paulinism requires historical explanation. If the only adequate explanation takes one beyond merely human history and into the mysterious realm of direct divine activity in earthly affairs, then that simply demonstrates the limitations of historical scholarship.[26]

The scholarly essays of 1912, taken together, constitute a clear and public announcement that a decisive corner had been turned in Machen's intellectual and spiritual journey. They signalled the dispersion of his confusion and doubt, and announced that he had become an unqualified adherent of the historic faith, the supernatural and redemptive Christianity of ancient creed and Reformation testimony. Furthermore, the essays proclaimed Machen's presence on the intellectual scene not only as an adherent but also as a defender of supernatural Christianity. At the higher levels of scholarship, it is not to be doubted that proponents and defenders of the historic faith were becoming a proportionately decreasing number; with these essays Machen joined that number. Indeed, his concern to defend supernatural Christianity seemed at this time to overshadow his solicitude for Princeton's Calvinism, but he was later to modify his stance on this question. Finally, the essays marked Machen's emergence as a New Testament scholar to be reckoned with. In an unusual move, Adolf Harnack, whose views Machen had challenged in his two articles on Luke, reviewed Machen's articles in *Theologische Literaturzeitung* in January 1913 (scholars did not ordinarily review journal articles). While Harnack naturally expressed disagreement with Machen's thesis, he pronounced the studies "admirable" and "deserving of every attention." Such public notice from the most eminent New Testament scholar of the day, as Stonehouse suggests, served to give standing to Machen's work and to reinforce his self-confidence. In sum, it appears that Machen's convictions were now solidified, his abilities confirmed, and his direction for the future clear.[27]

Christianity and Culture

The impression that Machen had reached a decisive point is given confirmation by an address which he delivered in the fall of 1912. On 20 September Machen spoke on "Christianity and Culture" at the opening exercises of Princeton Seminary's 101st year. In what was intended as a popular message to the academic community rather than as a scholarly essay, Machen issued a ringing call for a Christian response to the cultural trends of the day. Several emphases of this address are noteworthy.[28]

In the first place, Machen began clearly to express his belief concerning the nature of the modern ideological opposition to Christianity. Machen suggested that there were three alternative models for viewing the relationship between culture and Christianity: the subordination of Christianity to culture, the destruction of culture by Christianity, and the Christian consecration of culture to divine ends. The third alternative was that which Machen supported: let Christians cultivate the arts and sciences "with all the enthusiasm of the veriest humanist, but at the same time consecrate them to the service of our God." Such consecration required Christian engagement with modern intellectual and cultural currents in order both to enjoy beauty and the acquisition of knowledge and also to appropriate what might be helpful to the cause of the gospel and oppose whatever is contrary to biblical Christianity. The second solution, the destruction of culture by Christianity, Machen considered to be illogical, unbiblical, and at bottom anti-intellectual. But the first alternative was worse, for it involved the destruction of Christianity altogether. Machen described this option in the following words:

> In the first place, Christianity may be subordinated to culture. That solution really, though to some extent unconsciously, is being favored by a very large and influential portion of the Church today. For the elimination of the supernatural in Christianity – so tremendously common today – really makes Christianity merely natural. Christianity becomes a human product, a mere part of human culture.

In writing that "Christianity may be subordinated to culture," it is unclear whether Machen meant that Christianity may be subordinated to ancient culture by its being construed as a mere product of that culture, or that Christianity may be subordinated to modern culture by its being interpreted according to contemporary categories of analysis, by which it is made a mere product of ancient culture (the latter understanding seems more likely, since he was discussing the relationship of Christianity to modern culture). In either case the outcome was the same: Machen saw the assumptions of historicism at work in the elimination of the supernatural from Christianity and in the reinterpretation of the Christian faith which rendered it merely the product of natural cultural and historical forces – "Christianity becomes a human product, a mere part of human culture." In claiming that this historicizing spirit had invaded the church, Machen seems to have been defining theological liberalism as an expression of historicism. This understanding of liberalism is in accord with the position advanced by Machen in his 1923 book, *Christianity and Liberalism*, and by later historians such as William Hutchison and Sydney Ahlstrom. Machen clearly repudiated this historicist interpretation of Christianity with its rejection of the supernatural and its implication of cultural relativism. "In subordinating Christianity to culture we have really destroyed Christianity, and what continues to bear the old name is a counterfeit." Here Machen also continued to maintain his insistence on the radical disjunction of Christianity and liberalism.[29]

In the second place, Machen located the chief obstacle to acceptance of the Christian faith "in the intellectual sphere. Men do not accept Christianity because they can no longer be convinced that Christianity is true." This suggests that Machen recognized the difficulty that was being thrown in the pathway of Christian advance by the varied but widespread acceptance of the historicist outlook, especially in the academic world; he specifically mentioned the defection from Christianity among students at American and European universities. Although he did not explicitly identify the intellectual difficulties in view, he had described the historicist mentality earlier in this address, and he was quite likely referring to it here in more general terms. "The thought of the day, as it makes itself most strongly felt in the universities, is profoundly opposed to Christianity, or at least it is out of connection with Christianity." Even the spirit of indifference, which he believed accounted for much of the defection from Christianity, was due to an "intellectual atmosphere" which would not allow the Christian faith even to gain a hearing in many instances.[30]

In the third place, Machen held that the task of analyzing modern thought and assimilating it to Christianity was a task for the scholar who is "a regenerated man," one who had been renewed in his soul by the power of God and who would yield to no one "in the intensity and depth of his religious experience." Machen did not here amplify the point, but it does suggest that he posited an absolute distinction between the scholar who had known the biblical experience of regeneration and the one who had not. Understood in this way, his position would imply something of a break with the philosophy of Common Sense Realism and a commitment to a more presuppositional approach.[31]

In the fourth place, it is apparent that Machen was attempting to maintain the unity of truth in the face of forces which were tending toward fragmentation. While his entire address was a protest against the dichotomy between intellect and religion which he perceived as characterizing modern life, in some places the protest became explicit. He exclaimed: "What wonder that after such training" as divided Christianity from all matters of intellectual endeavor "we came to regard religion and culture as belonging to two entirely separate compartments of the soul, and their union as involving the destruction of both?" This concern seems to have been a fundamental one for Machen, and it was to reappear in his later writings.[32]

The testimony of "Christianity and Culture," when added to that of the four major essays of 1912, not only reinforces the impression that Machen had resolved his intellectual difficulties, but also provides evidence that he believed he had discerned the character of Christianity's greatest ideological opposition and called for a vigorous campaign of intellectual engagement with it. Though he of course did not use the language of later intellectual historians, it seems likely that Machen saw that the explanatory assumption of historicism, with its naturalistic implications, was that principle which provided the foundation both for theological liberalism and for biblical scholarship as it was commonly practiced. It now remains to review the culminating events of Machen's intellectual growth during the decisive years of his life, when he made this insight explicit.

CHAPTER 7

MACHEN'S NEW TESTAMENT SURVEY, ORDINATION, AND INSTALLATION, 1913–1915

No later than the early summer of 1913, J. Gresham Machen set in motion a series of events which would bring to a close what may be regarded as the decisive period of his life. For at that time Machen determined to seek ordination to the Christian ministry. The process involved several steps, including coming under care (supervision) of presbytery, licensure, and finally ordination itself, all of which transpired in 1913 and 1914. This process was punctuated by another, that of Machen's nomination to the regular faculty of Princeton Seminary in May 1914 and his installation a year later. The juncture of Machen's faculty installation in May 1915 and the expression of his maturing thought in an address he delivered on that occasion may properly be regarded as marking the culmination of the decisive years of his life, a period which saw the gradual resolution of his intellectual problems and the development of an open and unqualified commitment to the content and goals of the Princeton theological tradition.[1]

At the same time that Machen was moving toward ordination and installation, he was also engaged in a major writing project, the production of a survey of New Testament history and literature. This effort demanded a considerable portion of Machen's time and energy for a full year. Because this piece of work sets forth many of Machen's conclusions regarding the Bible in general and New Testament studies in particular, it is worthy of attention.

A New Testament Survey

Early in 1914 Machen was invited by the editorial secretary of the Board of Christian Education of the Northern Presbyterian Church to prepare a one-year series of Sunday School lessons. The series would constitute an elective course for young people, and would cover the history and literature of the apostolic age. Machen accepted the offer only with hesitation. He was aware of the arduous labor that such an undertaking would require and that meeting the weekly deadlines would be burdensome. Yet he wanted conservative theology to be heard in the church and feared that the assignment might go to a theological liberal if he turned it down. He began the work early in March 1914 and submitted weekly lessons for the next fifty-two weeks. Although at times he expressed dissatisfaction with the editing that was performed on his work, generally he considered the effort a beneficial experience.[2]

Machen was actually required to produce two pieces of work, for he had to write a student's book and a teacher's manual for each lesson. These were both published in separate booklets which contained lessons for thirteen weeks or one quarter of the year. The teacher's manuals were naturally written at a somewhat more advanced level than the student's books, incorporating more detail and suggestions for further reading, but both were pitched on a relatively high literary and pedagogical plane. The four teacher's manuals, taken together, constitute a rather complete survey of the New Testament, and run to nearly three hundred pages of small type. The title of the work was provided by the stated theme for the year: *A Rapid Survey of the Literature and History of New Testament Times.*[3]

The arrangement of material was somewhat dictated by the format for which it was being produced. The fifty-two lessons were presented under six major topics which were distributed over the four quarters of the year. The first quarter covered the historical background of Christianity in its Roman, Greek, and Jewish aspects, and the early history of the Palestinian church. The second quarter surveyed the ministry and writings of the apostle Paul, while the third treated the rest of the New Testament literature, including the Gospels, the general epistles, and Revelation. The fourth quarter's lessons sought to apply New Testament teachings to several issues relating to the church's life and ministry in the modern world. While even a brief analysis of so comprehensive a work would surpass the limitations of the present study, several observations may be made concerning pertinent features of Machen's work.

First, it was clearly the case that Machen's treatment was historically grounded. His introduction to the student's book emphasized the historical nature of New Testament study and disclosed as well Machen's pedagogical philosophy:

> This book is primarily historical. It should be studied like a historical
> course in school. In the study of history the first step is to learn the
> facts. . . . Biblical history is not different in this respect from any
> other history. The Bible, after all, is a record of events; the gospel is
> good news about something that has happened. . . . The sacredness of
> the history, however, does not prevent it from being history; and if it
> is history, it should be studied by the best historical method which
> can be attained.

Machen went on to explain his goal in preparing a historical study of
the New Testament: "The purpose of the present book is to ground
Christian piety more firmly in historical knowledge." He was
convinced that a historical study of the Bible would "show that the
extension of the gospel was a real movement in a real world," and
would "strengthen the conviction that the historical movement was
no mere product of human effort . . . but an entrance into human life
of the divine power, working permanently for the salvation of men."
Therefore, "Historical study is absolutely necessary for a stalwart
Christianity." Thus for all Machen's affirmation of the need for
historical study of the New Testament, he was far from capitulating
to historicism. What he advocated was the study of the New Testament
in its full historical context and with an appreciation of its historical
character. His survey consequently included chapters on the Greek,
Roman, and Jewish aspects of the environment in which early
Christianity was born, and he treated the advance of Christianity and
the development of the New Testament literature in a historical fashion
as opposed to the canonical order of the books. Yet while he was
vitally concerned with history, the naturalistic assumptions of
historicism were foreign to his historical method; on the contrary, he
seemed to expect that the historical examination of the New Testament
would confirm the supernatural origin of Christianity, at least for the
Christian young people who constituted his audience.[4]

A second notable feature of Machen's New Testament survey was
its emphasis on the authority of the Bible. In Machen's earlier writings,
which were admittedly of a different nature than this, the Bible's
authority as the Word of God had been given little attention; only in a
1909 book review had he as much as mentioned the doctrines of
biblical inspiration and authority. But here the case was different. In
his initial chapter, dealing with the nature of the New Testament,

Machen broached the subject of the authority of the New Testament writings. Their authority, he argued, lay ultimately in the authority of Jesus, who not only reverenced the Old Testament and received it as the authoritative divine word but also claimed for his own teaching an authority equal to that of the Old Testament. Jesus' authority was continued in the early church by the authority of his apostles, an authority which was not personally or inherently theirs but which was derived from the apostolic commission received from Jesus himself. It was this apostolic authority which the early and post-apostolic church recognized in the writings that eventually were included in the New Testament. Thus in accord with the traditional Princeton doctrine of scripture, Machen was not only affirming the unique authority of the Bible but was also – and crucially – linking the divine authority of the New Testament writings to their apostolic origin. He wrote:

> . . . the decisive test for determining whether a book was to be regarded as authoritative was found by the early Church in the genuineness of its 'apostolicity.' Only those books were received by the Church which were written by apostles, or at least – as was the case with the writings of Mark and Luke – were given to the Church under apostolic sanction.

This stance – which with regard to the question of the criteria of canonicity in the early church is not novel – placed stringent limits on the functioning of historical and literary criticism, limits which scholars such as Charles A. Briggs had sought to overthrow. Briggs in the 1880s and 1890s had objected to the practice of linking canonicity (and thus inspiration and authority) to authenticity of apostolic authorship. Such an *a priori* commitment, Briggs argued, would demand the rejection of critical conclusions before the arguments were even considered.[5]

The linking of canonicity to apostolicity had been problematic since the early days of historical criticism of the New Testament and constitutes a recurring theme in Werner G. Kümmel's history of the discipline. J. D. Michaelis in the eighteenth century had connected canonicity to apostolicity, and finding no reason on historical grounds for accepting the apostolic origin of Mark, Luke, and Acts, had rejected their canonicity and questioned several other books as well. The problem arose again in the early work of F. C. Baur, who also linked the two concepts, with negative results for the canonical authority of some New Testament books. This is a course which is "fraught with peril," according to Kümmel, because it

> required of historical criticism that it answer the *theological* question of the canonical validity of the New Testament writings as the Word of God, with the consequence that the negative result of such criticism carries with it a denial of the canonical worth of a New Testament book. And over against this, naturally, the defense of the traditional ascriptions of authorship must become at the same time a preservation of the canonical worth of the New Testament books.

In Machen's mind the notions were certainly connected but with different results than Michaelis and Baur had reached. While Machen operated with a broader conception of apostolic origin than the others, he at the same time allowed biblical ascriptions of authorship to carry definitive authority, with the resulting affirmation of apostolicity and canonicity. Michaelis and Baur gave priority to historical criticism and allowed it to render some New Testament writings uncanonical by virtue of non-apostolic authorship. Beginning with the same premise (that of the connection between apostolicity and canonicity), Machen gave supremacy to the authority of scripture, Michaelis and Baur to historical scholarship. In common with Michaelis and Baur, and over against Kümmel, Machen refused to divorce theological from historical considerations.[6]

Thirdly, and not surprisingly in light of the foregoing point, Machen consistently adopted conservative positions on critical questions. Two principles seem to have guided Machen in his discussions and decisions on questions of authorship of New Testament books: first, the self-testimony of the document is paramount; second, in cases of anonymous writings, the tradition of the early church is to be given great weight. The result was that Machen generally affirmed – not indeed without careful treatment of the evidence, but nevertheless affirmed – either the named or the traditional authorship of the various New Testament books. In cases where the author is purportedly identified in the document itself, as in the Pauline epistles, that identification was upheld. In cases where the tradition of the early church presents a strong testimony, as regarding the authorship of the Gospels for example, that testimony was usually received as trustworthy – though Machen was content to leave the Epistle to the Hebrews as an anonymous production. Machen's skill lay not in simply defending traditional views of authorship, though he did that quite ably, but also in expounding the documents and cogently explaining their distinctive features as products of the circumstances in which they originated, assuming the correctness of the conservative view.

Machen's position on critical questions stood in contrast to the prevailing thought in academic theology. Typical of a moderate criticism were the positions adopted by Edgar J. Goodspeed of the University of Chicago. Goodspeed's survey of critical questions pertaining to the various New Testament writings, published at nearly the same time as Machen's work, revealed that different conclusions were commonly reached by those who had little regard for any supposed authority of the Bible. Goodspeed denied the Pauline authorship of the Pastoral Epistles; expressed doubts about the Pauline authorship of Colossians, Ephesians, and Second Thessalonians; questioned the unity of Romans, Second Corinthians, and Philippians; doubted the apostolic authorship of the Gospels of Matthew and John; and assigned late dates to Hebrews and First and Second Peter. Such positions were not considered radical in many scholarly circles at the time and serve to illustrate by contrast the quite conservative nature of the stance taken by Machen, who would have disagreed with Goodspeed on each of the points mentioned.[7]

A fourth aspect of Machen's thought which expressed itself strongly for the first time in his New Testament survey was his Presbyterian confessionalism. Several times throughout the book Machen cited or referred to the Westminster confessional standards as providing the best statement of biblical teaching on a particular topic. This emphasis may have been a reflection of the recent necessity to engage in a careful study of the standards in preparation for his licensure and ordination examinations; or it may have reflected his consciousness of writing for an official Presbyterian publication; or it may simply have represented a renewed feeling of comfortableness with an old theological friend, the catechism he had memorized in childhood (his citations were always from the Westminster Shorter Catechism). Whatever the root of Machen's practice here, it affirmed his commitment to the historic theological standards of Presbyterianism and to confessional orthodoxy in general.

A particularly telling illustration of Machen's use of the

Westminster Catechism is found in his discussion of "the Jesus of the Gospels." Claiming that "departure from the Gospel conception [of Jesus] has often brought disaster," he mentioned specific kinds of doctrinal error in the history of the church: acceptance of Christ's divinity while denying his humanity; affirmation of his humanity while rejecting his divinity; or denial of both the humanity and deity of Christ. He continued:

> From all such errors, the Church must turn ever anew to the Gospels. 'The only Redeemer of God's elect is the Lord Jesus Christ, who, being the eternal Son of God, became man, and so was, and continueth to be, God and man in two distinct natures, and one person, for ever.' (Westminster Shorter Catechism, 21.) Such, in brief, is the Gospel account of Jesus. Every clause of that definition was wrought out, originally, in bitter controversy; every clause contains an essential element of Gospel teaching; and every clause has been tested and approved in the long centuries of the Church's life.

This example is significant because it expresses Machen's resolution of one of the central issues with which he had been wrestling, namely, the supernaturalness of Christ. But he cited or alluded to the Catechism not only when handling such fundamental questions which define the very nature of the Christian faith but also when dealing with narrower issues. Among these were the possibility of confidence when praying, the nature of the "intermediate state" between death and the resurrection, and the spiritual and moral goal of the resurrection. It seems that by this time in Machen's life the phrases of the Westminster standards (especially the Shorter Catechism) had so worked their way into the fabric of his thinking that his views were often adequately expressed in and by the formulations of the standards. Yet he regarded the standards as possessing no independent authority, but as useful only as they accurately reflected the teaching of the Bible. Thus concerning the intermediate state he wrote, "On the whole, no better statement of the apostolic teaching about the 'intermediate state' can be formulated than that which is contained in the Westminster Shorter Catechism, Q. 37. . . ." Although Machen was manifesting a strong confessional strain in his thinking, it appears that for him the authority of the standards was derived and always subordinate to the "apostolic teaching" and the authority of scripture.[8]

A final noteworthy feature of Machen's New Testament survey

was his forthright application of biblical teaching to the contemporary church and the world scene. The entire sixth division of his treatment, one quarter of the lessons, was devoted to modern application of the New Testament message. For purposes of the present study, two of Machen's emphases here are especially significant. First, he spoke emphatically in behalf of "the Christian use of the intellect," the title of the fiftieth lesson in the series. Careful intellectual effort is necessary, Machen argued, for several reasons: in order to acquire a knowledge of the facts about Jesus, which is accomplished through patient study of the Gospels; in order to grasp the Bible's explanation of these facts, which provides the content of sound theology; in order to refute error; in order to properly interpret the Bible generally; and in order to understand modern culture from a Christian perspective. It was this last task which he considered perhaps the most urgent, and he concluded the chapter with an appeal reminiscent of his 1912 address on Christianity and culture, calling for vigorous Christian intellectual engagement with contemporary thought. He then reached perhaps to the very heart of the crucial problem of relating Christianity to modern culture – a culture which was being increasingly dominated by historical consciousness – in some of the closing words of the chapter.

> Men cannot be convinced of the truth of Christianity so long as the whole of their thinking is dominated by ideas which make acceptance of the gospel logically impossible; false ideas are the greatest obstacles to the reception of the gospel. And false ideas cannot be destroyed without intellectual effort.

It is impossible to say whether Machen had in mind the "false ideas" embodied in historicist assumptions, but it is not unlikely, given his own intellectual history to this time. Machen went on to affirm the inadequacy of intellectual argument apart from the renewing work of the Holy Spirit, but he also denied that this made argumentation unnecessary.[9]

Throughout this chapter Machen seems to have been combatting what he perceived as a pervasive anti-intellectualism, the spirit of which he saw active not only in the world at large but also within professing Christianity. His later writings reveal that what he had in view was the anti-intellectualistic strain discernible in theological liberalism. From his perspective, liberalism was anti-intellectual in that it had largely given up any distinctly Christian theological content. Furthermore, liberalism had certainly not engaged in a constructive Christian critique of current thought, but rather had capitulated to it – which indeed it had, to the extent that it was dominated by historicist modes of thought.[10]

A second point of application was really an extension of the first: Machen called for a Christian theology of substantial (and biblical) content. This emphasis was also directed against theological liberalism, which he believed to be promoting both a dilution of traditional Christian teaching and a spirit of agnosticism because of its tolerant attitude toward heterodox teaching. Machen's response was twofold: he affirmed the necessity of theology, and he sought to clarify the content of that message which the church was obligated to proclaim. First, in his chapter on the Christian use of the intellect, Machen affirmed the necessity and value of Christian theology. Theology, he claimed, is nothing other than "thinking about God." Since every Christian must think about God, it follows that every Christian will be a theologian; "the only question is whether he is to be a bad theologian or a good theologian." If the Christian derives his thinking about God from his feelings or bases it on preconceived notions, he will be a poor theologian. But if he draws it from an intimate acquaintance with the Bible's teaching about God and with the great acts of God which the Bible records, he will be a good theologian. Such a theology need not even bear the name, nor need it be technical; "but whatever it is called and however it is expressed, it is absolutely necessary for a genuine Christianity." A Christianity without such substantial theological content is not Christianity at all.[11]

And what exactly is that content? In an earlier chapter of the book, entitled "The Christian Message," Machen spelled out the content of the apostolic preaching. Based on a study of the evangelistic speeches in the early chapters of Acts, Machen's analysis of the apostolic *kerygma* or message to some degree anticipated the findings of New Testament scholars several decades later. He argued that there were three essential elements in the apostolic church's proclamation: first, the story of Jesus' earthly ministry; second, the narration and explanation of Jesus' death; third, the proclaiming of the resurrection of Jesus. Machen implied that this content of the primitive gospel was normative and authoritative for the contemporary church. In this message alone was to be found true spiritual power, and its abandonment left the church without its good news. When in a later chapter on the relief of the poor Machen applauded the modern church's renewed concern for the needy, he also added a warning. The church was coming to a new realization of her duty to help the poor, he said, in an obvious reference to the social gospel. "It is useless to give a man a sermon when he needs bread"; poverty "sometimes prevents the gospel even from being heard." But,

> material benefits were never valued in the apostolic age for their own sake, they were never regarded as substitutes for spiritual things. That lesson needs to be learned. Social betterment, though important, is insufficient; it must always be supplemented by God's unspeakable gift.

For Machen the essential message of the gospel must not be obscured by other aspects of the church's life and work. To an uncomfortable degree, in his view, just such an obfuscation was being accomplished in contemporary Christianity, and his antidote was a return to the New Testament message.[12]

Machen's *Rapid Survey* disclosed the direction in which his views were maturing. He was convinced of the necessity and legitimacy of historical study of the New Testament, but he had not adopted the naturalistic assumptions of historicism. He had by this time come to accept a view of the Bible which regarded it as uniquely authoritative; and while as yet he had formulated no precise doctrine of inspiration (at least he had not expressed one), he did allow the claims of the New Testament itself to exercise definitive authority over critical questions such as authorship of the documents. But he was also convinced on historical and literary grounds that a conservative position on critical questions was not only tenable but best explained the internal and external evidence. He was becoming more openly oriented toward the historic confessions of the church, especially the Westminster standards. And he recognized in the current intellectual climate of the West a crisis which urgently needed to be addressed by an intellectually and theologically energetic Christianity.

Licensure, Ordination, and Installation
Even as Machen was engaged in writing his *Rapid Survey*, events were unfolding which would formally ratify his commitment to the

redemptive and supernatural Christianity for which he was becoming a spokesman. The decision to seek ordination was apparently made in the early summer of 1913. After a trip to Europe for several weeks of Alpine mountain climbing, intended to benefit his health, he took the first step toward ordination in the fall of 1913. In November he came under care of the Presbytery of the Potomac, the Southern Presbyterian Church court which held jurisdiction over his home church in Baltimore, where he still retained membership. The Potomac presbytery thus assumed oversight of his further preparation for the ministry, and Machen did not move his membership to the Northern Presbyterian denomination until just prior to his ordination. Coming under care required Machen to state his intention to seek the ministerial office and to give a satisfactory account of his religious experience and of his motives for entering the ministry. As Stonehouse observes, this step was a simple yet solemn one for Machen, a step which because it had been so long delayed was now filled with all the more significance.[13]

The second step of the process was somewhat more demanding. Prior to his licensure examinations, scheduled for April 1914, Machen was required to prepare a sermon, a lecture, a critical exegesis, and a Latin thesis. The latter he wrote on the birth of Christ, and given his classical training and his experience as a teacher and a scholar, neither this nor any other of the requirements was a great burden for him though he was somewhat apprehensive about his performance. On 22 April Machen underwent what was reputed to be a rigorous battery of oral examinations before the presbytery committees, and he preached that evening. Although he afterward made light of the demands placed upon him and of his performance also, accounts of the event rendered by others who were present indicate that he performed outstandingly. There have survived no accounts of the act of licensure itself, according to Stonehouse, although Machen's taking of the licensure vows would have been the most meaningful part of the day's events. Especially significant was his readiness at last to affirm publicly that he believed "the Scriptures of the Old and New Testaments to be the Word of God, the only infallible rule of faith and practice," and to acknowledge the Westminster Confession and Catechisms "as containing the system of doctrine taught in the Holy Scriptures." His long intellectual and spiritual struggle now formally came to an end as he publicly confessed the faith he had fought so hard to win.[14]

After Machen's licensure, the Southern Presbyterian Church sent his credentials to the New Brunswick Presbytery of the northern body, in which Machen would be ordained and hold membership (Princeton Seminary was an institution of the northern church). On 23 June 1914 Machen was examined and ordained, and preached a sermon on Psalm 2:11. The fact that only ninety minutes were scheduled for both the examination and sermon suggests that his admission to the ministry of the northern body was regarded as more a formality than an ordeal.[15]

Running parallel with the stages in Machen's ordination process were the corresponding steps in his promotion to full faculty status at Princeton Seminary. Since official ministerial standing was a prerequisite to faculty membership, it was necessary that the process leading toward ordination be under way before Machen could seriously be considered for promotion. After his licensure in April 1914 he became eligible for such consideration, and in May the Princeton faculty unanimously recommended to the board of directors that Machen be appointed Assistant Professor of New Testament (he had held the rank of Instructor ever since his original appointment in 1906). He was given voting privileges in the faculty immediately but, apparently because of the heavy burden imposed by the writing of the *Rapid Survey* lessons, Machen felt constrained to postpone his installation for several months until such a time when he would be relieved of that burden. Accordingly, the installation service was set for 3 May 1915. On the occasion of his installation Machen was not only formally inducted into the faculty but was also expected to deliver an address. This he did on the subject "History and Faith."[16]

History and Faith

Machen prefaced his inaugural address with words of appreciation for the "precious personal associations" which his years of affiliation with Princeton had provided him. He singled out for special mention Professor William Park Armstrong and President Francis L. Patton. Machen extolled Armstrong's learning and scholarship, and acknowledged that "the assistance he has given me in the establishment of my Christian faith has been simply incalculable." Of Patton, who delivered the charge that day to the new professor, Machen said that "without his sympathy and help you may be very sure that I should not be standing before you today." Machen thus openly acclaimed the two scholars who had undoubtedly been the most helpful in his long intellectual struggle. It was perhaps fitting on this occasion, which marked the end of that earlier era of his life and the beginning of a new, that he should give due recognition to his two most beloved mentors.[17]

The impression given by Machen's discourse "History and Faith" is that he was attempting to steer a middle course between the views of history offered by theological liberalism and radical historicism. On the one hand was liberalism, which was indifferent to history, or which at least attempted to transcend history by deriving eternal ideas and ethical principles from the Bible while at the same time handing the Bible over to destructive criticism. Machen, as Stonehouse suggests, may have been reflecting on the views of his theological teacher in Germany, Wilhelm Herrmann, who had powerfully represented the view that "faith might be valid regardless of one's conclusions concerning the history of Jesus Christ." While sitting under Herrmann, Machen had expressed puzzlement over how Herrmann could exude such a vibrant and Christ-centered religious aura while holding "the views that he does about the accounts of Christ in the New Testament" (see above, Chapter IV). Early in his intellectual journey Machen had recognized the disjunction between faith and history which lay at the heart of liberalism; now he declared its invalidity. By divorcing faith from history, Machen claimed, liberalism was attempting to make religion "independent . . . of the uncertainties of historical research." But this attempt was a failure; it was flawed in its very conception of the gospel and provided an unstable foundation for liberalism. For, argued Machen, "Give up history, and you can retain some things" – such as an abstract belief in God or a high ethical ideal.

> But be perfectly clear about one point – you can never retain a gospel. For gospel means 'good news,' tidings, information about something that has happened. In other words, it means history. A gospel independent of history is a simple contradiction in terms.

For Machen, no history meant no gospel.[18]

Not only was the foundation of liberalism fatally flawed, its entire superstructure was full of holes. Machen claimed that for several reasons the liberal reconstruction of Jesus was a failure. In the first place, it was impossible to separate the "natural" from the supernatural elements in the Gospel accounts of Jesus, as liberal scholars had sought to do; the two are inextricably intertwined. In the second place, assuming that the former feat could be accomplished, what remains is a Jesus who is an impossible figure historically, for he still retains his messianic consciousness. The meek and mild Jesus of liberalism thought himself a heavenly being who would judge the world; this places a contradiction at the very center of Jesus' personality. In the third place, it is impossible to explain how the natural, human Jesus (granting that such a person could ever be contrived) came to be regarded as a supernatural, superhuman being by his closest associates and his contemporaries. And it was impossible to explain, further, how this case of mistaken identity among Jesus' deluded followers ever gave rise to the great edifice and overwhelming force of the Christian church. The liberal Jesus is simply inadequate to account for the historical origin of Christianity.[19]

On the other hand, and in some ways at the other extreme, was the radical historicist alternative, which Machen found just as unacceptable as liberalism. Machen thought he could discern cracks in the scholarly support for the historical reconstruction of Jesus which provided the basis of liberalism. Some students of the New Testament were recognizing that the liberal Jesus could never account for the origin of Christianity. Their solution was to completely historicize Jesus and the early Christian movement. Machen observed:

> Radical thinkers are drawing the conclusion. Christianity, they say, was not founded upon Jesus of Nazareth. It arose in some other way. It was a syncretistic religion; Jesus was the name of a heathen god. Or it was a social movement that arose in Rome about the middle of the first century.

Others had concluded that Jesus was insane, or that he never existed. To Machen, such conclusions were historically more consistent than the liberal reconstruction, but they were essentially absurd. However, their very absurdity at least constituted a decisive refutation of the liberal Jesus: it was becoming clear that such a person never existed. But the radical reconstructions themselves were merely futile attempts to fill the historical void left by the demise of the liberal Jesus.[20]

Although theological liberalism and radical historicism might reach different conclusions, Machen recognized at the root of both the same intellectual soil: the naturalistic assumptions which underlay the modern historicist outlook. He wrote:

> A supernatural person, according to modern historians, never existed. That is the fundamental principle of modern naturalism. The world, it is said, must be explained as an absolutely unbroken development, obeying fixed laws.

Here Machen fairly accurately summarized the central elements of historicism as it had developed to 1915. According to Wacker, that outlook included an explanatory component which saw all "patterns of belief and value" as "created in the matrix of history"; a developmental component which understood history as "a process of continuous development"; and a directional component which regarded the processes of history as "propelled by directional laws that are essentially extrahistorical in nature." Machen may be taken as referring explicitly to all three of these components, sometimes using the very language by which Wacker described them. The world (including human beliefs and values, such as belief in the existence of a supernatural person) must be "explained" by reference to a process of historical "development" according to fixed "laws". And this entire historical process is conceived as a naturalistic one, since its development occurs in "absolutely unbroken" fashion. This statement of Machen's indicates that he had discerned the intellectual temper of the era and realized that the battle was to be waged on the broad front of philosophical assumptions concerning the nature of history rather than in the narrower sphere of the truthfulness of any particular Christian doctrine. Earlier in his address he had stated the issue as he saw it: was "Jesus a product of the world, or a heavenly being come from without?" Was he a natural product of the unbroken process of historical development, or a supernatural savior sent by God? This was the question indeed, and it involved at its core the very nature of history.[21]

Closely connected in Machen's mind (and in the immediate context) with this central issue was a subsidiary one, the authority of the Bible. It was the Bible's faithfulness to reality in its portrayal of Jesus that provided the ultimate criterion for determining its authority more generally:

Here is the real test of Bible authority. If the Bible is right here, at the decisive point, probably it is right elsewhere. If it is wrong here, then its authority is gone. The question must be faced. What shall we think of Jesus of Nazareth?

The truthfulness of the Bible's representation of Jesus, as Machen had determined it historically, served to substantiate for him the authority of the Bible as a whole. Toward the end of the address Machen returned to the issue of biblical authority. The Bible, he concluded – on the basis of historical evidence and the confirmation offered by Christian experience – was correct at the crucial point: it was true in its account of the person of Jesus. It will not do, therefore, to be indifferent to the Bible (which is at the foundation of Christianity and which presents Christ to the contemporary believer) or to biblical criticism (which in naturalistic hands was undermining that foundation). The reason is simple. "The Bible is at the foundation of the Church. Undermine that foundation, and the Church will fall." For Machen there could be no disjunction between history and faith, between the historical truthfulness of the Bible and the continuance of Christianity in its historic form. The Christian faith is based upon the Bible as historically true; to reject the latter – and thus, by implication, to reject the Bible's authority – is to destroy Christianity.[22]

Also toward the end of the address Machen briefly explained the relationship between history and faith, undoubtedly drawing upon his own experience during his long intellectual and spiritual struggle. The resurrection of Jesus provides the only adequate historical explanation for the existence of Christianity, he argued, and therefore may be accepted as historical fact. But historical research does not lead to certainty. "The historical evidence for the resurrection amounted only to probability; probability is the best that history can do." What then? Is faith at the mercy of historical scholarship? "Must we stake our salvation upon the intricacies of historical research?" he asked. "Is the trained historian the modern priest without whose gracious intervention no one can see God? Surely some more immediate certitude is required." That certitude is provided by Christian experience. Accepting the Easter message enough to make trial of it, enough to approach the risen Christ in faith, leads one to experience its truthfulness for oneself. "Christian experience cannot do without history, but it adds to history that directness, that

immediateness, that intimacy of conviction which delivers from fear."
Apart from such experience, faith "will probably never stand the fires
of criticism." Perhaps here Machen was speaking directly out of his
own experience. For him, history and faith were intimately connected.
History provides the objective foundation for faith, and faith in turn
provides the experiential confirmation of history. In genuine Christian
faith, the two cannot be separated but are bound indissolubly together;
history and faith walk hand in hand. For the God of the Bible is a God
who has revealed himself not in an abstract way, but concretely in
history. He is "a God who from the heaven of His awful holiness has
of His own free grace had pity on our bondage, and sent His Son to
deliver us from the present evil world and receive us into the glorious
freedom of communion with Himself." In Machen's conception, faith
meant seeking acceptance with God on the basis of what God himself
had done in history through the incarnation, death, and resurrection
of Jesus. History could no more be divorced from this conception of
faith than it could be eliminated from the Bible itself.[23]

"History and Faith" provided the capstone and marked the
culmination of Machen's intellectual and spiritual maturation, not
only for the years 1913 to 1915, but also for that whole period of his
life which was consummated with his installation at Princeton in his
thirty-fourth year. It is a major element in the argument of the present
study that Machen's intellectual formation was substantially complete
by 1915, and that his later work, his co-belligerency with the
fundamentalist movement as well as his New Testament scholarship,
was an expression or natural extension of positions he had reached by
1915. Attention now turns to a brief consideration of the labor of his
mature years.[24]

PART FOUR

THE MATURE YEARS,
1915–1937

CHAPTER 8

MACHEN'S LATER WORK AND ITS RELATIONSHIP TO HIS EARLIER SCHOLARSHIP, 1915–1937

During the later years of Machen's life, from his installation at Princeton Seminary in May 1915 until his death in January 1937, his professional activities found two centers of focus besides his regular teaching at Princeton. These were his continued scholarly work in New Testament criticism, resulting in the production of two major books in this field, and his involvement in an unsuccessful attempt to exclude theological liberalism from the teaching and ministerial offices of the Northern Presbyterian Church. A comparison of the work of Machen's mature years with the scholarly labors of his early manhood reveals sharp lines of continuity between the two periods. The views to which Machen had begun to give forceful public expression in the years 1912 to 1915 provided the unifying ideological foundation for both his scholarly work and his ecclesiastical activities during his later years. More precisely, it was Machen's opposition to the historical naturalism which was operating both in historicist attempts to explain the origin of Christianity and in liberal or modernist attempts to bring contemporary Christianity into conformity with historicist thinking that gave direction and impetus to his work after 1915. The purpose of the present chapter is to draw attention to some of those lines of ideological continuity which unite the earlier and later periods of his life.

Questions of New Testament Criticism
Machen's mature years saw the publication of two major contributions in the field of New Testament studies. *The Origin of Paul's Religion* appeared in 1921, *The Virgin Birth of Christ* in 1930, both published by the Macmillan Company of New York. Both volumes also treated questions with which he had long been concerned.

Machen's first book, *The Origin of Paul's Religion*, had a long lineage, reaching back nearly a decade. In 1912 he had published his essay on "Jesus and Paul," exhibiting then what was probably already a well-established interest in the topic. Then in 1915 came an invitation to deliver a series of lectures at Union Theological Seminary in Richmond, Virginia, with the proposed date for the lectures being some time in 1920 or 1921. Machen accepted the invitation and determined to lecture on the historical relationship of Paul to Jesus. After American entry into World War I, he volunteered to serve with the YMCA in Europe, and this interruption, along with many other pressures, delayed his starting on the preparation of the lectures. In December 1919, several months after his return to the United States, he found himself burdened over the immense amount of labor to be completed before January 1921, when the lectures were now scheduled to be delivered. Utilizing opportunities to get away from Princeton, he often wrote in the seclusion of hotel rooms in Boston or New York. By December 1920 he had produced a series of eight lectures which he delivered at Union Seminary in early January 1921. From the beginning of the project Machen intended to publish the lectures in book form. After negotiations with Macmillan had produced a shortened manuscript and an agreement by Machen to purchase four hundred copies of the book (because he was an unknown author), it appeared in print in October 1921.[1]

In the opening pages of *The Origin of Paul's Religion* Machen forthrightly described the issue he was addressing: it was nothing less than "the problem of the origin of Christianity." He specifically had in mind the supernaturalness of Christian origins, and he claimed that this was an important question historically and practically. The problem was important historically because Christianity had been extremely influential in the Western world, and the founding documents of the movement claimed for it a supernatural origin. It is important practically, he argued, because "Christian experience has ordinarily been connected with one particular view of the origin of the Christian movement; where that view has been abandoned, the experience has ceased."[2]

Machen began by explaining the distinctive significance of the apostle Paul as the first disciple of Jesus fully to delineate the character of Christianity as a religion of redemption based on recent historical events involving a supernatural person. In the attempt to account for the phenomenon of Paulinism, two classes of answer had been put forth. "There is first of all the supernaturalistic explanation, which simply accepts at its face value what Paul presupposes about Jesus" –

namely, that Jesus was a heavenly being who willingly came to earth as a man in order to redeem sinful humanity through his death, resurrection, and exaltation. "If this representation be correct, then there is really nothing to explain; the religious attitude of Paul toward Jesus was not an apotheosis of a man, but recognition as divine of one who really was divine."[3]

The second class of explanation could be subdivided into three distinct views, but they all possessed the common characteristic of rejecting supernaturalism as an explanation: "they all deny the entrance into human history of any creative act of God, unless indeed all the course of nature be regarded as creative." These three explanations "all agree, therefore, in explaining the religion of Paul as a phenomenon which emerged in the course of history under the operation of natural causes." This latter sentence constitutes a fair description of the conclusions demanded by historicism, reflecting as it does the explanatory and developmental assumptions which it incorporated. Here Machen clearly defined, as he had done in 1915 (in "History and Faith") and probably by 1912 (in "Christianity and Culture"), the nature of the ideological opponent at which he was taking aim. That opponent was essentially a philosophy of history which allowed no room for the historical operation of those divine influences to which the origin of Christianity had traditionally been attributed by Christians in the past.[4]

In attempting to vindicate the supernatural origin of Christianity, this book had an ideological as well as a genetic connection with Machen's 1912 article "Jesus and Paul." The book treats the same broad theme in a more comprehensive way, arguing that there was a supernatural Jesus at the basis of Paul's religion. It also explicitly refers back to the earlier article and incorporates most of its argument. In several places Machen directed the reader's attention to those pages in "Jesus and Paul" where he treated similar or related ideas; and the substance of that essay was largely reproduced in Chapter IV of the book, entitled "Paul and Jesus." The topic had therefore claimed Machen's attention for a decade or longer. The historical origin of Paul's beliefs about and relationship to Jesus was one of the crucial foundational issues that he had wrestled with and resolved during his period of questioning and doubt. Now he considered it worthwhile to address the issue in a comprehensive fashion for a larger public audience.[5]

Over against the supernaturalistic approach to the question, Machen discerned three logically distinct antisupernaturalistic explanations. The first, for want of a better term, he called the "liberal" view, represented by Adolf Harnack. At its foundation was the purely human Jesus of liberalism, who urged men to take himself as an example of faith in God, but who certainly never offered himself as the object of faith. Jesus was raised to the status of deity and made an object of faith by his earliest disciples; the resurrection appearances were merely hallucinations induced by the power of Jesus' personality. Paul then carried the process further, building a whole theology upon the conception of Jesus as a divine savior; but, this view held, it is possible to preserve the kernel of Paul's religion while discarding the chaff of his theology. A second view, represented by Wilhelm Wrede, sought for the origin of the Pauline portrayal of Christ in the pre-Christian Jewish conception of Messiah as a transcendent, heavenly, apocalyptic figure. The third variety of explanation, as represented by Wilhelm Bousset, found the origin of the Pauline theology in the concepts of oriental and Hellenistic mystery religions. Bousset argued that while the Jewish Christians of Palestine viewed Jesus as the heavenly Son of Man who would come to judge the earth, Greek-speaking Gentile Christianity developed a belief in Jesus as the Lord who was now present with his church, an idea derived from the mystery religions of the ancient Hellenistic world. Paul adopted this Hellenistic conception of Jesus as Lord and brought it into connection with his idea of the Spirit. In the first of these reconstructions of early Christianity there is some historical connection between Paul and the figure of Jesus, even if only an impression left by the Master's powerful personality. In the latter two there is none; the Pauline theology is constructed entirely of elements alien to Jesus' teaching, derived either from Judaism or paganism. After discussing the primary sources available for a critical examination of Paul's life and thought, Machen devoted the rest of his book to a refutation of these three views.[6]

The first component of Machen's argument was a treatment of the life of Paul, occupying the second through the fourth chapters of the book. Here Machen sought to outline Paul's life, dealing with critical problems along the way. He also presented a general vindication of the historical trustworthiness of the data relating to Paul in the book of Acts, observing that the trend of recent scholarship had been toward a more respectful attitude toward the reliability of Acts. Machen's fourth chapter, as noted above, reiterated the substance of his 1912 article on Jesus and Paul, with extensive additions, seeking to show that Paul was a true disciple of the supernatural Jesus who is portrayed in the Gospels. The establishment of this argument constituted a refutation of the liberal view of the origin of Pauline Christianity.[7]

Machen devoted the last four chapters of the book to a refutation of the remaining two explanations of the rise of Paulinism. In a single chapter he disposed of the view of Wrede and others that the Pauline conception of Christ derived from contemporary Judaism. Here Machen contended that the Jewish apocalyptic doctrine of Messiah, even if Paul could be shown to have held to it (which is questionable), is insufficient to account for Paul's conception of Christ, on three counts. First, it could not account for Paul's view of the activity of Messiah in the creation of the universe, nor Paul's conception of the warm personal relationship between the believer and Christ, nor his doctrine of the deity of Christ, all of which were important components of the Pauline doctrine as presented in his epistles. Second, supposing that Paul did adhere to the pre-Christian Jewish apocalyptic view of Messiah, it had not been satisfactorily explained how he came to attach this view to the person of Jesus of Nazareth. Third, adequate explanation was lacking for the close conformity of Paul's teaching and character to those of Jesus, had he not based his views on the historical Jesus himself. The explanation which seeks for the roots of the Pauline doctrine in apocalyptic Judaism fails, therefore, because it does not account for the historical phenomena.[8]

Occupying more space was Machen's treatment of the third variety of historical explanation for Paul's religion, that which sought to derive it from pagan sources. This was the method of the history of religions school and was particularly in vogue at the time Machen wrote (he referred to it as the comparative religion school). Machen's refutation of this view proceeded along two lines. First he laid the groundwork in his sixth chapter by offering a historical survey of ancient Greek religion and eastern and Hellenistic mystery religions. Here he maintained that the similarity between Christianity and the pagan religions of antiquity had been greatly exaggerated. Machen also observed that the documentary sources used by scholars to reconstruct the mystery religions were of post-Christian origin. He entered a protest against the all-too-common impatience of scholars with questions of chronological priority, and against the "lordly disregard of dates" which "runs all through the modern treatment of the history of religion in the New Testament period."[9]

Then in chapters seven and eight, Machen engaged in a point-by-point examination of the evidence which was put forward to show the similarity between Paul's thought and pagan ideas. He began by stating two reservations, one a reminder of the lack of proof that the kind of religion attested by the later sources actually existed in the time of Paul, the other making the point that it had not been shown that there existed any adequate channel or mechanism for the entrance of pagan ideas into Paul's thinking. He then took up the alleged points of correspondence between the pagan religions and Paul's theology. An examination of the evidence put forward by Bousset and Reitzenstein to show Paul's dependence on pagan ideas with respect to his views of salvation, the sacraments, and the person and work of Christ revealed the weakness of their argument. Machen endeavored to show that the claimed similarities were only superficial and were not founded on an accurate interpretation of the historical evidence.[10]

Machen took special aim at Bousset's argument regarding the alleged transformation of Jesus from the apocalyptic Son of Man in Palestinian Christianity to the ever-present Lord of the Hellenistic Gentile churches, from which source Paul supposedly derived his doctrine. Machen termed Bousset's reconstruction "brilliant," and claimed that not since the work of F. C. Baur had there appeared such an "original, comprehensive, and grandly conceived rewriting of early Christian history" as that found in Bousset's *Kyrios Christos*. "The only question," Machen wrote, "is whether originality, in this historical sphere, is always compatible with truth." He concluded that in this case it was not. The central thrust of Machen's argument against Bousset's hypothesis was that it was historically untenable: it was not possible to interpose a Gentile Christian link between Paul and the Jerusalem church; it could not be proven that Palestinian Christians did not use the title "Lord" in reference to Jesus or that they did use "Son of Man"; it had not been shown that Paul's doctrine was dependent on pagan conceptions of a dying and rising god; nor could Bousset's theory account for the warm personal response of love which Paul exhibited toward Jesus.[11]

Machen concluded his argument with the assertion that Paulinism differed profoundly from contemporary religion, for it was neither a philosophy nor a cult; at its heart Paul's teaching was "an account of something that had happened," an account, namely, of the death and resurrection of Jesus. "If the account was true, the origin of Paulinism is explained; if it was not true, the Church is based upon an inexplicable error." The refusal to accept the explanation which lay on the surface of the New Testament – that Jesus is what Paul and the Gospels represent him to be, the eternal Son of God come to earth for the redemption of man – this refusal "has left an historical problem which so far has not been solved." Having shown the untenableness of the alternative historical explanations, Machen invited his readers to accept with him the only explanation remaining – recognizing that it flies full in the face of modern thought – that Paul's religion was founded on true historical events, on the historical but supernatural person of Jesus.[12]

This survey of Machen's argument in *The Origin of Paul's Religion* serves to demonstrate its historical nature. In common with his earlier work on the subject, and reflecting his personal intellectual struggle, he did not argue for the validity of Christianity from any presumed authority of the Bible, but argued rather from the historical testimony presented by the conversion, life, and writings of Paul of Tarsus. That testimony, Machen concluded, pointed decisively toward the supernatural reality of Jesus.

Other features of Machen's first book in the field of New Testament scholarship are worth noting, but before doing so it will be well to examine the argument of his second such book, and then to consider both volumes together. *The Virgin Birth of Christ* was published in 1930, and brought to consummation Machen's research on this aspect of New Testament studies, a topic which had occupied his scholarly attention for a quarter-century. His preface indicates that the substance of the book had been delivered as lectures at Columbia Theological Seminary in the spring of 1927, but that the book presented the material in greatly expanded form and made use of his earlier published studies.[13]

The extent of Machen's indebtedness to his earlier work is suggested by the very form of his argument, which was similar to that of his first published work on the virgin birth, the student essay of 1905. He began with the undeniable fact that the historic Christian church has universally believed Jesus to have been conceived by the Holy Spirit and born of the virgin Mary without a human father. The historical fact of the church's belief in the virgin birth may be explained in two different ways. First, "it may be held that the Church came to believe in the virgin birth for the simple reason that the virgin birth was a fact." Second, "it may be held that the virgin birth was not a fact, but that the Church came to accept it as a fact through some sort of error." But "if the idea of the virgin birth is not founded on fact, how did that idea originate?" Machen thus asked for a historical explanation of a historical fact, namely, the church's belief in the virgin birth. The book then falls into two broad sections: chapters one through eleven take up the possibility that belief in the virgin birth was based on fact, and evaluate the positive testimony in support of that view as well as objections that had been brought against it; chapters twelve through fourteen consider the hypothesis that belief in the virgin birth was not founded on fact, and examine the various theories which attempt to account for that belief on the supposition that it had no factual basis. This twofold division of Machen's treatment is identical to that adopted in his student essay on the virgin birth published in 1905 and 1906. The book may thus rightly be regarded as an expansion of the argument presented in that early essay. Since then, of course, Machen had gone through the fires of intellectual testing and had pursued a quarter-century of research on the topic. His knowledge had grown and his judgment had matured in the intervening twenty-five years, but he nevertheless found no reason to abandon his earlier position, and he treated the subject in the same manner as he had then.[14]

Any adequate summary of *The Virgin Birth of Christ*, a volume of some four hundred pages, would carry this discussion beyond the bounds of the present study. A brief survey will suffice to indicate the nature of Machen's argument and to draw attention to noteworthy features of the volume.

The first chapter establishes the strength of early Christian belief in the virgin birth by examining the second-century testimony to that tradition. This historical survey, with a thorough discussion of critical questions, brought up to date Machen's 1912 treatment of the same topic and concluded in the same way: there was "a firm and well-formulated belief in the virgin birth" in the early part of the second century, while denials of the virgin birth during this era were probably based on dogmatic or philosophical considerations rather than on any creditable historical tradition.[15]

The next five chapters deal with Luke's testimony to the virgin birth. Of these, the fourth chapter, "The Hymns of the First Chapter of Luke," is dependent on Machen's 1912 article of the same title, and the other chapters incorporate material from the other early essay on Luke, "The Origin of the First Two Chapters of Luke." The earlier treatments were updated by reference to recent literature. In all these chapters Machen's concern was to affirm the literary integrity and historical credibility of the Lucan account.[16]

Machen devoted one chapter to Matthew's narrative of the virgin birth, and then four chapters to a discussion of the Lucan and Matthean accounts taken together. Here he treated the relationship between the two accounts, their inherent credibility, and their relationship to secular history and to the rest of the New Testament. Finally he turned to a consideration of the alternative theories of the origin of the idea of the virgin birth of Jesus, spending a chapter each on general preliminary considerations, theories of Jewish derivation, and theories of pagan derivation. In the fifteenth and concluding chapter Machen discussed the consequences of one's attitude toward the doctrine of the virgin birth of Jesus.[17]

Machen revealed something of the nature of his argument concerning the virgin birth tradition as he summarized that argument at the beginning of his final chapter (assuming the two major divisions of the book):

We have shown, under the former head, that in the early patristic period no gradual formation of the tradition can be traced, but that the tradition appears just as firmly established at the beginning of the second century as at the close. We have shown that in the New Testament it does not appear as a late addition, but had an original place in the First and Third Gospels and was plainly attested in Palestinian sources, oral or written, underlying those Gospels. We have shown that the two infancy narratives containing it are independent but not contradictory. We have shown that it is not contradicted by the rest of the New Testament and that it is as strongly attested as we should expect it to be on the assumption that it is true.

Under the second head, we have shown that if the virgin birth tradition is not true the efforts at explaining the origin of it have so far resulted in failure. It did not originate on the basis of Jewish ideas or in order to show fulfillment of a misunderstood prophecy. It was no mere reflex among Gentile Christians of the pagan notions about children begotten by the gods. It was no ancient pagan idea already

naturalized in the pre-Christian Jewish doctrine of the Messiah. The
advocates of one of these theories are often the severest critics of the
advocates of another; and none of the theories has obtained anything
like general assent.[18]

Several observations with respect to Machen's position as
expressed in *The Virgin Birth of Christ* are relevant to the present
study. First, as in his earlier work on the subject, Machen argued
historically. His entire approach sought for a historical solution to a
historical problem: How did belief in the virgin birth of Jesus originate?
He argued that all attempts to explain its origin had been shown to be
inadequate, except for one. The one adequate explanation is that belief
in the virgin birth arose because the belief was true: Jesus was indeed
born of a virgin. This answer alone accounts for the phenomena of
the New Testament and of later history. It is clear that in employing
this argument Machen differed from other scholars in what he was
willing to accept as historical explanation. What he regarded as
"historical" was not what naturalistic scholars would consider
"historical," for their historicist assumptions excluded *a priori* any
immediate divine activity in the external world and required
"historical" to be defined wholly in terms of natural phenomena. As
will be noted below, Machen recognized the influence of such
presuppositional considerations, but that did not keep him from
pressing his case. His argument appealed to historical evidence, and
the fact that his explanation would most likely be rejected by those
adhering to the modern naturalistic outlook did not detract in the least
from its historical viability, in his view.

Second, Machen believed that the doctrine of the virgin birth was
important both intrinsically and as an index of one's attitude toward
Jesus Christ and the Bible. The virgin birth, he argued in his concluding
chapter, is intrinsically important because the event itself fixes the
time and mode of the Incarnation. A knowledge of the fact of the
virgin birth gives the Christian an awareness of that time and that
mode, thus providing important details in the Christian view of Christ
and forestalling erroneous views. Furthermore, he claimed that in the
modern context the doctrine of the virgin birth constitutes an effective
test of one's view of the person of Christ. Here Machen distinguished
between the naturalistic and supernaturalistic views of Jesus, founded
on two different world views, and then queried, "what question may

be asked to determine whether a man holds a naturalistic or a supernaturalistic view of Jesus Christ?" Questions concerning certain aspects of Christ's person and ministry – relating, for example, to his deity, his resurrection, or the Incarnation – are capable of vague, ill-defined, or equivocating responses which appear to give an affirmative answer and yet do not mean at all what traditional Christian teaching has meant by these terms. The doctrine of the virgin birth allows for less ambiguity: "men who reject the virgin birth scarcely ever hold to a really Christian view of Christ." Finally, Machen argued that the doctrine of the virgin birth also makes manifest one's attitude toward the Bible. One cannot reject the biblical teaching about the mode of Christ's entrance into the world and at the same time affirm the infallibility of the Bible in any meaningful sense. If forced to choose between two current views which rejected the virgin birth, Machen by far preferred the one which said that the Bible is not infallible and is wrong about the virgin birth to the one which denied the virgin birth and yet held that the Bible is infallible when it speaks in the sphere of religious truth. For the latter position Machen had no regard: it was dishonest, a mere trifling with words, and involved a denial of the gospel, which is an account of real events in the external world. If we are going to reject the Bible's teaching concerning the birth of Christ, he argued, it is far better to admit that "we can no longer depend on the Bible *as such*." If we reject certain parts of the Bible, then "our belief in the authority of the Bible is gone," and the fact should be honestly faced.[19]

From this it is evident, in the third place, that Machen was attempting to maintain something which radical historical relativism and its theological offspring had given up, the unity of all knowledge. Returning to a theme he had first enunciated in his 1912 address "History and Culture," he expressed his unwillingness to divorce "religious" truth from historical truth. In what may be regarded as one of the more significant passages of the entire book, Machen explicitly rejected such a dichotomous view of truth:

> We are often told, indeed, that if the virgin birth is accepted, it can only be accepted as a matter of "faith," and that decision about it is beyond the range of historical science. But such a distinction between faith and history is, we think, unfortunate.

He went on to acknowledge that in order to believe in the virgin birth of Christ one must evaluate the documentary evidence "in connection with a sound view of the world" and of human nature. But he did not believe that a sharp separation between one's theistic presuppositions and the documentary evidence was conducive to scientific history, for all historical study is conducted on the basis of presuppositions; "the important thing is that the presuppositions shall be true instead of false." From Machen's viewpoint, it constituted an "unwarranted narrowing of the sphere of history" to confine history to natural events and to exclude from purview those events which arise from the immediate, creative activity of God, such as the virgin birth.

> The true sphere of history is the establishment of all facts, whatever they are, that concern human life – the establishment of these facts and the exhibition of the relations between them. So if the virgin birth is a fact at all, by whatever means it may be established, it is a fact of history.

Machen lodged a protest against the compartmentalization of truth into "scientific" or "religious." "If we are to be truly scientific," he wrote, "there must be a real synthesis of truth." Distinctions between kinds of truth are only provisional or temporary: "all truth, ultimately, is one."[20]

In contrast to many of the proponents of historicism, who, according to Wacker, had by about 1930 given up "the possibility of '*a priori* synthetic' knowledge of any sort," Machen was seeking to maintain the unity of all knowledge, and he regarded the creation of a synthesis of knowledge to be a primary goal of human intellectual endeavor. This was no abstract intellectual exercise for Machen, but, as he argued in his final chapter, involved the very nature of Christianity itself. The grounding of the Christian faith in history was a matter of primary concern to Machen, and he saw the effort to divorce Christian belief from historical events as ultimately destructive of genuine Christianity, however well-intentioned such an effort might be. One of the central tenets of theological liberalism with respect to the Bible – that the Bible is authoritative in the spheres of religion and ethics but not in that of external history – may serve to protect the Bible from historical criticism, but it also makes Christianity independent of historical events. Why then is Jesus necessary at all? Is not the logical effect of this position, he asked, "to make the authority of the Bible and to make the Christian religion independent of the question whether such a person as Jesus ever lived upon this earth?" If the assertion that "Jesus lived in Palestine nineteen hundred years ago" cannot logically be upheld as a central element in biblical teaching and in Christianity because this affirmation lies in the realm of external history, then "even the very existence of Jesus is unnecessary to this sublimated religion that is independent of events in the external world." Although some modern men were willing to accept this logical result of their position, most are not, Machen observed, and they abide in the utterly illogical and intellectually precarious position of demanding that their Christianity and the authority of the Bible be independent of the realm of external history, while yet basing both in some ways on external events.[21]

Such a halfway house would not do for Machen, and he noted the inherent instability of the liberal stance: some moderns were indeed moving toward a "Christless Christianity," dependent on no historical Jesus at all. This simply served to demonstrate the validity of his argument. By capitulating to historicist thinking, by turning the Bible over to historical criticism without regard for the outcome in the sphere of external history, liberalism was giving up the grounding of the Christian faith in history. And by thus divorcing the Christian faith from the events of external history, liberalism was not just giving up certain specific teachings of the Bible and of Christianity, it was putting the whole edifice in jeopardy. These convictions concerning the unity of truth and the historical grounding of Christianity help to explain two aspects of Machen's work. They help explain his writing of such scholarly books as *The Virgin Birth of Christ* and *The Origin of Paul's Religion*, which attempted to demonstrate the historical tenability of the New Testament events (given theistic presuppositions) and to show the untenableness of critical reconstructions. They also explain his staunch opposition to theological liberalism, which he believed at its heart was sacrificing the historical grounding of the faith on the altar of modern naturalistic assumptions about history.[22]

In the fourth place, Machen's comments regarding presuppositions reveal his continuing awareness of the impact of philosophical commitments on the formation of historical judgments. His statements make at least two distinct affirmations. First, he acknowledged that all historical study proceeds on the basis of presuppositions: "scientific history as well as other branches of science rests upon presuppositions." Again: "A science of history that shall exist by itself, independent of presuppositions, is an abstraction to which no reality corresponds." Whatever assumptions Machen may have been making about the scientific nature of historical investigation, he recognized that historians cannot be presumed to operate on a purely objective basis, apart from prior philosophical commitments. Second, he believed that one's presuppositions will most definitely affect the direction which one's historical judgments take. With regard to the virgin birth, "one needs to take the documentary evidence in connection with a sound view of the world and with certain convictions as to the facts of the human soul." He perhaps differed from other scholars in believing that it is not essential for a Christian to separate his theistic presuppositions from his historical investigations; indeed, it cannot be done, for all science proceeds on the basis of the fundamental assumptions of the investigator. Since presuppositions must be present, therefore, "the important thing is that the presuppositions shall be true instead of false." More specifically, "the Christian gospel has as its necessary presupposition that particular view of the world which is called, in the fullest sense, 'theistic'" (which Machen defined as assuming the existence of a personal creator and of a real order of nature). This recognition of the place of presuppositions is simply a continuation of an emphasis found in Machen's scholarly works from the very beginning, and suggests an acknowledgment on his part that to a limited extent human knowledge is historically conditioned.[23]

It is now possible to offer a general assessment of Machen's two major scholarly works of New Testament criticism, *The Origin of Paul's Religion* and *The Virgin Birth of Christ*. Both books were the products of his mature scholarship, but both were also the continuation and culmination of work begun years earlier on the questions that Machen addressed. In both, he was concerned to establish the historical tenability of the New Testament account of the supernatural origin of Christianity; he considered the historicity of these events to be intimately related to the questions of both the historical nature and the truthfulness of Christianity. In neither book did Machen argue from a doctrine of holy scripture; this he knew would be unacceptable to his scholarly opponents and at any rate would not adequately deal with the historical problems involved (although in *The Virgin Birth* he did argue toward a doctrine of scripture, as noted above). Instead he argued entirely from historical evidence, seeking historical answers to historical problems. In both books Machen treated the advocates of opposing views with respect and restraint, honoring what he regarded as their genuine achievements (even if he strongly disagreed with them: he called Bousset's work "brilliant"), considering their arguments carefully and answering them fully, engaging in no *ad hominem* attacks. In both books he acknowledged the importance of presuppositions in scholarly work. And in both (more explicitly in *The Origin of Paul's Religion*) he discerned at the basis of the arguments of his scholarly opponents a philosophy of history which incorporated the assumptions of historicism, a philosophy which excluded, therefore, the possibility of God's activity in the external world and sought to explain the origin of Christianity as "a phenomenon which emerged in the course of history under the operation of natural causes." Having reached such conclusions in the scholarly sphere, it is perhaps no matter for surprise that Machen sought to apply them in the ecclesiastical.[24]

Machen's Critique of Liberalism

It is not necessary here to present a full-scale treatment of Machen's struggle to exclude theological liberalism from the teaching offices of the Northern Presbyterian Church and from a rightful place in Christianity at large. This story has been told often and well, for it is the aspect of Machen's life which is usually given greatest prominence in historical studies. Indeed, the struggle against liberalism occupied a large portion of Machen's energy during his mature years. After serving as a YMCA secretary in France during the First World War, Machen returned to Princeton and almost immediately began to oppose, on theological grounds, an effort mounted in 1920 and 1921 to unite the Presbyterian Church with several other church bodies in a loose federation. Then from the early to the middle 1920s he supported an unsuccessful conservative attempt to gain control of the ecclesiastical machinery of the Presbyterian Church. In the later 1920s he became involved in a struggle to maintain conservative control of Princeton Seminary. When that effort failed and Princeton was reorganized in 1929, Machen resigned and with others founded an independent institution, Westminster Theological Seminary in Philadelphia. In the meantime, his longstanding opposition to liberalism in the Presbyterian missionary agencies was coming to a

head, and finding no satisfaction from the denomination, he formed
an independent mission board in 1933. Machen spurned
denominational demands that he desist from such activity, as a result
of which he was subjected to a series of ecclesiastical court proceedings
and was finally suspended from the ministry of the Northern
Presbyterian Church in 1936. Thus being cut off by his own
denomination, Machen was instrumental in the formation of a new
Presbyterian body in 1936, first called the Presbyterian Church of
America and later the Orthodox Presbyterian Church. He was laboring
to see this new denomination become firmly established when he
died on 1 January 1937 while on a speaking tour in North Dakota.[25]

The present study is not concerned with the details of Machen's
ecclesiastical campaign against theological liberalism, but rather with
the ideological underpinnings of that campaign, particularly as they
relate to the historical study of the Bible. Machen set forth his case
against liberalism in his 1923 book entitled *Christianity and
Liberalism*. Most of his other writing on the topic, chiefly in the form
of periodical articles and public addresses, was simply a reiteration
of the points he made in this volume, which was itself developed
from earlier articles and addresses. This book not only has become
perhaps Machen's best-known work, but is also widely regarded as
the most incisive conservative polemic against theological liberalism.
Several of its salient features may be noted.[26]

First, it is most significant that Machen defined theological
liberalism in terms of its view of history. In the opening chapter of
Christianity and Liberalism, after observing that there were different
varieties of liberalism, Machen proceeded to describe the guiding
impulse which united all of them: "the many varieties of modern liberal
religion are rooted in naturalism – that is, in the denial of an entrance
of the creative power of God (as distinguished from the ordinary course
of nature) in connection with the origin of Christianity." The unitive
force which underlay all forms of theological liberalism, Machen
argued, was a philosophy of history which allowed for no operation
of the immediate power of God in the external world, including even
in the origination of the Christian movement in the first century (and,
implicitly, in its progress since then).[27]

Machen discerned at the root of liberalism the philosophical
commitment which was implicit in all the assumptions of historicism:
a naturalistic view of history. In its explanatory, epistemological, and

developmental assumptions, historicism insisted on an *a priori* denial of the activity of God in the external events of history, in acts of human cognition, and in the process by which history moves and the end toward which it is moving. Liberals commonly expressed their beliefs in traditional theological language, thus maintaining the aura of a theistic system; and various forms of liberalism might alter one or more of these assumptions, especially the latter, perhaps extensively. But at its most consistent level – which was the level at which Machen was interested in arguing – modernistic liberalism had incorporated these notions into the foundation of its system of beliefs. Thus liberals or modernists commonly held that the rise of Christianity is to be explained as due to the result of natural historical forces; that religious experience is the product of human insight and that it issues in continually changing doctrinal expressions; that the revelation of God and the coming of God's kingdom are to be found in the process of human cultural development. Liberalism had made all of Christianity – its foundational events, the revelation of God and the coming of his kingdom, and the experience of God's goodness – captive to natural historical processes. Machen detected in this theology the influence of what may now be identified as the historicist mode of thinking; and Sydney Ahlstrom's declaration that historical modes of thought "very nearly succeeded in determining both the strategies and the content of liberal theology" suggests that Machen may not have been far wrong.[28]

The liberal deemphasis or elimination of the historical accomplishment of redemption for fallen humanity through the death and resurrection of Jesus, as over against the supposed universal ethical ideals of Jesus, meant that history as the stage for the unfolding drama of divine redemption could be given up. History as such no longer possessed the decisive redemptive significance which it possessed in the biblical scheme; it served only as the scene of gradual human cultural development and of man's progressively developing religious insight – which were thought to constitute the coming of the kingdom of God. The liberal emphasis on the immanence of God meant that because God is thought to be active in all of history, he is no longer regarded as acting supremely in specific redemptive events of history. Thus it became a matter of relative indifference whether the New Testament accounts of the life of Jesus and the origin of the Christian movement were true or not.

Second, Machen continued in his earlier insistence that liberalism was not Christianity. The burden of *Christianity and Liberalism* was that "despite the liberal use of traditional phraseology modern liberalism not only is a different religion from Christianity but belongs in a totally different class of religions." This conclusion followed quite logically from the character of liberalism as a religion of self-redemption through ethical and religious conformity to Jesus, in contrast to Christianity, which proclaimed divine redemption through the gracious act of God in Jesus. Here was to be found "the most fundamental difference between liberalism and Christianity – liberalism is altogether in the imperative mood, while Christianity begins with a triumphant indicative; liberalism appeals to man's will, while Christianity announces, first, a gracious act of God." Christianity and liberalism differed in both their view of history and their means of redemption. Machen's persuasion of this radical disjunction between Christianity and liberalism was not a new element in his intellectual growth, but represented a conviction he had reached at least as early as 1906, expressed at that time in his conversation with Professor Heitmüller, and often afterwards.[29]

In the third place, Machen saw liberalism's attitude toward history reflected in its view of the Bible. According to the traditional Christian view, the Bible is unique as divine revelation because it alone narrates the events upon which redemption rests and through which man's reconciliation to God is effected: the life, death, and resurrection of Jesus Christ. Machen portrayed liberalism as deserting this view of the Bible by attempting to cut Christianity loose from history:

> Must we, it is said, depend on what happened so long ago? Does salvation wait upon the examination of musty records? . . . Can we not find, instead, a salvation that is independent of history, a salvation that depends only on what is with us here and now?

Machen's response was to point out that salvation does indeed depend on what happened long ago, but that it also has effects in the present as the believer experiences forgiveness of sin and fellowship with the risen Christ. But, he hastened to add, religious experience alone is not enough. Christians cannot by resorting entirely to experience make themselves "altogether independent of the results of Biblical criticism" so that it becomes a matter of indifference what kind of person Jesus actually was or whether he in fact lived and died and rose again. This is not possible in genuinely Christian experience, Machen insisted, because "Christian experience depends absolutely upon an event." The Christian who seeks for acceptance with God on the basis of the death and resurrection of Christ will acknowledge that his Christian life "depends altogether upon the truth of the New Testament record." Christian experience serves to confirm the documentary evidence, but it can never stand by itself; it is always grounded in the events narrated by the Bible.[30]

At this point in his argument Machen introduced the doctrine of biblical inspiration, in what must be one of the earliest expositions of that doctrine to be found in his writings. As Machen expounded it, the function of divine inspiration was simply to secure the truthfulness of the Bible's account of redemptive events by preserving the biblical writers from error. The authority of the Bible then rests upon its truthfulness. The doctrine of inspiration, in Machen's words, "means that the Bible not only is an account of important things, but that the account itself is true, the writers having been preserved from error, despite a full maintenance of their habits of thought and expression, that the resulting Book is the 'infallible rule of faith and practice.'" He objected to the distorted representation of this doctrine which portrayed it as involving mechanical dictation; this, he claimed, was a caricature, a straw man. The doctrine of "plenary inspiration" (the term he applied to his definition) does not "deny the individuality of the Biblical writers," nor "ignore their use of ordinary means for acquiring information," nor "involve any lack of interest in the historical situations which gave rise to the Biblical books. What it does deny is the presence of error in the Bible." In accord with the traditional Princeton doctrine of scripture, Machen's view allowed for the operation of ordinary historical factors in the production of the Bible, while at the same time its authors were divinely superintended so that what they wrote was preserved from error and provided an accurate account of the revelatory and redemptive events which it records.[31]

The divinely secured truthfulness of the Bible establishes its authority, making it an "infallible rule of faith and practice." Machen contrasted this conception of biblical authority with the view of authority which obtained in liberalism. In that system the authority of Jesus was not really observed, despite claims to the contrary, for only those elements in the teaching of Jesus were received which were in agreement with modern thought. Rather, "the real authority, for liberalism, can only be 'the Christian consciousness' or 'Christian experience.'" But this quickly dissolves into "individual experience," which is "no authority at all." The result of this vacuum is "an abysmal skepticism."[32]

In Machen's view, the denial of specific teachings of the Bible had broad ramifications. Such denial constituted not only a rejection of essential elements of Christian doctrine, which was bad enough in itself, but also a denial of biblical authority, which left modern man (including modernistic religion) with no firm epistemological ground on which to stand. The loss of biblical authority meant the loss of all stable authority in life, and left modern man gazing into the abyss of skepticism. Machen did not elaborate this theme here, but he indicated clearly the direction of his thinking.

In the fourth place, Machen argued that liberalism should be excluded from the professing Christian church. This position followed logically upon the demonstration of his thesis in *Christianity and Liberalism* that liberalism was different from Christianity in its views of history, God and man, the Bible, Jesus Christ, and salvation. It was simply a matter of definition, then, to conclude that liberalism had no rightful place in the Christian church:

> . . . liberalism is not Christianity. And that being the case, it is highly undesirable that liberalism and Christianity should continue to be propagated within the bounds of the same organization. A separation between the two parties in the Church is the crying need of the hour.[33]

Furthermore, it was merely a matter of simple honesty for liberal ministers to exclude themselves from the church. Machen carefully distinguished between church members who were confused or troubled by doubts concerning the truthfulness of Christianity and those persons who positively denied the faith and yet sought to occupy positions as ministers or teachers within the church. For the former he expressed nothing but sympathy (having endured the same ordeal himself). For the latter he suggested a specific course of action: they were free to leave the evangelical churches with whose doctrine they disagreed and to unite themselves with other church bodies with which they were in agreement. Such a course of action might be difficult, but it had one overriding advantage: it was honest. While pursuing this line of reasoning, Machen specifically referred to the ordination vows of the Presbyterian Church, and cited the questions concerning the scriptures and the confession of faith to which candidates for the ministry were required to give affirmative answers. One page later he wrote:

> Whether it be desirable or not, the ordination declaration is part of the constitution of the Church. If a man can stand on that platform he may be an officer in the Presbyterian Church; if he cannot stand on it he has no right to be an officer in the Presbyterian Church.

It is not difficult to imagine Machen recalling, as he wrote such words, his own affirmative response to those questions on the occasion of his ordination nearly a decade earlier, and recalling as well the anguished intellectual struggle which troubled him for a decade before he was able in good conscience to make that affirmation. The standards of intellectual integrity and ecclesiastical honesty that he applied so stringently to himself he was now applying in the same measure to others. He could hardly be expected to do less.[34]

The three books examined here serve to demonstrate the substantial lines of continuity which run between Machen's early development and his mature views. There is one other volume which is worthy of consideration at this point, however, because of its treatment of several themes relevant to the current study.

The Nature of Faith
Machen authored another book in a popular vein which was published in 1925 bearing the title *What Is Faith?*. The book originated as a series of lectures delivered at Grove City Bible School in the summer of 1925 and utilized material previously published in periodicals. This work, perhaps more than the others surveyed here, serves to reveal Machen's essential intellectual position since, in Stonehouse's words, "it constituted a summary treatment of considerable portions of Christian doctrine." One of its central purposes was "to combat the anti-intellectualism of contemporaneous modernism, with its false separation of faith and knowledge," and thus it "may be thought of as a sequel to *Christianity and Liberalism*, though its theme was somewhat less comprehensive." The book was so highly regarded by John B. Hutton, editor of *The British Weekly*, that he ran a series of eight responses to the book by British theologians in 1926. *What is*

Faith? may in some ways have a claim to be the most significant book to have been produced by Machen because of its treatment of certain broad themes.[35]

It may first be observed that Machen clearly indicated that form of Christianity with which he identified himself: it was "evangelical Christianity," "supernatural Christianity," or "historic Christianity." It is not without significance that at the height of the "fundamentalist-modernist controversy" (the John T. Scopes trial occurred in the summer of 1925), Machen identified himself with the historic tradition of supernatural and evangelical Christianity rather than with fundamentalism. This was Machen's consistent position. He made himself a co-belligerent with the fundamentalists, and he from time to time served as a spokesman for the conservative position under the label of fundamentalism, but he typically rejected the term as a means of identifying himself, preferring rather to occupy the ground of orthodox or historic or supernatural or evangelical Christianity.[36]

Second, Machen also clearly identified the ideological opponent he was confronting: it was the philosophical position he termed "modern naturalism." Machen used the terminology "naturalism" or "naturalistic" at least eleven times in various combinations during the course of this book. He did not elaborate on the meaning of the term but made it clear by his usage (naturalistic "principles," "reconstructions," "historians") that he had in mind that set of assumptions which discounted the possibility of any supernatural divine activity in earthly history and thus ruled out the supernatural origin of Christianity as set forth in the New Testament. He was thus pointing out the fundamental assumption which lay at the foundation of consistent historicism, the assumption which prohibited *a priori* even a consideration of the possibility that divine action was involved in Christian origins.[37]

Third, as might be expected, Machen devoted a good deal of attention to the nature and characteristics of Christian faith. He claimed that historical events provided the basis of Christian faith, just as they were at the center of the New Testament. Therefore faith has an intellectual content, namely knowledge of those historical events and of the nature of God and of Jesus Christ as revealed in such events and in the Bible as a whole. It is in this connection that he protested the divorce between religion and theology which he found to characterize much of modern religious thought. Indeed, Machen rejected the intellectual reductionism which characterized both religious liberalism and fundamentalism: "we prefer, instead of seeing how little of Christian truth we can get along with, to see just how much of Christian truth we can obtain."[38]

Faith is born of God's grace and the work of the Holy Spirit, yet on the human side faith is a venture, with "no rigidly mathematical proof" supporting it but with "at least certitude enough to cause us to risk our lives." Faith involves becoming convinced of the truth of the testimony of the scriptures to Jesus Christ, a persuasion that comes from becoming "personally acquainted with the writers who give us the testimony," and then coming "to have an overpowering impression that they are telling us the truth." Machen seems to advocate here a view of scripture which acknowledges its self-authenticating authority and is far from a mechanical approach. He uses the Gospels of Mark and of John as illustrations of how doubts as to the truthfulness of the records can be overcome by the force and power of the documents themselves.[39]

Fourth, Machen to a limited extent described what he meant by the concept of scientific method. He deplored the current "abandonment of scientific historical method," by which "the Biblical writers should be allowed to speak for themselves" through the historian's use of "grammatico-historical exegesis." True practice of scientific method will give due consideration to the testimony of others (e.g., the biblical authors), and conclusions reached by this means will be no less adequate because of it. "It is not true that convictions based on the word of others must necessarily be less firm and less scientific than convictions based on one's own calculation and observation." Both theology and chemistry may be considered as scientific "because they are both concerned with the acquisition and orderly arrangement of a body of truth." If this latter statement is to be taken as Machen's understanding of what is meant by science – "the acquisition and orderly arrangement of a body of truth" – then there is little here which, when taken alongside his other comments, could not be described by Ernst Breisach's account of what was considered "scientific" history at the turn of the century: "reverence for written sources, strict evidence, text criticism, archives, and seminars." Machen seems to have possessed no unbridled confidence in "scientific method" when applied to history, especially when it is noted that he claimed that "no historian can be altogether without presuppositions," and with reference to one historian in particular, "he finds what he expects to find."[40]

Furthermore, faith itself has epistemological or scientific (with "science" taken in its basic sense of "knowledge") implications. Machen cites Hebrews 11:1 where he sees faith "regarded as contributing to the sum of human knowledge." In this sense "faith is just as scientific as astronomy. The future is predicted by means of faith when one depends for one's knowledge of the future on the word of a personal being." Machen seems to be suggesting here that believing the testimony of the biblical authors (or believing God speaking through the biblical authors) can result in knowledge that is just as secure as that attained through believing the testimony of a scientist (an astronomer, for example).[41]

It is in this connection that Machen made two statements that are important in evaluating his intellectual dependence on the philosophy of Scottish Common Sense Realism. The first of these affirms the primacy of spiritual regeneration (or lack thereof) in determining the orientation of one's intellectual outlook. Machen claimed that "no one can be truly scientific who ignores the fact of sin" and that "in humanity as it is actually constituted, an intellectual conviction of the truth of Christianity is always accompanied by a change of heart and a new direction for the will." This does not imply a relativism in which something (such as Christianity) may be true for some people but not for others; truth is universally and objectively true. "But," Machen continued,

> for a thing to be true is one thing and for it to be recognized as true is another; and in order that Christianity may be recognized as true by men upon this earth the blinding effects of sin must be removed. The blinding effects of sin are removed by the Spirit of God; and the Spirit chooses to do that only for those whom He brings by the new birth into the Kingdom of God. Regeneration, or the new birth, therefore, does not stand in opposition to a truly scientific attitude toward the evidence, but on the contrary it is necessary in order that that truly scientific attitude may be attained; it is not a substitute for the intellect, but on the contrary by it the intellect is made to be a trustworthy instrument for apprehending truth.

This statement is significant for several reasons. (1) By distinguishing between the truth of a thing and the apprehension of its truth, Machen acknowledged a subjective element in the act of apprehending truth. (2) He claimed that sin has a blinding effect which must be removed in order for Christianity to be recognized as true, thus affirming a Calvinistic understanding of human sin and inability. (3) He asserted that the blinding effects of sin are removed only by regeneration effected by the Spirit of God, thereby attributing a noetic effect to regeneration. (4) He claimed that such regeneration is necessary to a "truly scientific attitude," for by this means the intellect becomes a "trustworthy instrument for apprehending truth," therein positing an absolute distinction between the regenerate and the unregenerate. (5) Machen supports his position by going on to cite the Westminster Shorter Catechism on effectual calling, which describes God's work in effecting regeneration, thus bolstering his position by appeal to standard Reformed doctrine. The affirmation by Machen which this passage sets forth compels the recognition that whatever his adherence to Common Sense Realism, he was discriminating in his use of this philosophy; he did not allow it to control his theology. Indeed, at certain crucial points – as here – Machen's Calvinism overruled any claims made by Common Sense Realism, for example as to a single human consciousness or the ability of the human intellect.[42]

Another important statement relates to the presuppositions of a genuinely scientific outlook. In referring to the testimony of the New Testament writers to events which purportedly occurred in first-century Palestine, Machen says:

> That testimony may conceivably be true and it may conceivably be false; but to say beforehand that it cannot be true is to fall into a very serious intellectual fault. If the testimony is true, then the rejection of it is just as unscientific and the acceptance of it just as scientific as the rejection or acceptance of assured results in the field of the laboratory sciences.

Machen here labels as "unscientific" the rejection of specific potential conclusions in advance of undertaking an investigation of the evidence. It may well be that "to say beforehand" that the New Testament accounts "cannot be true" is demanded by the naturalistic assumptions of a consistent historicism, but it is "a very serious intellectual fault." It is neither scientific nor scholarly, Machen is arguing, to eliminate some conclusions from consideration on the basis of prior philosophical commitments. And yet that is precisely what modern naturalistic criticism does.[43]

It appears that Machen comes very close in this passage to exposing what he would evidently regard as the central problem of modern biblical criticism conducted along historicist lines: "If the testimony is true, then the rejection of it is . . . unscientific," and by implication the method by which that testimony is rejected is unscientific as well, for on the basis of its presuppositions it has no means for determining the truthfulness of the documents should they indeed be true. There is at bottom only one conclusion allowed by the assumptions and methods of historicist biblical criticism: it is that the New Testament documents are not true in their description of the supernatural origins of Christianity. But what is even worse, from Machen's perspective, is that this approach is incapable of ascertaining that the documents are true should it be the case that they are; there could hardly be a more "serious intellectual fault" than this. The method of historicist biblical criticism is thus shown not to be scientific (in the sense of being truly critical, open to all the evidence, and capable of leading to reliable knowledge) and, insofar as it incorporates naturalistic assumptions, must be pronounced intellectually bankrupt. Its conclusions are determined by its presuppositions.[44]

Fifth, Machen in this book was voicing a protest against the relativism which he perceived was becoming pervasive in American culture and religious life. In contrast to the historical, epistemological, and cultural relativism fostered by the historicist approach, Machen maintained the objectivity, permanence, and universality of truth. Machen objected, for example, to modern creeds which were "intended to 'interpret' Christianity in the 'thought-forms' of the twentieth century." The great difference between the recent creeds and those they were intended to replace was that "the historic creeds, unlike the modern creeds, were intended by their authors or compilers to be true." This, he thought, was "the most necessary qualification of a creed." He continued: "if theology is not even intended to be permanently and objectively true, if it is merely a convenient symbol in which in this generation a mystic experience is clothed, then theologizing, it seems to me, is the most useless form of trifling in which a man could possibly engage." On the basis of the modern "pragmatist" approach, there could be no progress in theology because there is no "objective norm of truth" at which to aim; in contrast, "believers in historic Christianity maintain the objectivity of truth" and thus hold out the possibility of progressing toward ever closer approximations of the truth.[45]

It was here, regarding the objectivity of truth, that there occurred, in Machen's view, "the really important divergence of opinion in the religious world of the present day." The great divide concerned not particular doctrines, as important as they might be, but the loss of the possibility of attaining any objective theological truth. "The modern depreciation of theology results logically in the most complete skepticism"; "all is denied, because all is affirmed merely as useful or symbolic and not as true." In drawing attention to the loss of the concrete possibility of objective truth in modern thought, Machen put his finger on what was perhaps the crucial, the defining epistemological problem of the twentieth century. But this was no mere reflection of Princeton's alleged adherence to Common Sense Realism, for Machen at the same time distinguished between objective truth and the subjective apprehension of truth: "the facts are one thing, and the recognition of the facts is another." The objective truth for which Machen was contending was not something that was self-evident to the impartial observer (since no one can receive Christianity as true apart from the regenerating work of God), but it was objective truth nevertheless. "The facts of the Christian religion remain facts no matter whether we cherish them or not." Christianity involves objective truth which is subjectively appropriated under the influence of the Spirit of God.[46]

Alongside his affirmation of the objectivity of truth, Machen affirmed as well the universality of truth. He objected to the application of the "pragmatist attitude" to "simultaneously existing nations and races," according to which there is "no possibility that anything in the sphere of doctrine can be permanently and universally true." He denied that Christianity can be true for some people and not true for others (though it may not be recognized as true by some); "on the contrary," he claimed, "it is true, we think, even for the demons in hell as well as for the saints in heaven, though its truth does the demons no good."[47]

This book, *What Is Faith?*, serves to demonstrate not only lines of continuity with Machen's earlier work, but also shows his views probably reaching substantially complete maturation by 1925 and his engagement with some of the prominent intellectual tendencies of his day, including the implications of historicist thinking. It remains now to draw some final conclusions.

CHAPTER 9

CONCLUSION

The conclusions which may be drawn from the foregoing investigation fall into three categories. The first concerns the primary interest of this study, the development of Machen's views concerning the Bible, historical scholarship, and Christianity. The second is an extension of the first, relating to the nature of the conservative Christian movement in the 1920s. The third, of broader scope, involves reflections on the direction of American intellectual and religious culture.

The Development of Machen's Views Concerning the Bible and Historical Scholarship

First, it is clear that in his early manhood J. Gresham Machen experienced a profound and unsettling disturbance of his beliefs concerning the Bible. Having inherited the traditional Protestant reverence for the Bible as the inspired and infallible Word of God, he was thrown into doubt and confusion by his exposure to the modern historicist understanding of the Bible and to a liberal theology which had incorporated the historicist approach. The central question at issue in Machen's mind was the supernaturalness of the person of Jesus Christ and of the origin of Christianity in the first century. That supernaturalness was denied by historicist biblical criticism, which sought to explain Jesus and the Christian movement as natural historical products of the first-century environment in which they arose. Machen was particularly disturbed by the implications of the historicist approach which suggested that neither Jesus nor the Christian movement were of divine origin, and that supernaturalistic, redemptive Christianity as historically maintained was therefore not true. This disturbance of Machen's beliefs not only caused him considerable intellectual turmoil for the better part of a decade but also left him uncertain regarding his professional calling. He was clearly gifted for and most naturally drawn to the scholarly study of the Bible, but his great scrupulousness would not allow him to consider entering the Christian ministry in any capacity while he entertained doubts about the truthfulness of the Christian faith. Only with difficulty was he finally convinced to become an instructor at Princeton Seminary in 1906.

Second, it is equally clear that although Machen's doubts were occasioned by historical criticism of the Bible, yet he did not oppose but forcefully advocated a rigorous historical method in biblical study. He utilized such a method himself, applying the full weight of his impressive classical training to the tasks of interpreting the New Testament text, elucidating its historical environment, and investigating the circumstances connected with the production of its documents. His book reviews reveal that he criticized those who may have held to conservative theological views but did not adequately address the historical problems connected with the interpretation of the Bible. Furthermore, it is likely that Machen would claim to have resolved his intellectual difficulties by means of his own historical study of the Bible. His brief dispute with his mother in the fall of 1906 gave eruptive expression to his demand for intellectual freedom and his insistence on intellectual integrity; only through a full and fair investigation, he believed, could he arrive at assured and settled convictions in the matter. It need not be doubted that Machen gave the question the full hearing which he insisted was his right and duty to perform. His investigation led him to conclude, perhaps as early as 1909, that the historical evidence favored the supernatural origin of Christianity.

Third, Machen's insistence on a historical approach to the Bible did not mean that he accepted the historicist assumptions regarding the nature of history. Indeed, it was in his rejection of those assumptions that he departed most markedly from the scholarly norms of his day. The difference between Machen and historicist or liberal scholars was the way in which they defined history; the latter would not allow for direct divine action in the external events of history (even though some of them might see a divine purpose behind natural historical processes) while Machen would. For the consistent historicists, "historical" meant "natural," while for Machen "historical" referred to all events occurring in the external world, whether naturally or supernaturally caused. While the historicist view of history was defined by its naturalistic assumptions, Machen's philosophy of history was shaped by the Bible and by his Reformed theological heritage.

This led him to distinguish – as does the Westminster Shorter Catechism, Question 8 – between the mediate, providential working of God in all of history, and the immediate, creative activity of God in specific redemptive events, a distinction which liberal theology did not possess. The evidence presented by Machen's more popular addresses, "Christianity and Culture" in 1912, and "History and Faith" in 1915, indicates that by these dates he recognized that this difference in philosophy of history lay at the bottom of the divergence of historicist and liberal thought from traditional Christianity. Thus Machen's resolution of the dilemma presented by biblical criticism was to adhere to an approach to the Bible that was historical without being historicist.[1]

Fourth, Machen believed that the divergence of liberalism from traditional Christianity – especially in the sphere of philosophy of history – was so great as to preclude the former from being identified as Christianity and to exclude it from a rightful place within the Christian church. Machen had expressed as early as 1906 his conviction that the difference between the liberal and orthodox theologies affected the very essence of Christianity. As he gradually reached firmer intellectual ground himself, and as he came to recognize the difference between the two as lying in their respective views of history, this conviction did not diminish. He expressed it most forcefully in 1923 in *Christianity and Liberalism*, where he explicitly defined liberalism in terms of its historicist philosophy of history. Machen rejected the identification of liberalism as Christian because of its denial of the historical reality of those divinely-caused supernatural events which are at the heart of the biblical message: the incarnation, death, and resurrection of Jesus as the divine redeemer. He believed that in giving up a historically-grounded message of redemption, liberalism had given up the gospel (which Machen consistently defined as good news about something that had happened) and had forfeited the right to be reckoned as Christianity. As a consequence, he argued, liberalism should no longer be afforded a place of respect within the traditional Christian church; liberals or modernists should voluntarily withdraw, in the interests of clarity and honesty. Although Machen's mature convictions regarding the nature of liberalism and its place in the church were not fully expressed until 1923, it is evident that those convictions were the fruit of long reflection on the matter, reflection which had begun perhaps two decades earlier. Some recent scholars have acknowledged the correctness of Machen's judgment here: "J. Gresham Machen was right. What we have in the Enlightenment tradition of criticism is nothing less than another religion that supplants biblical faith."[2]

Fifth, not only was Machen's attitude toward liberalism in the 1920s a product of his earlier development, so also was his New Testament scholarship during this decade. Mark Noll has stated that "Machen's New Testament work was the high point of conservative evangelical scholarship in the 1920s,"[3] as indeed it undoubtedly was; but the foundations of that scholarship were laid in the previous decades. Both *The Origin of Paul's Religion* and *The Virgin Birth of Christ* had their beginning much earlier in Machen's life when he was wrestling with these questions in order to find answers for his own mind's illumination and his soul's well-being. These books may fairly be understood to embody the historical considerations which aided Machen himself in the resolution of his own intellectual struggles and in the attainment of a measure of spiritual certainty.

Sixth, it is likely that Machen's mature convictions regarding the most effective way to defend Christianity against contemporary attacks were powerfully affected by his own experience. He had moved from doubt to certainty by means of a resolution of the historical problems connected with Christian origins. And by the time he produced "Christianity and Culture" in 1912 and his *Rapid Survey* in 1914 and 1915, he was arguing that it is necessary for Christians to address the pressing intellectual problems which kept the Christian faith from even gaining a hearing in modern academic circles. It can hardly be doubted that he had in mind the problem of history and historical evidence; and a 1912 book review revealed his characteristic emphasis on the logical priority of historical evidence over Christian experience in establishing the truthfulness of the Christian faith. His conviction of the need for such an approach remained strong; in 1925 he wrote, "It is one of the root errors of the present day to suppose that because the philosophical and historical foundations of our religion are insufficient to produce faith, they are therefore unnecessary." Machen's strong advocacy of a historical apologetic, for which he has been criticized in some quarters (though he in fact did not neglect the work of the Holy Spirit in conversion), is probably a reflection of his own experience, his perception of having become convinced on the basis of historical evidence.[4]

Seventh, Machen certainly allowed for the influence of philosophical presuppositions in the formation of historical judgments. He did not believe, as is evident from his early essays on the virgin birth, that the historical evidence in itself is necessarily compelling. The evidence could be misinterpreted, or it could be evaluated from the standpoint of a presuppositional bias against the supernatural. He continued to demonstrate this attitude in his major scholarly books of the 1920s. At any rate, as he acknowledged in "History and Faith," historical scholarship was incapable of demonstrating that Christianity is true, for Christianity deals with matters which historical investigation cannot touch. He recognized that there are limits beyond which historical research cannot go and that historical scholarship renders judgments only in terms of probability. The attainment of certainty is achieved only through the exercise of faith in Jesus Christ, faith which receives Christ as he is set forth in the New Testament. Such faith is produced only by the Spirit of God, who may nevertheless utilize historical argumentation to induce a conviction of the truth. Such emphases in Machen's theology suggest that he may not have been so captive to Scottish Common Sense Realism as some historians have contended. He believed that there is a subjective element in human knowledge; that philosophical presuppositions may influence one's evaluation of historical evidence; that the evidence in itself is not necessarily convincing; and that the human mind is incapable of attaining to truth (in the sense of recognizing the truthfulness of Christianity) or of exercising faith by its own power, but that for these ends the operation of the Holy Spirit is necessary.[5]

Eighth, Machen developed his doctrine of scripture only gradually and as a secondary element in his view of the Bible. Prior to 1914 he had made only the slightest mention of a doctrine of scripture in any of his writings (a 1909 book review), and in 1914 his emphasis was entirely on the authority of the Bible, with no discussion of the dynamics or function of inspiration. His view of biblical authority was indeed firm by the time he wrote the *Rapid Survey*, for in this work the authority of the New Testament was bound up with apostolic authorship (or sanction) and exercised definitive control over critical questions. When Machen first expounded his view of biblical inspiration in the early 1920s, divine inspiration served in his thought as a mechanism for securing the accuracy of the biblical account of God's redemptive activity. The inspiration of the Bible was not for

Machen an end in itself, but was important because it subserved the divine purposes in the redemption of fallen humanity. Inspiration safeguarded the objective truthfulness of the revelation contained in the Bible; the revelation was intended to lead men to God himself in forgiveness and in positive fellowship through Christ. Machen's view of the Bible also consistently allowed for a high degree of divine accommodation to the limitations of the recipients of revelation. The same allowance of accommodation to human limitations which was noted in Machen's student essay of 1905 is evident throughout his treatment in *The Virgin Birth of Christ* twenty-five years later.[6]

It should be noted that Machen's doctrine of scripture served a preservative function that was not available, for example, to Charles A. Briggs. Briggs's experience shows that once the lion of criticism is let out of the cage with no inherent limitations on its power, it cannot be contained. Briggs's criticism relativized some of Christian history while seeking to leave some of it absolute; his successors went on to relativize all. If everything is not to be cut adrift, there must be invoked a principle by which some stable or absolute points can be maintained; for Machen that principle was the historic Protestant doctrine of Holy Scripture which maintains that God has guaranteed the truthfulness of the New Testament writings. Thus once Machen had demonstrated the literary and historical possibility of the truthfulness of the New Testament accounts of the origin of Christianity (in his scholarly work, conducted on a presuppositional base allowing for divine supernatural activity in earthly history), he went on to affirm the actual truthfulness of the accounts in all they assert as a result of the operation of divine inspiration (a position taken in faith). This was an option that was not open to Briggs and others who had rejected the historic view of scripture. Their position was inherently untenable and unstable because they could not draw a line beyond which criticism could not go.[7]

Ninth, it appears from the evidence presented in this study that Machen's commitment to a specifically Reformed theological position also developed gradually. During the decade of the 1900s, Machen's chief concern was the historical truthfulness of the biblical account of Christian origins, with little attention given to distinctively Reformed concerns. During the early 1910s, he seems to have been growing in his appreciation of Reformed emphases and theological traditions, as evidenced by his Calvinistic attitude toward culture in

1912 and his citation of the Shorter Catechism in the *Rapid Survey*. By the mid-1920s Machen was convinced that a thoroughgoing Reformed stance was the best vantage point from which to defend supernatural Christianity; when offered the presidency of Bryan Memorial University in 1927 he declined on such grounds.[8]

Tenth, at bottom, Machen was concerned for the historical grounding of the Christian faith and for the unity of truth. He consistently defined the gospel as good news about something that had happened in history, referring to the life, death, and resurrection of Jesus. "Redemption was accomplished, . . . according to the New Testament, by an event in the external world, at a definite time in the world's history, when the Lord Jesus died upon the cross and rose again." He saw historicist biblical criticism as denying that historical grounding by rejecting the historicity of these events, and liberalism as ignoring that historical grounding by its indifference to these events. His own spiritual and intellectual struggle was concerned with the establishment of the historical grounding of the faith on a scientific and scholarly basis, and when he had resolved the matter satisfactorily for himself, it provided the central unifying element in his opposition to the naturalistic implications of the historicist position as manifested both in biblical scholarship and in the church. This conclusion is supported by Harrisville and Sundberg, who claim, "The external grounding of the Christian proclamation in the narrative integrity of the biblical record is the core of Machen's argument." The strength of his conviction as to the historical nature of the Christian message gave a vigorous and uncompromising quality to his response to historicist scholarship and theological liberalism, for he perceived both as overturning the historical groundedness of the Christian faith.[9]

Machen also opposed the compartmentalization of knowledge into "scientific" and "religious" or any dichotomy between intellectual and spiritual truth. He insisted that the events and documents which lay at the foundation of the Christian faith were fully historical and susceptible to historical investigation by ordinary means, and that such investigation did not disprove their essential historicity and truthfulness. His desire to uphold the historical nature of the faith, combined with his conviction that the historical tenability of the New Testament could be demonstrated, gave impetus to his scholarly work and imparted to his books an imposing intellectual force. George Marsden has rendered the judgment that Machen's "impressive demonstrations in his academic works that, at the least, traditional understandings of the Bible could be defended on just the grounds they were so widely attacked – their empirical reliability as historical accounts – were certainly among the most remarkable intellectual achievements of the era." Those works were impressive precisely because in them Machen sought to preserve the unity between intellectual and spiritual knowledge. The principle he enunciated in 1925 had motivated his entire intellectual enterprise for the preceding two decades: "ultimately there ought to be a real synthesis of truth."[10]

If this study of J. Gresham Machen offers any distinctive contribution it is likely to be found in its analysis of Machen's early writings, which are interpreted against the background of the rise of historical consciousness; and in its conclusions that probably by 1912, definitely by 1915, Machen came to believe (without using this terminology) that the assumptions of historicism underlay both theological liberalism and much practice of biblical criticism; that while Machen affirmed the historical study of the Bible, he rejected the assumptions of historicism insofar as they demanded a naturalistic explanation for the origin of Christianity; and that Machen's responses to biblical criticism and theological liberalism during the 1920s were expressions of views he reached in resolving his own confrontation with historicism. Thus the period of Machen's intellectual struggle and its resolution may be regarded as the crucial and decisive era of his life, laying the foundation for all that followed.

An additional and broader conclusion to emerge from this study is that for the earnest enquirer faced with the current practice and results of biblical criticism, it is true now as it was for Machen in his struggle: presuppositions count. Indeed, presuppositions – the philosophical bias, theological commitments, or historical assumptions with which one approaches the investigation of the origins of Christianity – may exercise greater influence than any other single factor in conditioning or determining the outcome of the investigation, for they control what kinds of conclusions are even considered possible or allowable. As philosopher C. Stephen Evans has observed, "For the defender of the narrative, the problem is not critical study of the Bible *per se*, but the conclusions and assumptions of particular critics."[11]

The Nature of Fundamentalism

Machen's personal pilgrimage serves to illuminate the nature and concerns of the American fundamentalist movement. That movement has sometimes been portrayed as one of the aberrant social manifestations of the 1920s, properly classified along with nativism, the Ku Klux Klan, the prohibition movement, and anti-urbanism as part of the anti-progressive social tendency of the decade. Such is the picture presented by William E. Leuchtenburg in his popular volume, widely used as a textbook, *The Perils of Prosperity, 1914-32*, where he treats all these phenomena in a single chapter entitled "Political Fundamentalism." If Machen is to be regarded as a fundamentalist, then clearly such a representation of the movement must be revised, for the description of fundamentalism which Leuchtenburg offers (chiefly of the anti-evolution crusade) bears little resemblance to the concerns expressed by Machen. Such a revisionist process has indeed already been initiated, led primarily by Ernest Sandeen's *The Roots of Fundamentalism* (1970) and George Marsden's *Fundamentalism and American Culture* (1980). These scholars see the movement growing out of several distinct religious traditions in American Protestantism, each with long historical roots and strong ideological concerns. Sandeen gives special emphasis to the roots of the movement in nineteenth-century premillennialism and the Princeton doctrine of scripture, lending his portrayal of fundamentalism a distinctly theological cast. Marsden includes other strands of tradition along with these, and defines the movement as a religious one, possessing indeed a particularly theological world view but also arising out of genuine concern for the proper relationship of men to God through Jesus Christ. More recently, in his provocative volume *Religious Outsiders and the Making of Americans* (1986), R. Laurence Moore has affirmed the interpretative approaches of both Sandeen and Marsden, recognizing that "both stress the importance of religious issues in shaping the Fundamentalist mentality."[12]

The findings of the present study tend to confirm this recent historiographical trend in the interpretation of fundamentalism. Machen's opposition to modernism was religiously rather than socially based, for he believed that historicist biblical scholarship and theological liberalism hindered the propagation and reception of the truth embodied in historic Christianity and thus kept men from coming to a true knowledge of the living God. Furthermore, it is most

significant that Machen's views had been substantially formulated
by 1915, a time when, according to Marsden, fundamentalism had
not yet become a self-conscious movement, and well before the
controversy of the 1920s. Machen's response to liberalism in the
1920s, therefore, and his co-belligerency with self-proclaimed
fundamentalists (Machen himself consistently disavowed the term),
while indeed a reflex of the developing situation in the churches, was
no mere reaction to the post-war social climate but the expression of
theological views developed a decade earlier. If Machen is to be
regarded as a fundamentalist, then that movement must be so defined
as to acknowledge as its paramount concern the intellectual question
of the naturalistic assumptions of historicism.[13]

But in light of Machen's intellectual development and theological
stance, it may well be asked whether he should be regarded as a
fundamentalist at all. Would it not serve the progress and clarity of
historical analysis to acknowledge that Machen was not a fundamentalist but a confessional Calvinistic Presbyterian of the Old School
tradition who allied himself with fundamentalists in a common cause?
The theological stance which Machen had adopted by 1915 differed in
no significant way from that of his nineteenth-century Princeton
predecessors. And if Machen ever had a theological mentor or hero,
it was B. B. Warfield, the Princeton apologete and a traditional Calvinistic scholar of the first rank. Machen's militancy can even be regarded
as a continuation of Princeton's vigorous apologetic tradition extending
from far back in the nineteenth century. When these considerations
are taken in conjunction with the facts that historians commonly recognize that Machen was atypical of the fundamentalists and that Machen
himself consistently rejected his being identified as a fundamentalist
(although he was willing to be aligned with them when the lines were
drawn), then it appears appropriate to ask whether a reassessment of
that identification is not in order. Would it not be helpful to recognize
at least two categories of opponents to theological liberalism: the
fundamentalists and their evangelical allies or co-belligerents? Such
an analysis would promote clarity and consistency of definition, for
then the term fundamentalist could be reserved for those who claimed
that title and who exhibited a more or less distinctive set of common
characteristics. Such characteristics would include not only militancy,
but also other theological or intellectual attributes not shared by
Machen, such as premillennialism, anti-evolutionism, ecclesiastical

separatism, super-patriotism, theological reductionism, and lack of concern to engage in scholarly debate. It may readily be admitted that the fundamentalists made use of Machen and his case against liberalism. But this may well have been an instance partially analogous to the usage which later fundamentalists made of the person and writings of C. S. Lewis (1898-1963), the eminent British literary scholar and Christian writer; in both cases self-acknowledged fundamentalists claimed the work of one who was not really their own.[14]

The present study also supports the contention of George Marsden, Grant Wacker, and Mark Massa that at the bottom of the conflict between theological conservatives and liberals was a difference in beliefs about the nature of history. If Machen is to be taken as a leading spokesman for the conservative or even the fundamentalist cause (which he could well have been even though not personally a fundamentalist), then some credence must be given to his 1915 declaration, reaffirmed in 1923, that the central issue was the naturalistic view of history – and specifically of Christianity – that was implied in historicist assumptions. Wacker has put the matter aptly in claiming that the "dynamite in the crevices" of nineteenth-century biblical civilization – the force behind the liberal movement –

> was not the reconstruction of this or that particular doctrine. It was not the denial of the virgin birth of Jesus, not the assertion of future probation for the heathen. Nor indeed was it the development of historical-critical method itself. Rather the dynamite that ultimately exploded the entire edifice was the assumption that knowledge of divine things, like knowledge of ordinary things, must be found squarely within the historical process or not at all.

Conservatives, on the other hand, including Machen, "typically claimed that some parts of God's self-revelation escaped the grip of history," that is, were not entirely determined by the historical process and environment. This stance may properly be regarded as the characteristic feature of the conservative movement. "Indeed," Wacker concludes, "it could be argued that this insistence that the method and content of revelation were not a function merely of historical processes stood at the core of what came to be known, especially in the United States, as fundamentalism." Thus what Machen had in common with the fundamentalists was the conviction that the ultimate question at issue was the historical reality of divine activity in the external events of the world; and he regarded specific doctrines such as the virgin birth as useful indicators of whether one held to a historicist or a biblical view of history and of the person of Christ.[15]

The Direction of American Culture

Machen's experience and convictions are also relevant to the direction of American religious and intellectual culture during the twentieth century.

In the first place, it may be argued that events subsequent to Machen's lifetime have served to vindicate his judgment that historic Christianity ceases to exist apart from confidence in the historical truthfulness of the Bible. "The authoritative Bible," he declared in 1909, "has been and is to-day the very foundation of popular Christianity . . . the Christianity that does without it has never exhibited the power to become anything more than a religion of the few." Historian Winthrop Hudson, who is by no means a fundamentalist, has described the history of Protestantism in the late-nineteenth and early-twentieth centuries as a "loss of identity." In the ninth chapter of his *American Protestantism*, whose chapter title includes the suggestive phrase just cited, Hudson claims that during this era "Protestantism . . . was losing its identity and no longer possessed to any great degree the indispensable leverage of an independent theological position," having given up any normative theology of distinctively Christian content. As a result, liberal Protestantism after 1940 entered a period of decline relative to more conservative evangelical groups, a decline which has accelerated rapidly since the publication of Hudson's book in 1961. This erosion of strength – both numerically and financially – in the liberal or "mainline" Protestant churches has extended through the 1960s and 1970s into the 1980s and beyond and has been amply documented in more recent studies, as has the corresponding resurgence of conservative evangelical bodies. To put the matter in the terms used in this study, those church bodies which accommodated themselves to historicist views of the Bible and adopted the liberal theology seem to be perceived by histor-ians such as Hudson and by the general populace as having lost their distinctively Christian character – which was precisely the contention advanced by Machen. The steady growth of evangelical bodies which uphold the authority of the Bible suggests, in spite of the superficiality and anti-intellectualism that is undoubtedly present in some strains of conservative Protestantism, that Machen was correct: historic Christianity is founded on the Bible received as historically true. These conservative churches and denominations (excluding heterodox sects such as Mormonism) have commonly affirmed not only the authority of the Bible but also the historic, orthodox supernaturalism of the ancient creeds and the Reformation confessions.[16]

In the second place, Machen's position provided him and his ideological followers with firm intellectual ground and preserved them from the relativism and skepticism that came to dominate American intellectual life. The intellectual stance finally adopted by Machen – the rejection of historicist assumptions concerning history and the acceptance of a historically true and authoritative Bible – provided an epistemological foundation for his view of reality and gave to it stable content as well. Such a position stood in sharp contrast to the epistemological skepticism and cultural relativism that was flooding American intellectual and academic circles in Machen's day and had overwhelmed the culture by the end of the century.[17]

Historian Henry Steele Commager, writing from the vantage point of the late 1940s, surveyed the changes that had occurred in American life since 1890 and declared that "the most important changes were . . . in the philosophical realm." While Commager acknowledged the inadequacy of generalization because of the diverse manifestations of American thought and the tentative nature of his conclusions, yet he offered a summary: "In a general way it could be said that the two generations after 1890 witnessed a transition from certainty to uncertainty, from faith to doubt, from security to insecurity, from seeming order to ostentatious disorder." This transition was in part the product of those intellectual forces whose progress Commager had traced – evolutionism, the scientific temper, the rejection of absolutism, and pragmatism – each of which contributed in its own way to the growing conviction that the meaning of human existence can be found and must be found within the natural flow of historical process. By his rejection of this central tenet of the historicist mentality, J Gresham Machen placed himself outside the mainstream of American intellectual life. But by this means he also enabled himself to pass from his personal experience of uncertainty, doubt, and insecurity toward the freedom of a sure faith. It is by no means clear that he was not better off than those who were moving in the opposite direction.[18]

SELECTED BIBLIOGRAPHY

1. Primary Sources by J. Gresham Machen

1. Published works by Machen (in chronological order; *PTR* = *Princeton Theological Review*)

"The New Testament Account of the Birth of Jesus," First Article. *PTR* 3 (1905):641-70.

"The New Testament Account of the Birth of Jesus," Second Article. *PTR* 4 (1906):37-81.

Review of *The Birth and Infancy of Jesus Christ According to the Gospel Narratives*, by Louis Matthews Sweet. *PTR* 5 (1907):315-16.

Review of *Der Zeugniszweck des Evangelisten Johannes nach seinen eigenen Angaben dargestellt*, by Konrad Meyer. *PTR* 6 (1908):142-43.

Review of *Des Paulus Brief an die Römer für höhere Schulen*, by Rudolf Niemann. *PTR* 6 (1908):144.

Review of *Des Paulus Epistel an die Römer: Abdruck der revidierten Übersetzung Luthers und Auslegung für Gymnasialprima*, by Rudolf Niemann. *PTR* 6 (1908):144.

Review of *The Virgin Birth of Christ*, by James Orr. *PTR* 6 (1908):505-508.

Review of *St. Paul's Epistles to the Thessalonians*, by George Milligan. *PTR* 7 (1909):126-31.

Review of *Interpretation of the Bible: A Short History*, by George Holley Gilbert. *PTR* 7 (1909):348-51.

Review of *PROS ROMAIOUS: Die Epistel Pauli an die Römer*, by G. Richter. *PTR* 7 (1909):351.

Review of *A Short Grammar of the Greek New Testament for Students Familiar with the Elements of Greek*, by A. T. Robertson. *PTR* 7 (1909):491-93.

Review of *The Johannine Writings*, by Paul W. Schmiedel. *PTR* 7 (1909):670-74.

Review of *The Irenaeus Testimony to the Fourth Gospel: Its Extent, Meaning and Value*, by Frank Grant Lewis. *PTR* 8 (1910):137-39.

Review of *Der Leserkreis des Galaterbriefes: ein Beitrag zur urchristlichen Missionsgeschichte*, by Alphons Steinman. *PTR* 8 (1910):299-300.

Review of *The Pauline Epistles: A Critical Study*, by Robert Scott. *PTR* 8 (1910):300-301.

Review of *Commentar über den Brief Pauli an die Römer*, by G. Stockhardt. *PTR* 8 (1910):490-91.

198

Review of *Selections from the Greek Papyri*, by George Milligan, ed. *PTR* 9 (1911):327-28.

Review of *The Bible for Home and School: Commentary on the Epistle of Paul to the Galatians*, by Benjamin W. Bacon. *PTR* 9 (1911):495-98.

Review of *The Childhood of Jesus Christ According to the Canonical Gospels*, by A. Durand. *PTR* 9 (1911):672-73.

"The Hymns of the First Chapter of Luke." *PTR* 10 (1912):1-38.

"The Origin of the First Two Chapters of Luke." *PTR* 10 (1912):212-77.

Review of *Christ and His Critics: Studies in the Person and Problems of Jesus*, by F. R. Montgomery Hitchcock. *PTR* 10 (1912):334-35.

"Jesus and Paul." In *Biblical and Theological Studies*, by The Members of the Faculty of Princeton Theological Seminary, pp. 545-78. New York: Charles Scribner's Sons, 1912.

"The Virgin Birth in the Second Century." *PTR* 10 (1912):529-80.

"Christianity and Culture." *PTR* 11 (1913):1-15. Reprinted in *What Is Christianity? and Other Addresses*, ed. Ned Bernard Stonehouse, pp. 156-69. Grand Rapids: Wm. B. Eerdmans Publishing Co., 1951.

A Rapid Survey of the Literature and History of New Testament Times. Student's Text Book, Parts I-IV. Teacher's Manual, Parts I-IV. Philadelphia: Presbyterian Board of Christian Education, 1914-1915. Edited and reprinted as *The New Testament: An Introduction to Its Literature and History*. Edited by W. John Cook. Edinburgh: The Banner of Truth Trust, 1976.

Review of *Die Apostelgeschichte*, by Hans Hinrich Wendt. *PTR* 13 (1915):292-95.

"History and Faith." *PTR* 13 (1915):337-51. Reprinted in *What Is Christianity? and Other Addresses*, ed. Ned Bernard Stonehouse, pp. 170-84. Grand Rapids: Wm. B. Eerdmans Publishing Co., 1951.

The Origin of Paul's Religion. New York: Macmillan Co., 1921.

Christianity and Liberalism. New York: Macmillan Co., 1923; reprint ed., Grand Rapids: Wm. B. Eerdmans Publishing Co., 1956.

What is Faith? New York: Macmillan Co., 1925; reprint ed., Grand Rapids: Wm. B. Eerdmans Publishing Co., 1969.

"The Relation of Religion to Science and Philosophy: A Review [of *Christianity at the Cross Roads*, by E. Y. Mullins]." *PTR* 24 (1926):38-66.

"What the Bible Teaches About Jesus." *The Evangelical Student* 3 (October 1928):4-11. Reprinted in *What Is Christianity? and other Addresses*, ed. Ned Bernard Stonehouse, pp. 24-36. Grand Rapids: Wm. B. Eerdmans Publishing Co., 1951.

The Virgin Birth of Christ. New York: Harper, 1930. 2nd ed., 1932; reprint ed., London: James Clarke & Co., 1958.

"Christianity in Conflict." In *Contemporary American Theology: Theological Autobiographies*, ed. Vergilius Ferm, 1:245-74. New York: Round Table Press, 1932.

2. Manuscript materials

Philadelphia, PA. Westminster Theological Seminary. Montgomery Library. Machen Archives. Letters from J. Gresham Machen to various members of his immediate family. Boxes "1904-06: Family"; "1907-08: Family."

2. Other Primary Sources

Bultmann, Rudolf. "Is Exegesis without Presuppositions Possible?" In *Existence and Faith: Shorter Writings of Rudolf Bultmann.* Selected, translated, and introduced by Schubert M. Ogden. Cleveland: World Publishing Co., 1960.

Briggs, Charles Augustus. *Whither? A Theological Question for the Times.* New York: Charles Scribner's Sons, 1889.

Clarke, William Newton. *Sixty Years with the Bible: A Record of Experience.* New York: Charles Scribner's Sons, 1909.

Goodspeed, Edgar Johnson, and Ernest DeWitt Burton. "The Study of the New Testament." In *A Guide to the Study of the Christian Religion*, ed. Gerald Birney Smith, pp. 180-200. Chicago: University of Chicago Press, 1916.

Green, William Brenton, Jr. Review of *Sociological Study of the Bible*, by Louis Wallis. *PTR* 11 (1913):119-22.

Harnack, Adolf. *What Is Christianity?* Translated by Thomas Bailey Saunders. Introduction by Rudolf Bultmann. New York: Harper & Brothers, 1957.

Hodge, A. A. *Outlines of Theology.* Reprint ed. Grand Rapids: Zondervan Publishing House, 1972.

Hodge, Archibald A., and Benjamin B. Warfield. *Inspiration.* Introduction by Roger R. Nicole. Grand Rapids: Baker Book House, 1979.

Hodge, Charles. *Systematic Theology.* 3 vols. Reprint ed., Grand Rapids: Wm. B. Eerdmans Publishing Co., 1975.

James, William. "The Will to Believe." In *The Will to Believe and Other Essays in Popular Philosophy*, pp. 1-31. New York: Longmans Green and Co., 1899.

Machen, Minnie Gresham. *The Bible in Browning, with Particular Reference to "The Ring and the Book."* New York: Macmillan Co., 1903.

Santayana, G[eorge]. "The Intellectual Temper of the Age." In *Winds of Doctrine: Studies in Contemporary Opinion*, pp. 1-24. New York: Charles Scribner's Sons, 1913.

Warfield, Benjamin B. "What Is Calvinism?" In *Selected Shorter Writings of Benjamin B. Warfield*, ed. John E. Meeter, 1:389-92. Nutley, NJ: Presbyterian and Reformed Publishing Company, 1970.

3. Secondary Sources

Ahlstrom, Sydney E. *A Religious History of the American People.* New Haven: Yale University Press, 1972.

Ahlstrom, Sydney E. "The Scottish Philosophy and American Theology. *Church History* 24 (1955): 257-72.

Baumer, Franklin L. *Modern European Thought: Continuity and Change in Ideas, 1600-1950.* New York: Macmillan Publishing Co., 1977.

Breisach, Ernst. *Historiography: Ancient, Medieval, & Modern,* 2nd ed. Chicago: University of Chicago Press, 1994.

Bromiley, Geoffrey W. *Historical Theology: An Introduction.* Grand Rapids: Wm. B. Eerdmans Publishing Co., 1978.

Brown, Colin. *Christianity & Western Thought: A History of Philosophers, Ideas & Movements,* vol. 1. Downers Grove, IL: InterVarsity Press, 1990.

Brown, Ira V. "The Higher Criticism Comes to America, 1800-1900." *Journal of the Presbyterian Historical Society* 38 (December 1960):193-211.

Bruce, F. F. "The History of New Testament Study." In *New Testament Interpretation: Essays on Principles and Methods,* ed. I. Howard Marshall, pp. 21-59. Grand Rapids: Wm. B. Eerdmans Publishing Co., 1977.

Bruce, F. F. "The New Testament and Classical Study." *New Testament Studies* 22 (1975-76):229-42.

Butterfield, Herbert. *Man on His Past: The Study of the History of Historical Scholarship.* Cambridge: Cambridge University Press, 1955.

Calhoun, David B. *Princeton Seminary.* 2 vols. Edinburgh: The Banner of Truth Trust, 1994, 1996.

Carter, Paul A. "The Fundamentalist Defense of the Faith." In *Change and Continuity in Twentieth-Century America: The 1920's,* eds. John Braeman, Robert H. Bremner, and David Brody, pp. 179-214. N.p.: Ohio State University Press, 1968.

Commager, Henry Steele. *The American Mind: An Interpretation of American Thought and Character Since the 1880's.* New Haven: Yale University Press, 1950.

Conkin, Paul K. *Puritans and Pragmatists: Eight Eminent American Thinkers.* New York: Dodd, Mead & Co., 1968.

Coray, Henry W. *J. Gresham Machen: A Silhouette.* Grand Rapids: Kregel Publications, 1981.

Cross, F. L., ed. *The Oxford Dictionary of the Christian Church.* London: Oxford University Press, 1958. S.v. "Herrmann, Wilhelm."

Cunningham, Richard B. *The Christian Faith and Its Contemporary Rivals.* Nashville: Broadman Press, 1988.

Dean, William. *American Religious Empiricism.* Albany: State University of New York Press, 1986.

Dean, William. *History Making History: The New Historicism in American*

Religious Thought. Albany: State University of New York Press, 1988.

Dennison, Charles G. "Machen, Culture, and the Church." *The Banner of Truth* 286 (July 1987):20-27, 32.

Dennison, James T., Jr., and Grace Mullin. "A Bibliography of the Writings of J. Gresham Machen, 1881-1937." In *Pressing Toward the Mark: Essays Commemorating Fifty Years of the Orthodox Presbyterian Church*, ed. Charles G. Dennison and Richard C. Gamble, pp. 461-85. Philadelphia: The Committee for the Historian of the Orthodox Presbyterian Church, 1986.

Dollar, George W. *A History of Fundamentalism in America*. Greenville, SC: Bob Jones University Press, 1973.

Douglas, J. D., ed. *The New International Dictionary of the Christian Church*. Grand Rapids: Zondervan Publishing House, 1974. S.v. "Bultmann, Rudolf," by R. E. Nixon; "Clarke, William Newton," by Darrel Bigham; "Harnack, Adolf," by Colin Brown; "Lake, Kirsopp," by W. Ward Gasque; "Lewis, C(live) S(taples)," by Joan Ostling; "Ritschl, Albrecht," by Colin Brown.

Duncan, J. Ligon III. "Common Sense and American Presbyterianism:An Evaluation of the Impact of Scottish Realism on Princeton and the South." M.A. thesis, Covenant Theological Seminary, 1987.

Edwards, Paul, ed. *The Encyclopedia of Philosophy*. New York: Macmillan Publishing Co. and The Free Press, 1967. S.v. "Harnack, Carl Gustav Adolf Von" by John Macquarrie; "Historicism," by Maurice Mandelbaum; "Reid, Thomas," by S. A. Grave.

Elwell, Walter A., ed. *Evangelical Dictionary of Theology*. Grand Rapids: Baker Book House, 1984. S.v. "Bultmann, Rudolf," by R. C. Roberts; "Lewis, Clive Staples," by R. N. Hein; "Liberalism, Theological," by R. V. Pierard; "Warfield, Benjamin Breckinridge," by Mark A. Noll.

Evans, C. Stephen. *The Historical Christ and the Jesus of Faith: The Incarnational Narrative as History*. Oxford: OxfordUniversity Press, 1996.

"From 'Mainline' to Sideline." *Newsweek*, 22 December 1986, pp. 54-56.

Fuller, Donald, and Richard Gardiner. "Reformed Theology at Princeton and Amsterdam in the Late Nineteenth Century:A Reappraisal." *Presbyterion: Covenant Seminary Review* 21, no. 2 (1995): 89-117.

Funk, Robert W. "The Watershed of American Biblical Tradition: The Chicago School, First Phase, 1892-1920." *Journal of Biblical Literature* 95 (1976):4-22.

Furniss, Norman. F. *The Fundamentalist Controversy, 1918-1931*. New Haven: Yale University Press, 1954.

Grant, Robert M., with David Tracy. *A Short History of the Interpretation of the Bible*. 2nd ed. Philadelphia: Fortress Press, 1984.

Gundry, Robert H. *A Survey of the New Testament*, 3rd ed. Grand Rapids: Zondervan Publishing House, 1994.

Harrisville, Roy A., and Walter Sundberg. *The Bible in Modern Culture: Theology and Historical-Critical Method from Spinoza to Kasemann.* Grand Rapids: William B. EerdmansPublishing Co., 1995.

Hart, Darryl G. "The Princeton Mind in the Modern World and the Common Sense of J. Gresham Machen." *Westminster Theological Journal* 46 (1984):1-25.

Hart, D. G. *Defending the Faith: J. Gresham Machen and the Crisis of Conservative Protestantism in Modern America.* Baltimore: Johns Hopkins University Press, 1994; GrandRapids: Baker Book House, 1995.

Hart, D. G., and John Muether. *Fighting the Good Fight: A Brief History of the Orthodox Presbyterian Church.* Philadelphia: The Committee on Christian Education andThe Committee for the Historian of the OrthodoxPresbyterian Church, 1995.

Hastings, James. ed. *Encyclopaedia of Religion and Ethics.* New York: Charles Scribner's Sons, 1928. S.v. "Ritschlianism," by Alfred E. Garvie; "Scottish Philosophy," by William L. Davidson.

Hatch, Nathan O. "*Sola Scriptura* and *Novus Ordo Seclorum.*" In Hatch and Noll, *The Bible in America*, pp. 59-78.

Hatch, Nathan O., and Mark A. Noll, eds. *The Bible in America: Essays in Cultural History.* New York: Oxford University Press, 1982.

Helm, Paul. "Thomas Reid, Common Sense and Calvinism." In *Rationality in the Calvinian Tradition*, ed. Hendrik Hart et al., pp. 71-89. Lanham, MD: University Press of America, 1983.

Hoffecker, W. Andrew. "Benjamin B. Warfield." In Wells, *Reformed Theology in America*, pp. 60-86.

Hofstadter, Richard. *Anti-intellectualism in American Life.* New York: Vintage Books, 1963.

Hudson, Winthrop S. *American Protestantism.* Chicago: University of Chicago Press, 1961.

Hutchison, William R. *The Modernist Impulse in American Protestantism.* Cambridge: Harvard University Press, 1976.

Iggers, Georg G. *The German Conception of History: The National Tradition of Historical Thought from Herder to the Present.* Revised ed. Middletown, CN: Wesleyan University Press, 1983.

Johnson, Allen. *Dictionary of American Biography.* New York: Charles Scribner's Sons, 1956.

Kelley, Dean M. *Why Conservative Churches Are Growing: A Study in Sociology of Religion.* New York: Harper & Row, 1972.

Kümmel, Werner Georg. *The New Testament: The History of the Investigation of Its Problems.* Translated by S. McLean Gilmour and Howard C. Kee. Nashville: Abingdon Press, 1972.

Lee, Dwight E., and Robert N. Beck. "The Meaning of Historicism." *American Historical Review* 59 (1954):568-77.

Leuchtenburg, William E. *The Perils of Prosperity, 1914-32*. Chicago: University of Chicago Press, 1958.

Linnemann, Eta. *Historical Criticism of the Bible: Methodology or Ideology?* Translated by Robert W. Yarbrough. Grand Rapids: Baker Book House, 1990.

Livingston, James C. *Modern Christian Thought: From the Enlightenment to Vatican II*. New York: Macmillan   Publishing Co., 1971.

Livingstone, William D. "The Princeton Apologetic as Exemplified by the Work of Benjamin B. Warfield and J. Gresham Machen: A Study of American Theology, 1880-1930." Ph.D. dissertation, Yale University, 1948.

Loetscher, Lefferts A. *The Broadening Church: A Study of Theological Issues in the Presbyterian Church since 1869*. Philadelphia: University of Pennsylvania Press, 1954.

Longfield, Bradley J. *The Presbyterian Controversy: Fundamentalists, Modernists, and Moderates*. New York:Oxford University Press, 1991.

Malone, Dumas, ed. *Dictionary of American Biography*. New York: Charles Scribner's Sons, 1934. S.v. "Patton, Francis Landey," by G. M. Harper.

Maring, Norman H. "Baptists and Changing Views of the Bible, 1865-1918." *Foundations* 1 (July 1958):52-75, and (October 1958):30-61.

Marsden, George M. "The Collapse of American Evangelical Academia." In *Faith and Rationality: Reason and Belief in God*, eds. Alvin Plantinga and Nicholas Wolterstorff, pp. 219-64. Notre Dame: University of Notre Dame Press, 1983.

Marsden, George M. "Everyone One's Own Interpreter?: The Bible, Science, and Authority in Mid-Nineteenth-Century America," in Hatch and Noll, *The Bible in America*, pp. 79-100.

Marsden, George M. *Fundamentalism and American Culture: The Shaping of Twentieth-Century Evangelicalism, 1870-1925*. New York: Oxford University Press, 1980.

Marsden, George M. "J. Gresham Machen, History and Truth." *Westminster Theological Journal* 42 (Fall 1979):157-75.

Marsden, George M. *The Evangelical Mind and the New School Presbyterian Experience: A Case Study of Thought and Theology in Nineteenth-Century America*. New Haven: Yale University Press, 1970.

Marsden, George M. *Understanding Fundamentalism and Evangelicalism*. GrandRapids: William B. Eerdmans Publishing Co., 1991.

Massa, Mark Stephen. *Charles Augustus Briggs and the Crisis of Historical Criticism*. Minneapolis: Fortress Press, 1990.

Masselink, William. "Professor J. Gresham Machen: His Life and Defense of the Bible." Th.D. dissertation, Free University of Amsterdam, 1938.

May, Henry F. *The End of American Innocence: A Study of the First Years of Our Own Time, 1912-1917*. New York: Alfred A. Knopf, 1959.

May, Henry F. *The Enlightenment in America*. New York: Oxford University Press, 1976.

Metzger, Bruce Manning. *The New Testament: Its Background, Growth, and Content*. Nashville: Abingdon Press, 1965.

Moore, R. Laurence. *Religious Outsiders and the Making of Americans*. New York: Oxford University Press, 1986.

Morris, Richard B., ed. *Encyclopedia of American History*. New York: Harper & Brothers, 1953.

Mowry, George E. *The Urban Nation, 1920-1960*. New York: Hill and Wang, 1965; revised ed., with Blaine A. Brownell, 1981.

Neil, William. "The Criticism and Theological Use of the Bible, 1700-1950." In *The Cambridge History of the Bible: The West from the Reformation to the Present Day*, ed. S. L. Greenslade, pp. 238-93. Cambridge: Cambridge University Press, 1963.

Neill, Stephen. *The Interpretation of the New Testament, 1861-1961*. London: Oxford University Press, 1966.

Niebuhr, H. Richard. *The Social Sources of Denominationalism*. Reprint ed.; Hamden, CN: Shoe String Press, 1954.

Noll, Mark, A. *Between Faith and Criticism: Evangelicals, Scholarship, and the Bible in America*. San Francisco: Harper & Row, 1986.

Noll, Mark, A. "Common Sense Traditions and American Evangelical Thought." *American Quarterly* 37 (1985): 216-38.

Noll, Mark, A. "The Princeton Theology." In Wells, *Reformed Theology in America*, pp. 15-35.

Noll, Mark, A, ed. *The Princeton Theology: 1812-1921*. Grand Rapids: Baker Book House, 1983.

Peterson, Walter F. "American Protestantism and the Higher Criticism, 1870-1910." *Transactions of the Wisconsin Academy of Sciences, Arts, and Letters* 50 (1961):321-29.

Reid, W. Stanford. "J. Gresham Machen." In Wells, *Reformed Theology in America*, pp. 102-118.

Richardson, Alan. "The Rise of Modern Biblical Scholarship and Recent Discussion of the Authority of the Bible." In *The Cambridge History of the Bible: The West from the Reformation to the Present Day*, ed. S. L. Greenslade, pp. 294-338. Cambridge: Cambridge University Press, 1963.

Roark, Dallas M. "J. Gresham Machen and His Desire to Maintain a Doctrinally True Presbyterian Church." Ph.D. dissertation, University of Iowa, 1963.

Rogers, Jack B., and Donald K. McKim. *The Authority and Interpretation of the Bible: An Historical Approach*. San Francisco: Harper & Row, 1979.

Rozier, John, ed. *The Granite Farm Letters: The Civil War Correspondence of Edgeworth and Sallie Bird*. Athens, GA: The University of Georgia Press, 1988.

Russell, C. Allyn. *Voices of American Fundamentalism: Seven Biographical Studies*. Philadelphia: Westminster Press, 1976.

Sandeen, Ernest R. *The Roots of Fundamentalism: British and American Millenarianism, 1800-1930*. Chicago: University of Chicago Press, 1970.

Sandeen, Ernest R., and Frederick Hale. *American Religion and Philosophy: A Guide to Information Sources*. American Studies Information Guide Series, vol. 5. Detroit: Gale Research Co., 1978.

Seligman, Edwin R. A., ed. *The Encyclopaedia of Social Sciences*. New York: Macmillan, 1931. S.v. "Fundamentalism," by H. Richard Niebuhr.

Stanford, Michael. *A Companion to the Study of History*. Oxford: Blackwell Publishers, 1994.

Stonehouse, Ned B. *J. Gresham Machen: A Biographical Memoir*. Grand Rapids: Wm. B. Eerdmans Publishing Co., 1955.

Tarnas, Richard. *The Passion of the Western Mind: Understanding the Ideas That Have Shaped Our World View*. New York: Harmony Books, 1991.

Tholfsen, Trygve R. *Historical Thinking: An Introduction*. New York: Harper & Row, 1967.

van Biema, David. "The Gospel Truth." *Time*, 8 April 1996, pp. 52-59.

Vander Stelt, John C. *Philosophy and Scripture: A Study in Old Princeton and Westminster Theology*. Marlton, NJ: Mack Publishing, 1978.

Voelkel, Robert T. "Introduction," in Wilhelm Herrmann, *The Communion of the Christian with God*, pp. xv-lxii.   Edited by Robert T. Voelkel. Philadelphia: Fortress Press, 1971.

Wacker, Grant. *Augustus H. Strong and the Dilemma of Historical Consciousness*. Macon, GA: Mercer University Press, 1985.

Wacker, Grant. "The Demise of Biblical Civilization." In Hatch and Noll, *The Bible in America*, pp. 121-38.

Weaver, Richard M. *The Southern Tradition at Bay: A History of Postbellum Thought*. Reprint ed. Washington, D.C.: Regnery Gateway, 1989.

Wells, David F., ed. *Reformed Theology in America: A History of Its Modern Development*. Grand Rapids: Wm. B. Eerdmans Publishing Co., 1985.

White, Morton G. *Social Thought in America: The Revolt Against Formalism*. New York: Viking Press, 1949.

Wiebe, Robert H. *The Search for Order, 1877-1920*. The Making of America Series. New York: Hill and Wang, 1967.

Wiener, Philip P., ed. *Dictionary of the History of Ideas*. New York: Charles Scribner's Sons, 1973. S.v. "Historicism," by Georg G. Iggers.

Woodbridge, John D. *Biblical Authority: A Critique of the Rogers/McKim Proposal*. Grand Rapids: Zondervan Publishing House, 1982.

Woolley, Paul. *The Significance of J. Gresham Machen Today*. Nutley, NJ: Presbyterian and Reformed Publishing Company, 1977.

REFERENCES

INTRODUCTION

[1] D. G. Hart, *Defending the Faith: J. Gresham Machen and the Crisis of Conservative Protestantism in Modern America* (Baltimore: Johns Hopkins University Press, 1994; Grand Rapids: Baker Book House, 1995). In this and subsequent notes, all references for a paragraph shall be entered in a single note and will follow the order in which the items appear in the paragraph unless otherwise stated.

[2] Citations from Grant Wacker, "The Demise of Biblical Civilization," in *The Bible in America: Essays in Cultural History*, ed. Nathan O. Hatch and Mark A. Noll (New York: Oxford University Press, 1982), pp. 125, 127. For a fuller treatment of historical consciousness, see below, Chapter I.

[3] David van Biema, "The Gospel Truth," *Time*, 8 April 1996, pp. 52-59.

[4] J. Gresham Machen, "Christianity in Conflict," in *Contemporary American Theology: Theological Autobiographies*, ed. Vergilius Ferm, vol. 1 (New York: Round Table Press, 1932), p. 261-62.

[5] Citation from J. Gresham Machen, *The New Testament: An Introduction to its Literature and History*, ed. W. John Cook (Edinburgh: The Banner of Truth Trust, 1976), p. 9. For a treatment of the "historical-critical method" as an ideological crusade, see Eta Linnemann, *Historical Criticism of the Bible: Methodology or Ideology*, trans. Robert W. Yarbrough (Grand Rapids: Baker Book House, 1990).

[6] Citation from J. Gresham Machen, *The Virgin Birth of Christ* (London: James Clarke & Co. Ltd., 1958; reprint of 1932 edition), p. 385.

[7] George M. Marsden, *Understanding Fundamentalism and Evangelicalism* (Grand Rapids: William B. Eerdmans Publishing Co., 1991), pp. 185-97.

[8] Roy A. Harrisville and Walter Sundberg, *The Bible in Modern Culture: Theology and Historical-Critical Method from Spinoza to Käsemann* (Grand Rapids: William B. Eerdmans Publishing Co., 1995), pp. 180-202; Bradley J. Longfield, *The Presbyterian Controversy: Fundamentalists, Modernists, and Moderates* (New York: Oxford University Press, 1991), pp. 28-53 and passim.

[9] D. G. Hart, *Defending the Faith*; George M. Marsden, *Understanding Fundamentalism and Evangelicalism*, pp. 182-201, and *Fundamentalism and American Culture: The Shaping of Twentieth-Century Evangelicalism, 1870-1925* (New York: Oxford University Press, 1980); C. Allyn Russell, *Voices of American Fundamentalism: Seven Biographical Studies* (Philadelphia: Westminster Press, 1976), pp. 135-61.

[10] Ned B. Stonehouse, *J. Gresham Machen: A Biographical Memoir* (Grand Rapids: Wm. B. Eerdmans Publishing Co., 1955); D. G. Hart and

John Muether, *Fighting the Good Fight: A Brief History of the Orthodox Presbyterian Church* (Philadelphia: The Committee on Christian Education and The Committee for the Historian of the Orthodox Presbyterian Church, 1995); George W. Dollar, *A History of Fundamentalism in America* (Greenville, SC: Bob Jones University Press, 1973), pp. 173-83; David B. Calhoun, *Princeton Seminary*, 2 vols. (Edinburgh: The Banner of Truth Trust, 1994, 1996); W. Stanford Reid, "J. Gresham Machen," in David F. Wells, *Reformed Theology in America: A History of its Modern Development* (Grand Rapids: William B. Eerdmans Publishing Co., 1985), pp. 102-118. For Machen's position on the question, see Calhoun, 2:343.

Chapter 2: THE RISE OF HISTORICAL CONSCIOUSNESS AND ITS IMPACT ON BIBLICAL STUDY IN EUROPE AND AMERICA

[1] Marsden, *Fundamentalism and American Culture*, p. 63; Wacker, "The Demise of Biblical Civilization," p. 125; Sydney E. Ahlstrom, *A Religious History of the American People* (New Haven: Yale University Press, 1972), p. 772. See also Mark Stephen Massa, *Charles Augustus Briggs and the Crisis of Historical Criticism* (Minneapolis: Fortress Press, 1960), p. 158: "It was the intellectual threat of historicism that informed and united the various religious battles of the period."

[2] The terminology applied to the various assumptions was devised by the present author; the definitions are from Wacker, *Augustus H. Strong*, p. 16, with all citations from this page. "Historicism" has been used in various senses; for a treatment, see Dwight E. Lee and Robert N. Beck, "The Meaning of Historicism," *American Historical Review* 59 (1954):568-77. An excellent discussion of historicism, with a full bibliography, is found in *The Dictionary of the History of Ideas*, s.v. "Historicism," by Georg G. Iggers; see also Iggers, *The German Conception of History: The National Tradition of Historical Thought from Herder to the Present*, rev. ed. (Middletown, CN: Wesleyan University Press, 1983), p. 3-13, 295-98, and "The Dissolution of German Historism," in Richard Herr and Harold T. Parker, eds., *Ideas in History: Essays Presented to Louis Gottschalk by His Former Students* (Durham, NC: Duke University Press, 1965), pp. 288-329; and *The Encyclopedia of Philosophy*, s.v. "Historicism," by Maurice Mandelbaum. Also worthy of note is the summary description offered by Massa, *Briggs*, "all notions of truth and value, even those ostensibly claiming transcendental warranty, were seen as products forged within the historical process," p. 5.

[3] Michael Stanford, *A Companion to the Study of History* (Oxford: Blackwell Publishers, 1994), p. 255.

[4] Massa, *Briggs*, p. 7.

[5] A synopsis of this process is found in Wacker, *Augustus H. Strong*, pp. 33-42, on which this summary is based; see also Iggers, "Historicism." I am reluctant to describe the prevailing Protestant view of the Bible, history, and

truth altogether in the terms set forth by such scholars as Marsden, Wacker, Massa, and others, for reasons which will appear later in this study. They have tended to define the Protestant intellectual outlook (especially that of Princeton Seminary) as one controlled by supernatural rationalism, common sense realism, Baconian inductivism, and complete ahistoricism. I question whether these categories may be applied wholesale to either Machen or the Princeton theology without qualification.

[6] Wacker, *Augustus H. Strong*, 33-35. The same material is treated in surveys of Western historiography; a worthwhile brief treatment, used here, is Trygve R. Tholfsen, *Historical Thinking* (New York: Harper & Row, 1967), Chapter 4, "Voltaire and the Historiography of the Enlightenment," pp. 93-136. For the beginnings of the changing view of history, see Franklin L. Baumer, *Modern European Thought: Continuity and Change in Ideas, 1600-1950* (New York: Macmillan Publishing Co., 1977), pp. 117-37; for its Enlightenment development, pp. 237-55.

[7] Wacker, *Augustus H. Strong*, pp. 36-37; Tholfsen covers the German tradition in *Historical Thinking*, pp. 127-85; see also Baumer, *Modern European Thought,* pp. 288-301, 327-29.

[8] Wacker, *Augustus H. Strong*, pp. 38-39; Baumer, *Modern European Thought*, 302-366.

[9] Morton G. White, *Social Thought in America: The Revolt Against Formalism* (New York: Viking Press, 1949), pp. 3-31; citations are from p.12.

[10] Wacker, *Augustus H. Strong*, pp. 37, 39-40; citations are from p. 39.

[11] See Ned B. Stonehouse, *J. Gresham Machen: A Biographical Memoir* (Grand Rapids: Wm. B. Eerdmans Publishing Co., 1955), pp. 178-82; and Chapter VI of the present study.

[12] White, *Social Thought in America*, pp. 107, 147; Henry F. May, *The End of American Innocence: A Study of the First Years of Our Own Time, 1912-1917* (New York: Alfred A. Knopf, 1959), especially pp. ix-xiv; on Beard, see White, pp. 107-27; Wallis's book was reviewed by William Brenton Green, Jr. in *Princeton Theological Review* 11 (1913):119-22; the Santayana citation is from G[eorge] Santayana, "The Intellectual Temper of the Age," in *Winds of Doctrine: Studies in Contemporary Opinion* (New York: Charles Scribner's Sons, 1913), p. 1.

[13] Wacker, *Augustus H. Strong*, pp. 40-41; citations from these pages. On the radical historicism of John Dewey (and William James), see William Dean, *History Making History: The New Historicism in American Religious Thought* (Albany: State University of New York Press, 1988), pp. 99-110. On the development of European thought along such lines, see Baumer, *Modern European Thought*, pp. 402-513.

[14] Wacker, *Augustus H. Strong*, pp. 31-33; immigration figures are given in Richard B. Morris, ed., *Encyclopedia of American History* (New York:

Harper & Brothers, 1953), pp. 446-47. On all these topics, and especially on the "distending" of American society, see Robert H. Wiebe, *The Search for Order: 1877-1920*, The Making of America Series (New York: Hill and Wang, 1967), pp. 1-163.

[15] On Göttingen and its faculty, see Herbert Butterfield, *Man on His Past: The Study of the History of Historical Scholarship* (Cambridge: Cambridge University Press, 1955), pp. 39-61; Tholfsen, *Historical Thinking*, pp. 142-51. On Semler and Michaelis, see Werner Georg Kümmel, *The New Testament: The History of the Investigation of Its Problems*, trans. S. McLean Gilmour and Howard C. Kee (Nashville: Abingdon Press, 1972), pp. 62-73, citation from p. 68; Stephen Neill, *The Interpretation of the New Testament, 1861-1961* (London: Oxford University Press, 1966), pp. 5-6.

[16] F. F. Bruce, "The History of New Testament Study," in *New Testament Interpretation: Essays on Principles and Methods*, ed. I. Howard Marshall (Grand Rapids: Wm. B. Eerdmans Publishing Co., 1977), p. 38.

[17] Surveys of the history of biblical scholarship are provided by Robert M. Grant with David Tracy, *A Short History of the Interpretation of the Bible*, 2nd ed. (Philadelphia: Fortress Press, 1984) and William Neil, "The Criticism and Theological Use of the Bible, 1700-1950," in *The Cambridge History of the Bible: The West from the Reformation to the Present Day*, ed. S. L Greenslade (Cambridge: Cambridge University Press, 1963), pp. 238-93.

[18] Ahlstrom, *A Religious History of the American People*, pp. 772-74; citation from Baumer, *Modern European Thought*, p. 356.

[19] On Baur's theory and its overthrow, see Neill, *Interpretation*, pp. 19-60, citation from p. 55; see also Kümmel, *The New Testament*, pp. 127-43; and Bruce, "History," pp. 42-43.

[20] On Ritschl, see Kümmel, *The New Testament*, pp. 162-67, 488; *Encyclopaedia of Religion and Ethics*, s.v. "Ritschlianism," by Alfred E. Garvie; *The New International Dictionary of the Christian Church*, s.v. "Ritschl, Albrecht," by Colin Brown.

[21] On Harnack and his views, see Neill, *Interpretation*, 130-36; Kümmel, *The New Testament*, pp. 178-84, 476; Geoffrey W. Bromiley, *Historical Theology: An Introduction* (Grand Rapids: Wm. B. Eerdmans Publishing Co., 1978), 390-97; *The Encyclopedia of Philosophy*, s.v: "Harnack, Carl Gustav Adolf Von," by John Macquarrie; *The New International Dictionary of the Christian Church*, s.v. "Harnack, Adolf," by Colin Brown; Adolf Harnack, *What Is Christianity?* trans. Thomas Bailey Saunders, with an Introduction by Rudolf Bultmann (New York: Harper & Brothers, 1957), pp. 1-74.

[22] On the pioneers of the history of religions school, see Neill, *Interpretation*, pp. 137-40, 153-59; Kümmel, *The New Testament*, 206-225; Pfleiderer citation is from p. 210.

[23] Neill, *Interpretation*, pp. 159-60; see also Kümmel, *The New Testament*, 255-57, 477.

[24] On the history of religions school generally, see Neill, *Interpretation*, pp. 160-67; Kümmel, *The New Testament*, pp. 245-80; 487, 468; Bruce, "History," pp. 48-50. On Lake, see also *The New International Dictionary of the Christian Church*, s.v. "Lake, Kirsopp," by W. Ward Gasque. On Bultmann, see Neill, pp. 222-23; Bruce, 51-52; *The New International Dictionary of the Christian Church*, s.v. "Bultmann, Rudolf," by R. E. Nixon; *Evangelical Dictionary of Theology*, s.v. "Bultmann, Rudolf," by R. C. Roberts.

[25] Rudolf Bultmann, "Is Exegesis without Presuppositions Possible?" in *Existence and Faith: Shorter Writings of Rudolf Bultmann*, selected, translated, and introduced by Schubert M. Ogden (Cleveland: World Publishing Co., 1960), pp. 289-96, citations from 291-92.

[26] On consistent eschatology, See Kümmel, *The New Testament*, 226-44, citation from pp. 226-27. On Schweitzer, see also Neill, *Interpretation*, 191-200.

[27] The Hodge citations are from *Systematic Theology*, I:152, 163; the Noll citation is from *Between Faith and Criticism*, p. 11. On the common nineteenth-century view of the Bible and its interpretation, see Nathan O. Hatch, "*Sola Scriptura* and *Novus Ordo Seclorum*," and Marsden, "Everyone One's Own Interpreter?" in Hatch and Noll, *The Bible in America*, pp. 59-78, 79-100.

[28] See Noll, *Between Faith and Criticism*, pp. 15-16; Ira V. Brown, "The Higher Criticism Comes to America, 1800-1900," *Journal of the Presbyterian Historical Society* 38 (December 1960):196.

[29] On the Briggs case, see Lefferts A. Loetscher, *The Broadening Church: A Study of Theological Issues in the Presbyterian Church Since 1869* (Philadelphia: University of Pennsylvania Press, 1954), pp. 48-62, citation from p. 62; Noll, *Between Faith and Criticism*, 16-18; Brown, "Higher Criticism," pp. 198-99; Walter F. Peterson, "American Protestantism and the Higher Criticism, 1870-1910," *Transactions of the Wisconsin Academy of Sciences, Arts, and Letters* 50 (1961):321-29; Massa, *Charles Augustus Briggs*, pp. 85-109.

[30] Loetscher, *The Broadening Church*, pp. 61, 63-68, 71-74.

[31] Maring, "Baptists and Changing Views of the Bible," Part II, p. 30, Part I, pp. 63-64; Noll, *Between Faith and Criticism*, pp. 27-28; Brown, "Higher Criticism," p. 205.

[32] On Harper, see Maring, "Baptists," II:30-33. On trends at the University of Chicago, see Robert W. Funk, "The Watershed of American Biblical Tradition: The Chicago School, First Phase, 1892-1920," *Journal of Biblical Literature* 95 (1976):4-22.

[33] Brown, "Higher Criticism," p. 207; Peterson, "American Protestantism," pp. 323-24.

[34] On the stature and influence of the Princetonians, see William R.

Hutchison, *The Modernist Impulse in American Protestantism* (Cambridge: Harvard University Press, 1976), pp. 199-206, citation from p. 199; Noll, *Between Faith and Criticism*, pp. 18-27, 47, 51-56.

[35] Noll, *Between Faith and Criticism*, pp. 32-34, citation from p. 33. Noll locates the watershed in the years 1900-1920. Peterson argues that the first decade of the twentieth century was the crucial era for the acceptance of biblical criticism, with a significant minority of American Protestant ministers adopting it by 1910, "American Protestantism," pp. 327, 329. Funk analyzes the situation somewhat differently, but places the critical period at "roughly 1890-1920," "The Watershed," p. 7.

[36] Noll, *Between Faith and Criticism*, pp. 34-36, citation from p. 35.

[37] Noll, *Between Faith and Criticism*, pp. 38-46, citations from p. 44. For other treatments of *The Fundamentals*, see Marsden, *Fundamentalism and American Culture*, pp. 118-23; Sandeen, *Roots of Fundamentalism*, pp. 188-207.

[38] Ahlstrom, *Religious History*, p. 774. Ahlstrom's entire analysis (on this page) is worthy of careful consideration as an explanation of the basic impulse which underlay theological liberalism.

[39] Hutchison, *Modernist Impulse*, pp. 2-4.

[40] Hutchison, *Modernist Impulse*, p. 2.

[41] Ahlstrom, *Religious History*, pp. 781-83. On the University of Chicago school of theological historicists and their influence, see Dean, *History Making History*, pp. 45-73. For a different taxonomy of theological liberalism, one based on the degree of historicizing taking place in the various camps, but which ends up with essentially the same categories, see William Dean, *American Religious Empiricism* (Albany: State University of New York Press, 1986), pp. 6-12. Hutchison would also seem to question the analysis of Ahlstrom, utilized above, in *Modernist Impulse*, pp. 7-9.

[42] The citations are from Archibald A. Hodge and Benjamin B. Warfield, *Inspiration*, with an Introduction by Roger R. Nicole (Grand Rapids: Baker Book House, 1979), pp. 23-24. The essay was first published in *Presbyterian Review* 2 (1881):225-60. For a discussion of this controversy and the literature it generated, see Nicole's Introduction, pp. vii-xiv; Noll, *Between Faith and Criticism*, pp. 15-22; and Mark A. Noll, ed., *The Princeton Theology: 1812-1921* (Grand Rapids: Baker Book House, 1983), pp. 218-20, with an excerpt of the essay, pp. 220-32.

[43] Hodge and Warfield, *Inspiration*, pp. 24-25, citation from p. 25.

[44] Hodge and Warfield, *Inspiration*, pp. 26-29, first citation from p. 26, the others from p. 28. Hodge's allowance for the historical conditioning of the Bible, along with his acceptance of limitations on its literalness and exactness, runs directly counter to Massa's description of his position as denying its "historically conditioned character" and as demanding "mathematical specificity," *Charles Augustus Briggs*, p. 59.

[45] Charles Augustus Briggs, *Whither? A Theological Question for the Times* (New York: Charles Scribner's Sons, 1889), pp. 63-90.

[46] For Briggs's assessment of the positive contributions of biblical criticism, see *Whither*, pp. 277-85.

[47] William Newton Clarke, *Sixty Years with the Bible: A Record of Experience* (New York: Charles Scribner's Sons, 1917; copyright 1909), citations from pp. 3, 4, 9.

[48] Clarke, *Sixty Years with the Bible*, pp. 11-249, citation from p. 68.

[49] Clarke, *Sixty Years with the Bible*, pp. 249-55, citations from pp. 253-54.

[50] Citation from Clarke, *Sixty Years with the Bible*, p. 176. On Clarke's career and influence, see *Dictionary of American Biography*, s.v. "Clarke, William Newton," by William H. Allison; and *The New International Dictionary of the Christian Church*, s.v. "Clarke, William Newton," by Darrel Bigham.

Chapter 3: MACHEN'S EARLY TRAINING AND THEOLOGICAL EDUCATION, 1881–1905

[1] The Bible League citation is from Machen, 'What the Bible Teaches About Jesus," originally published in the *Evangelical Student* 3 (October 1928): 4-11, reprinted in *What is Christianity? and Other Addresses*, ed. Ned Bernard Stonehouse (Grand Rapids: Wm. B. Eerdmans Publishing Co., 1951), p. 35; the second citation is from Machen, "Christianity in Conflict", p. 261.

[2] A description of Machen's ancestral heritage is found in Stonehouse, *J. Gresham Machen*, pp. 17-39. Stonehouse's biography of Machen will hereinafter be referred to simply by the author's name. On the pronunciation of the family name Gresham, see Stonehouse, p. 511 (the name is pronounced gress-am, with the "s" and "h" separated, and the "h" silent). The period of Machen's life covered in this chapter is treated in Hart, *Defending the Faith*, pp. 10-21.

[3] Stonehouse, pp. 34-38. The Civil War correspondence of Minnie's aunt Sarah Baxter Bird with her family, in which Minnie is mentioned frequently, has been published as *The Granite Farm Letters: The Civil War Correspondence of Edgeworth and Sallie Bird*, ed. John Rozier (Athens, GA: The University of Georgia Press, 1988). Longfield places heavy emphasis on Machen's Southern heritage, *The Presbyterian Controversy*, pp. 31-38. Machen himself comments on it in "Christianity in Conflict," pp. 248-49; Stonehouse, pp. 44-46. A treatment of the developing Southern outlook(s), with much of which Machen was evidently sympathetic, may be found in Richard M. Weaver, *The Southern Tradition at Bay: A History of Postbellum Thought* (reprint ed.; Washington, D.C.: Regnery Gateway, 1989).

[4] Stonehouse, pp. 38-39.

[5] Machen's comments on his father are in "Christianity in Conflict," pp.

246-47, from which the citations are taken. For other comments on the value of Machen's home training, see Stonehouse, p. 116.

[6] On Machen's mother and his home training, see his description in "Christianity in Conflict," pp. 248-50; Stonehouse, pp. 40-41. Machen's letter to his mother is given in Stonehouse, p. 41.

[7] Minnie Gresham Machen, *The Bible in Browning, with Particular Reference to "The Ring and the Book"* (New York: Macmillan, 1903), citation from p. 42; Stonehouse, pp. 77, 50.

[8] Stonehouse, pp. 42-47.

[9] Stonehouse, pp. 47-49.

[10] On Gildersleeve's stature and Machen's contacts with him, see Stonehouse, pp. 49-53; Machen, "Christianity in Conflict," pp. 250-51.

[11] Machen, "Christianity in Conflict," pp. 251-52. Machen claims here to have spent the summer of 1902 at the University of Chicago studying Greek under Paul Shorey, but the evidence presented by Stonehouse seems conclusive that this occurred in 1903. Perhaps as the result of a lapse of memory, Machen (writing three decades later) confused the activities of these two summers; according to Stonehouse, Machen was indeed at the University of Chicago in the summer of 1902, but was studying banking and international law, being uncertain at the time about his future career. See Stonehouse, pp. 58-59, 78-79.

[12] On nineteenth-century developments, see Winthrop Hudson, *American Protestantism* (Chicago: University of Chicago Press, 1961), pp. 96-109; on the differences between Old School and New School Presbyterians, see George M. Marsden, *The Evangelical Mind and the New School Presbyterian Experience: A Case Study of Thought and Theology in Nineteenth-Century America* (New Haven: Yale University Press, 1970), pp. 66-103.

[13] See Noll, *The Princeton Theology*, pp. 27-30; and "The Princeton Theology," in *Reformed Theology in America*, ed. David F. Wells, p 18-19; this and the following characteristics of the Princeton outlook are taken from Noll's treatment. For Warfield's position, see "What Is Calvinism?" in *Selected Shorter Writings of Benjamin B. Warfield*, ed. John E. Meeter, vol. I (Nutley, NJ: Presbyterian and Reformed Publishing Company, 1970), pp. 389-92, citations from pp. 389, 390. Noll's judgment as to the tendency of the Princetonians to view the various expressions of Calvinism as a unified whole, without a proper appreciation for historical context, diversity of thought, or internal development perhaps needs to be tempered by consideration of such statements as the following. Coming from A. A. Hodge: in listing those disciplines which are auxiliary to the study of theology, Hodge mentions first "Universal History" "as underlying and conditioning all knowledge" (A. A. Hodge, *Outlines of Theology*, reprint ed.; Grand Rapids: Zondervan Publishing House, 1972, p. 18); from Charles Hodge: "It cannot be denied that ever since the Reformation, more or less diversity in the

statement and explanation of the doctrines of Calvinism has prevailed in the Reformed Churches" (cited in Calhoun, *Princeton Seminary*, 1:217); and concerning Warfield: he did not "ignore the gradual progression of doctrinal knowledge that characterizes the study of historical theology" (Calhoun, *Princeton Seminary*, 2:245).

[14] Noll, *The Princeton Theology*, pp. 25-27; "The Princeton Theology," pp. 19-21. The citation is from Stonehouse, p. 63. Some historians have claimed that the Hodge-Warfield doctrine of scripture constituted an innovation and did not faithfully reflect the traditional Protestant view; see Sandeen, *The Roots of Fundamentalism*, pp. 114-31; and Jack B. Rogers and Donald K. McKim, *The Authority and Interpretation of the Bible: An Historical Approach* (San Francisco: Harper & Row, 1979), pp. 265-310. Others have argued with a good deal of persuasiveness that the concepts embodied in the Princeton doctrine antedated the work of Hodge and Warfield, who simply gave lucid and precise expression to views long held in more amorphous form; see, for example, John D. Woodbridge, *Biblical Authority: A Critique of the Rogers/McKim Proposal* (Grand Rapids: Zondervan Publishing House, 1982), pp. 119-40; Wacker, "The Demise of Biblical Civilization," p. 135, note 13; and Mark A. Noll, "Common Sense Traditions and American Evangelical Thought," *American Quarterly* 37 (Summer 1985),.p. 229; Calhoun, *Princeton Seminary*, 2:463-65, note 15.

[15] William L. Davidson, "Scottish Philosophy," in James Hastings, ed., *Encyclopaedia of Religion and Ethics* (reprint ed.; New York: Charles Scribner's Sons, 1958), 11:261-71; citations from p. 262; see also Colin Brown, *Christianity & Western Thought: A History of Philosophers, Ideas & Movements*, vol. 1 (Downers Grove, IL: InterVarsity Press, 1990), pp. 259-68.

[16] Henry F. May , *The Enlightenment in America* (New York: Oxford University Press, 1976), pp. 337-50; Sydney E. Ahlstrom, "The Scottish Philosophy and American Theology," *Church History* 24 (1955): 257-72; Mark A. Noll, "Common Sense Traditions and American Evangelical Thought," *American Quarterly* 37 (1985): 216-38; Noll, *The Princeton Theology*, pp. 30-33; "The Princeton Theology," pp. 21-23. For a sharp criticism of the Princetonians on this score, see John C. Vander Stelt, *Philosophy and Scripture: A Study in Old Princeton and Westminster Theology* (Marlton, NJ: Mack Publishing Company, 1978). On the other side of the question, John D. Woodbridge also lodges a warning against regarding the Princetonians as captives of Common Sense Realism. He cites Charles Hodge's express disagreement with Thomas Reid and William Hamilton (the chief Common Sense philosophers) concerning the role of human conscience and reason as guides to truth, and concerning the human will. Woodbridge points out other differences between the Princeton theologians and the Common Sense philosophy as well. See Woodbridge,

216 *Toward a Sure Faith*

Biblical Authority, pp. 135-38. Notice should also be taken of J. Ligon Duncan III, "Common Sense and American Presbyterianism: An Evaluation of the Impact of Scottish Realism on Princeton and the South," M. A. thesis, Covenant Theological Seminary, 1987; and Donald Fuller and Richard Gardiner, "Reformed Theology at Princeton and Amsterdam in the Late Nineteenth Century: A Reappraisal," in *Presbyterion: Covenant Seminary Review* 21, no. 2 (1995): 89-117. David Calhoun also offers a salutary warning against making too much of the Princetonians' adherence to Common Sense Realism, *Princeton Seminary*, 2:414. As an example of those who too facilely and simplistically assume a wholesale adoption of the Common Sense philosophy and all its implications by the Princeton theologians, see Mark S. Massa, *Charles Augustus Briggs*, passim. Although the Princetonians are frequently to be found advocating the tenets associated with Common Sense Realism, it should be recognized that (1) some of these tenets may be assumptions held in common with the biblical writers (and thus may reflect a dependence not on the philosophy but on the biblical outlook, e.g., belief in the existence of a universal truth applicable to all people); (2) some tenets may be assumptions without which ordinary discourse could not take place; (3) some tenets may be assumptions which are consistent with Calvinism; (4) individual adherents may modify or reject to varying extent those tenets which are not consistent with Calvinism. Some of these points are made by Paul Helm, "Thomas Reid, Common Sense and Calvinism," in Hendrik Hart et al., eds., *Rationality in the Calvinian Tradition* (Lanham, MD: University Press of America, 1983), pp. 71-89.

[17] Noll, *The Princeton Theology*, pp. 33-34; "The Princeton Theology," pp. 23-24.

[18] Stonehouse, pp. 58-61.

[19] Stonehouse, pp. 64-66; on Patton, see also the *Dictionary of American Biography*, s.v. "Patton, Francis Landey," by G. M. Harper; the Machen citation is from "Christianity in Conflict," p. 252.

[20] On Warfield, see Stonehouse, pp. 66-68, 310-311; Machen's comment is from p. 311. See also *Evangelical Dictionary of Theology*, s.v. "Warfield, Benjamin Breckinridge," by Mark A. Noll; Machen, "Christianity in Conflict," pp. 253-54. For Warfield's confidence in a scientific apologetic, see W. Andrew Hoffecker, "Benjamin B. Warfield," in *Reformed Theology in America*, pp. 70-71; and Noll, *The Princeton Theology*, pp. 230-31.

[21] Stonehouse, pp. 69-70; Machen, "Christianity in Conflict," pp. 252-53.

[22] Stonehouse, pp. 71-76, citation from p. 75. Hart's treatment of Machen's student years at Princeton is found in *Defending the Faith*, pp. 19-21, where he offers a decidedly less positive portrayal of Machen's experience at Princeton.

[23] Stonehouse, pp. 72-73, 78-79; Machen, "Christianity in Conflict," pp. 252, 254-55.

24 Stonehouse, pp. 80-81; the Machen citation is from p. 81. For Machen's later comment, see "Christianity in Conflict," p. 261.

25 Stonehouse, pp. 81-83.

26 Stonehouse, pp. 83-84.

27 Stonehouse, pp. 84-85. The citations and other information are taken from Machen's letters to Minnie G. Machen of 26 March 1905 (misdated 1904), 2 April 1905, and 7 May 1905. These and all letters subsequently referred to are housed at Westminster Theological Seminary (Philadelphia), Montgomery Library, Machen Archives, Boxes "1904-06: Family"; "1907-08: Family."

28 J. Gresham Machen, "The New Testament Account of the Birth of Jesus," First Article, *Princeton Theological Review* 3 (October 1905):641-70, citation from p. 6. Second Article, *Princeton Theological Review* 4 (January 1906):37-81.

29 Machen, "The New Testament Account," First Article, pp. 655-57, citations from pp. 655, 656.

30 Citations from Machen, "The New Testament Account," First Article, p. 654.

31 Citations from Machen, "The New Testament Account," Second Article, pp. 80-81. Machen here acknowledged that a person's judgment may to some degree be conditioned by factors other than simply hard evidence, recognizing the historical conditioning of human knowledge; and he insisted that the virgin birth of Jesus must be comprehended within the context of the biblical teaching as a whole, thus arguing from a principle of organic unity. For Warfield's use of one variety of presuppositional argument, see Hoffecker, "Benjamin B. Warfield," pp. 71-75.

32 Citation from Machen, "The New Testament Account," First Article, p.657.

33 These three instances are found in Machen, "The New Testament Account," First Article, pp. 667, 668-69, and 653, respectively. For the assertion that the idea of accommodation had no place in the Princeton tradition, see Rogers and McKim, *The Authority and Interpretation of the Bible*, p. 309; for their treatment of Machen, see pp. 362-68. These authors regard the whole Princeton tradition as "scholastic."

34 Machen, "The New Testament Account," First Article, pp. 665-66; the citations are from these two pages respectively.

Chapter 4: MACHEN AT MARBURG AND GÖTTINGEN, 1905–1906

1 Stonehouse, pp. 85-87. Hart's treatment of Machen's year of studies in Germany and its aftermath is found in *Defending the Faith*, pp. 21-26.

2 Stonehouse describes Machen's departure and travels, with lengthy excerpts from his letters, pp. 88-95. The citation regarding the letters is from p. 103; see also p. 145.

3 Machen's opinions of the scholars at Marburg are expressed in a letter

to Arthur W. Machen, Jr., 10 December 1905 (citations are from this letter); and in "Christianity in Conflict," pp. 257-59. See also Stonehouse, pp. 95, 104-105; and Kümmel, pp. 479, 494, and 467 for brief biographies of Jülicher, Weiss, and Bauer, respectively.

[4] Stonehouse, p. 105; Machen, "Christianity in Conflict," pp. 255-56, citation from p. 261. On Herrmann, see also *The Oxford Dictionary of the Christian Church*, s.v. "Herrmann, Wilhelm"; Robert T. Voelkel, "Introduction," in Wilhelm Herrmann, *The Communion of the Christian with God*, ed. Robert T. Voelkel (Philadelphia: Fortress Press, 1971), pp. xv-lxii.

[5] Machen, letter to Minnie G. Machen, 24 October 1905, Machen Archives, Westminster Theological Seminary, Philadelphia (all further references to Machen's letters are to those housed in this collection); letter to Arthur W. Machen, 28 October 1905. Portions of both these letters are given by Stonehouse, p. 106.

[6] Machen, letter to Arthur W. Machen, Jr., 2 November 1905; printed in Stonehouse, p. 107.

[7] Machen, letter to Arthur W. Machen, Jr., 10 December 1905; printed in Stonehouse, pp. 107-108.

[8] Armstrong's letters to Machen are given by Stonehouse, pp. 108-112. Stonehouse concurs in the interpretation of the incident which is presented here. Also worthy of note is Machen's letter to his father in which he reaffirmed his decision and stated that to have accepted the money "would have meant giving up the last vestige of my self-respect" (letter to Arthur W. Machen, 3 May 1906).

[9] See Stonehouse, pp. 113-14. The citation is from Machen, letter to Arthur W. Machen, 14 January 1906.

[10] The citation is from Machen, letter to Arthur W. Machen, Jr., 4 March 1906 (misdated 1905). Machen's correspondence with his family during this period is excerpted in Stonehouse, pp. 115-20.

[11] See Stonehouse's treatment and the letters excerpted, pp. 121-22 (the Stonehouse citation is from p. 122); Machen's comments are from a letter to Arthur W. Machen, Jr., 18 April 1906.

[12] Machen's opinions of the Göttingen faculty were expressed in a letter to Arthur W. Machen, Jr., 3 June 1906; see Stonehouse, pp. 122-25 for excerpts and other information.

[13] Machen, letter to Arthur W. Machen, Jr., 3 June 1906; excerpted in Stonehouse, p. 124.

[14] Machen, letter to Arthur W. Machen, Jr., 3 June 1906; see also the excerpts in Stonehouse, p. 125. For Machen's later comments on Bousset, see "Christianity in Conflict," pp. 260-61.

[15] Machen's conversation with Heitmüller is related in a letter to Minnie G. Machen, 29 July 1906; see Stonehouse, p. 128.

[16] Machen, letter to Minnie G. Machen, 22 July 1906; letter to Arthur W.

Machen, 25 February 1906; Stonehouse's comment is on p. 128.

[17] Machen, letter to Arthur W. Machen, Jr., 3 June 1906; see Stonehouse, p. 126.

[18] Stonehouse, pp. 130-34; the citations from the Armstrong letter are from p. 133.

[19] Machen, letters to Minnie G. Machen, 14 September 1906, and to a Mrs. Buchanan, 17 September 1906; Stonehouse, p. 135.

[20] Stonehouse's treatment of this controversy occupies pp. 135-44, with excerpts from the relevant letters; citations are from Machen's letter to Minnie G. Machen, 11 September 1906, emphasis in the original.

[21] Machen, letter to Minnie G. Machen, 14 September 1906; see Stonehouse, pp. 139-42.

[22] Mrs. Machen's letter is given in Stonehouse, pp. 144-45.

[23] Machen, letter to Arthur W. Machen, 14 September 1906; Stonehouse mentions this letter and cites one sentence, p. 142.

[24] Charles G. Dennison, "Machen, Culture, and the Church," *The Banner of Truth* 286 (July 1987):21. This essay was delivered as an address at the semi-centennial celebration of the Orthodox Presbyterian Church in 1986.

[25] For suggestive remarks on the value of classical studies as a preparation for New Testament scholarship, see F. F. Bruce, "The New Testament and Classical Study," *New Testament Studies* 22 (1975-76):229-42. Besides Armstrong, B. B. Warfield was also actively interested in recruiting Machen for Princeton; see Stonehouse, p. 133.

[26] Machen later indicated that his intellectual struggles had begun before his arrival in Germany: "It was not Germany, however, that first brought doubts into my soul; for I had been facing them for years before my German student days" ("Christianity in Conflict," p. 261).

[27] Machen's remarks are from "Christianity in Conflict,": pp. 261-62; see also his observations on the benefits of help from others in dealing with doubts, p. 250; for Stonehouse's comment, see p. 129.

[28] For a statement of Machen's mature position on ecclesiastical integrity, see, for example, "Christianity in Conflict," p. 272.

Chapter 5: MACHEN'S EARLY BOOK REVIEWS, 1907–1912

[1] Citations from Stonehouse, p. 145. For a later expression of Machen's view of the ministry and creedal commitment, see, for example, his 1923 book, *Christianity and Liberalism* (reprint ed., Grand Rapids: Wm. B. Eerdmans Publishing Co., 1956), p. 162. Events of these years of Machen's life are treated by Hart, *Defending the Faith*, pp. 24-30.

[2] Details in this paragraph were taken from Machen, letters to Minnie G. Machen, 15 September 1906, 23 September 1906, 21 October 1906, and 4 November 1906; and letter to Arthur W. Machen, 24 October 1906. See also Stonehouse, p. 170.

[3] See Stonehouse, pp. 147, 145 (citations are from letters excerpted on p.147). The present writer examined all of Machen's letters to his family during the 1906-1907 academic year and discovered no reference to his intellectual struggles except for the possible allusions cited here.

[4] J. Gresham Machen, review of *The Birth and Infancy of Jesus Christ According to the Gospel Narratives*, by Louis Matthews Sweet, in *Princeton Theological Review* 5 (1907):315-16. The title of this journal will hereinafter be abbreviated as *PTR*.

[5] J. Gresham Machen, review of *Der Zeugniszweck des Evangelisten Johannes nach seinen eigenen Angaben dargestellt*, by Konrad Meyer, in *PTR* 6 (1908):142-43, citation from p. 142.

[6] J. Gresham Machen, review of *The Virgin Birth of Christ*, by James Orr, in *PTR* 6 (1908):505-508, citation from p. 507. On Orr, see *Evangelical Dictionary of Theology*, s.v. "Orr, James," by D. F. Kelly.

[7] J. Gresham Machen, review of *Interpretation of the Bible: A Short History*, by George Holley Gilbert, in *PTR* 7 (1909):348-50, citations from pp. 349 and 350.

[8] Machen, review of Gilbert, *Interpretation of the Bible*, pp. 350-51, citations from p. 350.

[9] J. Gresham Machen, review of *PROS ROMAIOUS: Die Epistel Pauli an Die Römer*, by G. Richter, in *PTR* 7 (1909):351; review of *A Short Grammar of the Greek New Testament for Students Familiar with the Elements of Greek*, by A. T. Robertson, in *PTR* 7 (1909):491-93; review of *St. Paul's Epistles to the Thessalonians*, by George Milligan, in *PTR* 7 (1909):126-31; review of *The Johannine Writings*, by Paul W. Schmiedel, in *PTR* 7 (1909):670-74.

[10] Stonehouse, pp. 147-49, citation from p. 149.

[11] Stonehouse, pp. 149-53.

[12] Stonehouse, pp. 153-54, citation from p. 154.

[13] J. Gresham Machen, review of *Der Leserkreis des Galaterbriefes: ein Beitrag zur urchristlichen Missionsgeschichte*, by Alphons Steinman, in *PTR* 8 (1910):299-300; review of *The Pauline Epistles: A Critical Study*, by Robert Scott, in *PTR* 8 (1910):300-301, first citation from p. 300, the others from p. 301.

[14] J. Gresham Machen, review of *The Irenaeus Testimony to the Fourth Gospel: Its Extent, Meaning and Value*, by Frank Grant Lewis, in *PTR* 8 (1910):137-39.

[15] J. Gresham Machen, review of *Commentar über den Brief Pauli an die Römer*, by G. Stockhardt, in *PTR* 8 (1910):490-91, citations from p. 491.

[16] J. Gresham Machen, review of *The Bible for Home and School: Commentary on the Epistle of Paul to the Galatians*, by Benjamin W. Bacon, in *PTR* 9 (1911):495-98, citations from pp. 496-98.

[17] J. Gresham Machen, review of *Selections from the Greek Papyri*, by

George Milligan, ed., in *PTR* 9 (1911):327-28; review of *The Childhood of Jesus Christ According to the Canonical Gospels*, by A. Durand, in *PTR* 9 (1911):672-73, citation from p. 672.

[18] J. Gresham Machen, review of *Christ and His Critics: Studies in the Person and Problems of Jesus*, by F. R. Montgomery Hitchcock, in *PTR* 10 (1912):334-35, final citation from pp. 334-35, the others from p. 334.

[19] For Machen's 1910 remark, see Stonehouse, pp. 178-79.

Chapter 6: MACHEN'S PUBLIC EMERGENCE: THE MAJOR ESSAYS OF 1912

[1] For a discussion of Machen's and Princeton's positive approach to biblical criticism, as well as a treatment of these essays, see Hart, *Defending the Faith*, pp. 35-43.

[2] For the immediate issues, see J. Gresham Machen, "The Hymns of the First Chapter of Luke," *Princeton Theological Review* 10 (1912):1-2. Stonehouse's treatment of the three virgin birth essays is on pp. 178-80.

[3] Machen, "Hymns," pp. 2-4.

[4] Machen, "Hymns," pp. 4-18; citations from pp. 6-7, 18.

[5] Machen, "Hymns," pp. 18-38.

[6] See Machen's note to this effect in *The Virgin Birth of Christ* (reprint ed.; London: James Clarke & Co., 1958), p. 75.

[7] J. Gresham Machen, "The Origin of the First Two Chapters of Luke," *PTR* 10 (1912):212-58, citation from p. 255.

[8] Machen, "Origin," pp. 258-77, citations from p. 271.

[9] See Machen, "Hymns," p. 33.

[10] On the textual problem, see Machen, "Hymns," pp. 9-11; for the assessment of Harnack's conclusions, see "Origin," pp. 212-53.

[11] For a treatment of the consistently historicist scholars McGiffert, Smith, and Case, see Grant Wacker, *Augustus H. Strong and the Dilemma of Historical Consciousness* (Macon, GA: Mercer University Press, 1985), pp. 152-59; on Smith and Case, see William Dean, *History Making History: The New Historicism in American Religious Thought* (Albany: State University of New York Press, 1988), pp 58-60, 49-54.

[12] See Machen's comment at the beginning of the chapter, *The Virgin Birth of Christ*, p. 2.

[13] J. Gresham Machen, "The Virgin Birth in the Second Century," *PTR* 10 (1912), pp. 529-38.

[14] Machen, "Virgin Birth," pp. 538-74.

[15] Machen, "Virgin Birth," pp. 574-80, citation from p. 580.

[16] Machen's discussion of the disputed reading is in "Virgin Birth," p.548.

[17] The structure and entire argument of *The Virgin Birth of Christ* is founded on the need for historical explanation of the early Christian belief in this alleged event; see Machen's analysis of the historical problem in his

introduction to the book, p. 1. For Machen's view of the New Testament student as a historian, see his 1915 address, "History and Faith," in *What Is Christianity? and Other Addresses*, ed. Ned Bernard Stonehouse (Grand Rapids: Wm. B. Eerdmans Publishing Co., 1951), pp. 170-84, especially p.170.

[18] For Stonehouse's treatment of this essay, see pp. 180-82.

[19] See Stonehouse's account of the centennial celebration along with Machen's comments, pp. 182-86, citation from p. 184.

[20] J. Gresham Machen, "Jesus and Paul," in *Biblical and Theological Studies*, by The Members of the Faculty of Princeton Theological Seminary (New York: Charles Scribner's Sons, 1912), pp. 549-53, citation from p.549.

[21] Machen, "Jesus and Paul," pp. 553-66, citation from p. 557.

[22] Machen, "Jesus and Paul," pp. 566-71, citations from pp. 567, 568.

[23] Machen, "Jesus and Paul," pp. 571-77, first two citations from pp. 573 and 575 respectively, the last two from p. 577.

[24] Citations from Machen, "Jesus and Paul," p. 578.

[25] Machen's mature attitude toward liberalism in the church was expressed in *Christianity and Liberalism* (reprint ed.; Grand Rapids: Wm. B. Eerdmans Publishing Co., 1956), pp. 157-80.

[26] Citation from Machen, "Jesus and Paul," p. 577.

[27] For Harnack's response to Machen, see Stonehouse, pp. 179-80, citations from p. 180.

[28] For Stonehouse's treatment of this address, see pp. 186-89; see also Hart, *Defending the Faith*, pp. 30-34.

[29] J. Gresham Machen, "Christianity and Culture," in *What Is Christianity?*, citations from pp. 160, 158, 158-59. This address was first published in *PTR* 11 (1913):1-15.

[30] Machen, "Christianity and Culture," pp. 165-66, citations from p. 165.

[31] Machen, "Christianity and Culture," p. 164, citations from this page. For a later elaboration by Machen of the decisive difference introduced by regeneration, see below, pp. 180-81

[32] Machen, "Christianity and Culture," pp. 156-58, citation from p. 158.

Chapter 7: MACHEN'S NEW TESTAMENT SURVEY, ORDINATION, AND INSTALLATION, 1913–1915

[1] For the date of Machen's decision to seek ordination, see Stonehouse, p. 190.

[2] For Stonehouse's account, see pp. 202-205; see also Hart, *Defending the Faith*, pp. 43-44.

[3] These booklets were published in 1914 and 1915 in Philadelphia by the Board of Christian Education of the Presbyterian Church in the U.S.A. It is perhaps a matter of no mere bibliographical interest to observe that a publisher has recently issued these works for the first time in book form. The publisher, The Banner of Truth Trust, a British firm, engaged the editorial services of

W. John Cook, who blended elements of both the student's and teacher's lessons to form a harmonious and continuous treatment. A comparison of the resulting volume, now entitled *The New Testament: An Introduction to Its Literature and History* (1976), with the teacher's manual reveals that Cook incorporated rather more of the student's than of the teacher's lessons. For the sake of convenience of access for the general reader, reference will be made to the 1976 edition of Machen's *Rapid Survey* whenever possible.

[4] J. Gresham Machen, *The New Testament: An Introduction to Its Literature and History*, ed. W. John Cook (Edinburgh: The Banner of Truth Trust, 1976), pp. 9-10; all citations are from these pages.

[5] Machen, *The New Testament*, pp. 13-15, citation from pp. 14-15; on Briggs's position, see above, Chapter I. For a more recent affirmation, by a widely recognized scholar, of the criterion of apostolicity as a test for canon-icity in the early church, see Bruce M. Metzger, *The New Testament: Its Background, Growth, and Content* (Nashville: Abingdon Press, 1965), p.276.

[6] For Kümmel's discussions, see *The New Testament: The History of the Investigation of Its Problems*, trans. S. McLean Gilmour and Howard C. Kee (Nashville: Abingdon Press, 1972), pp. 69-70, 131-32, citations from pp. 131-32.

[7] For Goodspeed's positions, see Edgar Johnson Goodspeed and Ernest DeWitt Burton, "The Study of the New Testament," in *A Guide to the Study of the Christian Religion*, ed. Gerald Birney Smith (Chicago: University of Chicago Press, 1916), pp. 180-200. Goodspeed's later *Introduction to the New Testament* (Chicago: University of Chicago Press, 1937) became a standard work.

[8] The citations concerning the person of Christ are from Machen, *The New Testament*, pp. 231-32; references to the Catechism relating to prayer, the intermediate state, and the resurrection are on pp. 322, 382, and 381 respectively; the final citation is from p. 382. Machen also argued for the scripturalness of the presbyterian form of church government without referring to the standards, pp. 351-52.

[9] Machen, *The New Testament*, pp. 373-78, citation from p. 378. Machen's frequent emphasis on the necessity of the work of the Holy Spirit was an element in his thought which was inconsistent with a thoroughgoing commitment to Common Sense Realism; this aspect of Machen's theology, neglected in recent studies, merits a careful investigation.

[10] For Machen's later indictment of liberalism as anti-intellectual, see his 1925 book *What Is Faith?* (reprint ed.: Grand Rapids: Wm. B. Eerdmans Publishing Co., 1969), pp. 13-45. Machen here described Modernism as "a movement which really degrades the intellect by excluding it from the sphere of religion," p. 18.

[11] Machen, *The New Testament*, pp. 374-75; the first citation is from p.374, the latter two from p. 375.

[12] Machen, *The New Testament*, pp. 306-309; 345-46, citations from p.346. The results of later studies of the apostolic *kerygma* are summarized by Metzger, *The New Testament*, p. 177.

[13] Stonehouse, pp. 190-94.

[14] Stonehouse, pp. 194-97, citation from p. 197. Dallas M. Roark, in a dissertation on Machen, agrees in assigning "special significance" to the events connected with Machen's ordination, for largely the same reasons mentioned here; see Roark, "J. Gresham Machen and His Desire to Maintain a Doctrinally True Presbyterian Church" (Ph.D. dissertation, University of Iowa, 1963), pp. 59-61, citation from p. 59.

[15] Stonehouse, p. 197. Excerpts from Machen's ordination sermon and responses to it are given by Stonehouse, pp. 198-201.

[16] Stonehouse, pp. 202-203, 205-206.

[17] Stonehouse, pp. 208-209, first citation from p. 208, the latter two from p. 209. These remarks do not appear in the published copies of Machen's address; Stonehouse used Machen's original manuscript version. See also Hart, *Defending the Faith*, pp. 36-37, for a treatment of this address.

[18] Stonehouse's analysis of this address is on pp. 206-208, citation from p. 206; J. Gresham Machen, "History and Faith," in *What Is Christianity? and Other Addresses*, ed. Ned Bernard Stonehouse (Grand Rapids: Wm. B. Eerdmans Publishing Co., 1951), citations from pp. 170, 171. This address was first published in *PTR* 13 (1915):337-51.

[19] Machen, "History and Faith," pp. 172-81.

[20] Machen, "History and Faith," pp. 178, 180-82, citation from p. 181. On the radical scholars and their views, see Kümmel, *The New Testament*, pp. 281-308.

[21] Machen "History and Faith," first citation from p. 175, the question concerning Jesus is from p. 172; the Wacker citations are from *Augustus H. Strong and the Dilemma of Historical Consciousness* (Macon, GA: Mercer University Press, 1985), pp. 39-40. By the 1920s, as Wacker points out, many scholars had rejected the notion that history is directional or has a goal, and the "fixed laws" accordingly dropped out of the picture. But when Machen wrote these words, the First World War was only a few months old and had not yet done its work of destroying the assumption of inevitable progress in human affairs; see Wacker, p. 40. All things considered, Machen did a remarkable job of defining the convictions held by historicist scholars in the middle of the second decade of the twentieth century, assuming the accuracy of Wacker's account (or rather, Machen provides evidence substantiating the accuracy of Wacker's account). Machen's statement perhaps also reveals the need for revision of Mark Massa's assertion that neither side in the conflict understood or elucidated the real nature of the intellectual issues at stake (Massa, *Charles Augustus Briggs*, p. 157; Machen spoke these words just two years after Briggs' death).

[22] Machen, "History and Faith," pp. 172-73, 182-84, citations from pp.173, 184.

[23] Machen, "History and Faith," final citation from p. 184, all others from pp. 182-83. Machen's challenge to believe as described in this paragraph bears some superficial similarity to the argument set forth by William James in his essay "The Will to Believe." Machen's approach differed from James' in that Machen affirmed the objective nature of truth while James seemed to deny it. Machen also allowed logical priority and objective validity to historical evidence while James viewed all evidence as inconclusive. For Machen, experience provided a personal confirmation of the objectively true content of the Christian faith. Machen's point seems to be that historical evidence may in a given case be as conclusive as possible, and yet still only possess the quality of probability, whereas faith transcends rational assent to experientially grasp that to which one gives assent. This is not to deny that there is an element of tentativeness, of trial, or of a "leap" in Machen's conception of faith, but it is a leap toward perceived light rather than a leap in the dark. See the first two essays in William James, *The Will to Believe and Other Essays in Popular Philosophy* (New York: Longmans Green and Co., 1899); and Paul K. Conkin's treatment of James in *Puritans and Pragmatists: Eight Eminent American Thinkers* (New York: Dodd, Mead & Co., 1968), pp. 266-344.

[24] Machen also reviewed several books from 1913 to 1915, but these reviews do not add substantially to the information that may be gleaned from his major writings. Perhaps Machen's most expressive comment, relating directly to the naturalistic assumptions of a consistent historicism, and typical of this period in his life, was written for a 1915 review of *Die Apostelgeschichte*, by Hans Hinrich Wendt:

> There are only two really distinct views about the origin of Christianity. The one makes Christianity a product of the creative activity of the transcendent God, an entrance into the world of a new saving power, unlike the ordinary activities of God's providence; the other makes it a product of such forces – call them divine or not as you please – as were already here. The one is the view of the New Testament; the other is the view of modern naturalism. There is no real middle ground; the choice must be made.

PTR 13 (1915):292-95, citation from p. 295.

Chapter 8: MACHEN'S LATER WORK AND ITS RELATIONSHIP TO HIS EARLIER SCHOLARSHIP, 1915–1937

[1] Stonehouse's account of these events is found on pp. 235, 321-28; Hart's in *Defending the Faith*, pp. 47-58.

[2] J. Gresham Machen, *The Origin of Paul's Religion* (New York: Macmillan, 1921), p. 3, all citations from this page.

[3] Machen, *Origin*, pp. 4-24, citations from p. 24.

[4] Citations from Machen, *Origin*, p. 24.

[5] For references to "Jesus and Paul," see Machen, *Origin*, pp. 7, 17, 37; Chapter IV is introduced on p. 117 with a note of attribution to the earlier article.

[6] Machen, *Origin*, pp. 24-40.

[7] Machen, *Origin*, pp. 41-169.

[8] Machen, *Origin*, pp. 171-207.

[9] Machen, *Origin*, pp. 209-251, citation from p. 241.

[10] Machen, *Origin*, pp. 253-317.

[11] Machen, *Origin*, pp. 291-317; the "brilliant" statement is from p. 317, the other citations from p. 29.

[12] Machen, *Origin*, pp. 316-17, final citation from p. 312, the others from p. 316.

[13] See J. Gresham Machen, *The Virgin Birth of Christ*, 2nd ed. (reprint ed.; London: James Clarke & Co., 1958), p. vii. See also Hart, *Defending the Faith*, pp. 88-91.

[14] Citations from Machen, *Virgin Birth*, p. 1.

[15] Machen, *Virgin Birth*, pp. 2-43, citation from p. 43.

[16] Machen, *Virgin Birth*, pp. 44-168.

[17] Machen, *Virgin Birth*, pp. 169-397.

[18] Machen, *Virgin Birth*, p. 380.

[19] Machen, *Virgin Birth*, pp. 382-95, citations from pp. 387, 391, last two from p. 386.

[20] Machen, *Virgin Birth*, pp. 218-19; the first two citations are from p.218, the others from p. 219. Machen expressed a similar concern for the unity of truth in his 1926 article "The Relation of Religion to Science and Philosophy," *PTR* 24 (1926):38-66.

[21] The Wacker citation is from *Augustus H. Strong*, p. 41; Machen, *Virgin Birth*, pp. 383-84, citations from p. 384.

[22] Machen, *Virgin Birth*, pp. 383-84, citation from p. 384. The phrase "Christless Christianity" is B. B. Warfield's.

[23] Machen, *Virgin Birth*, pp. 218-19, citations from these two pages.

[24] Citations from Machen, *Origin*, pp. 317, 24. This work contains less emphasis on presuppositions than *The Virgin Birth*, but the question is not ignored; for one example, see p. 275.

[25] Treatments of Machen's ecclesiastical activities during these years are found in Stonehouse, pp. 298-508; Henry W. Coray, *J. Gresham Machen: A Silhouette* (Grand Rapids: Kregel Publications, 1981), pp. 70-128; C. Allyn Russell, *Voices of American Fundamentalism*, pp. 150-58; Lefferts A. Loetscher, *The Broadening Church*, pp. 108-155; Hart, *Defending the Faith*,

pp. 59-159; Bradley J. Longfield, *The Presbyterian Controversy*.

[26] For treatments of Machen's critique of liberalism (besides those mentioned in the previous note), see Stonehouse, pp. 335-50; George M. Marsden, *Fundamentalism and American Culture*, pp. 174-75; William R. Hutchison, *The Modernist Impulse in American Protestantism*, pp. 261-74; and Roy A. Harrisville and Walter Sundberg, *The Bible in Modern Culture*, pp. 180-202.

[27] J. Gresham Machen, *Christianity and Liberalism* (reprint ed.; Grand Rapids: Wm. B. Eerdmans Publishing Co., 1956), pp. 1-2, citation from p. 2.

[28] Sydney E. Ahlstrom, *A Religious History of the American People*, p.774. For Machen's concern to deal with liberalism as a logically consistent system, see *Christianity and Liberalism*, pp. 172-73. For a statement of the basic tenets of liberalism, see Hutchison, *Modernist Impulse*, especially pp.2-5; *Evangelical Dictionary of Theology*, s.v. "Liberalism, Theological," by R. V. Pierard; Ahlstrom, *A Religious History*, pp. 779-81.

[29] Machen, *Christianity and Liberalism*, citations from pp. 7, 47.

[30] Machen, *Christianity and Liberalism*, pp. 70-72, first citation from p.70, the last from p. 72, the others from p. 71.

[31] Machen, *Christianity and Liberalism*, pp. 72-74, citations from pp. 73, 74.

[32] Machen, *Christianity and Liberalism*, pp. 76-79, citations from p. 78.

[33] Machen, *Christianity and Liberalism*, citation from p. 160.

[34] Machen, *Christianity and Liberalism*, pp. 162-72, citation from p. 164.

[35] Stonehouse, pp. 394-400, citations from 394-95. The chapters after the Introduction treated various aspects of Christian faith: "Faith in God," "Faith in Christ," "Faith Born of Need," "Faith and the Gospel," "Faith and Salvation," "Faith and Works," and "Faith and Hope." J. Gresham Machen, *What Is Faith?* (reprint ed., Wm. B. Eerdmans Publishing Co., 1969). See Hart, *Defending the Faith*, 91-95; the evaluation of the book presented here differs somewhat from that offered by Hart.

[36] Citations from Machen, *What Is Faith?*, p. 17. Machen's position with respect to the fundamentalist label is set forth in Stonehouse, pp. 336-38; Calhoun, *Princeton Seminary*, 2:343; Hart and Muether, *Fighting the Good Fight*, 12-14.

[37] Machen's use of the terms naturalism or naturalistic is found in *What Is Faith?*, pp. 31, 62, 63, 65, 97, 99 (twice), 100, 103, and 132 (twice).

[38] See Machen, *What Is Faith?*, pp. 149, 151; 194; chap. II passim; chap. III passim; chap. I passim; citation from pp. 159-60.

[39] See Machen, *What Is Faith?*, pp. 194-96, 198, 203; 180; 238-240; citations from 180, 238.

[40] Machen, *What Is Faith?*, pp. 23-24; 237, 240-241; 33; 63; citations from 23-24; 237; 63. Ernst Breisach, *Historiography: Ancient, Medieval, & Modern*, second ed. (Chicago: University of Chicago Press, 1994), p. 288.

[41] Citations from Machen, *What Is Faith?*, pp. 230; 233.

[42] Citations from Machen, *What Is Faith?*, p. 135. George Marsden, in *Fundamentalism and American Culture*, presents an extended treatment of Common Sense Realism and the relation to it of Princeton theologians, pp.110-16. In his discussion of B. B. Warfield's apologetic method, he offers a description of an alternative approach. "In the traditions of Augustine, Calvin, and Jonathan Edwards the Fall was often regarded as having so blinded the human intellect that natural knowledge of God had been suppressed and therefore no one could have true understanding without receiving the eyes of faith. A version of this approach had recently been revived by conservative Calvinists in the Netherlands, including Herman Bavinck and Abraham Kuyper" (p. 115). Machen's statement as cited above appears to closely approximate the Augustinian-Calvinistic-Edwardsean-Dutch tradition that Marsden seems to favor. This passage in *What Is Faith?*, curiously neglected by students of Machen, is noted by Calhoun, *Princeton Seminary*, 2:421; it is misquoted by Hart, *Defending the Faith*, p. 94.

[43] Citation from Machen, *What Is Faith?*, pp. 237-38.

[44] Note the following statement by New Testament scholar Robert H. Gundry: "A truly scientific attitude will keep open the possibility of supernaturalism and test the claims to supernatural events in past history by searching questions." *A Survey of the New Testament*, 3rd ed. (Grand Rapids: Zondervan Publishing House, 1994), p. 115.

[45] Citations from Machen, *What Is Faith?*, pp. 28-29, 32-33.

[46] Citations from Machen, *What Is Faith?*, pp. 33-34, 249. By "facts" Machen often seems to have meant something like "events that actually occurred." For the necessity of both the means of encouraging faith and the work of the Holy Spirit to produce it, see pp. 197-98.

[47] Citations from Machen, *What Is Faith?*, pp. 30-31, 135. Machen's emphasis on the objectivity, permanence, and universality of truth in this book of 1925 suggests that he was battling by the mid-1920s a chief feature of what became known as postmodernism, namely, a collapse into complete relativism.

CONCLUSION

[1] The generalizations of this paragraph are not made without an awareness of the range of responses to historicist thought in American religious circles; for a classification of those responses into four categories, see Grant Wacker, *Augustus H. Strong and the Dilemma of Historical Consciousness* (Macon, GA: Mercer University Press, 1985), pp. 139-59. However, Machen's response, as presented in this study, displays considerebaly greater nuance and sophistication than those of others characterised by Wacker as "consistent ahistoricists," suggesting that perhaps Machen does not fit neatly into this category (e.g., Machen did not make the kind of claims that C.W. Hodge

did, pp. 140-41; Wacker's description on pp. 11-12 is likewise too overdrawn to represent Machen's position, which eventuates in a similar outcome regarding divine revelation but posits a different process in its delivery). Hart also comments on Machen's sensitivity to the historical circumstances of the origin of Christianity, *Defending the Faith*, pp. 50-51.

George Marsden also sees crucial significance in the difference between Machen's view of history and the view commonly held by twentieth-century historians; see Marsden, "J. Gresham Machen, History, and Truth," *Westminster Theological Journal* 42 (Fall 1979):161-68. For an examination of naturalism as an unproven and unprovable assumption, see Richard B. Cunningham, *The Christian Faith and Its Contemporary Rivals* (Nashville: Broadman Press, 1988), pp. 74-94.

[2] Harrisville and Sundberg, *The Bible in Modern Culture*, p. 268.

[3] Citation from Mark A. Noll, *Between Faith and Criticism*, p. 54.

[4] Machen's apologetic has been criticized, for example, by Marsden, in "J. Gresham Machen, History, and Truth." Citation from Machen, *What Is Faith?*, p. 249.

[5] For the opposing viewpoint, see Marsden, "J. Gresham Machen, History, and Truth," pp. 168-75. The disagreement with Marsden is in some ways a matter of emphasis. There can be little doubt that Machen gave priority to the objective grounds of faith, but Marsden's contention that Machen minimized subjective elements in religious faith seems an overstatement, pp. 168-69. It may be the case, as Marsden claims, that Machen did not consider the presuppositions of the Christian view of reality to be "the starting point in his apologetic" (p. 174, note 34); but for evidence to the contrary, see Machen's statements in *What Is Faith?*, p. 135, e.g., "no one can be truly scientific who ignores the fact of sin"; regeneration "is necessary in order that that truly scientific attitude may be attained"; by regeneration "the intellect is made to be a trustworthy instrument for apprehending truth." Machen's position is aptly described by Calhoun's comments on the Princeton theology generally, *Princeton Seminary*, 2:414.

Machen's work seems to reflect the "Augustinian tradition of historical criticism" as described by Harrisville and Sundberg: "Historical criticism limits itself to a verification of the verifiable, to a demonstration of the demonstrable – facts, objectifiable history, occurrences, whatever can be known or ascertained by dint of sheer logic and mental effort. . . . Faith, on the other hand, is the appropriation of an event which includes not merely fact but its interpretation, not merely the historical but its significance, not merely occurrence but its meaning" (*The Bible in Modern Culture*, p. 272). I am unaware of any claim by Machen such as Marsden attributes to him, that "one should be able to *demonstrate* that" the Christian faith "is historically true," "J. Gresham Machen, History, and Truth," p. 168 (emphasis his); indeed, Machen asserts the contrary in "History and Faith," pp. 182-83.

Machen's mention of Common Sense philosophy (*What Is Faith?*, p.27) should not be taken to indicate unqualified adherence to Common Sense Realism in all its tenets. He states in the immediate context its function in his thought: it stands opposed to the view that "the intellect is not reliable," to "a pragmatist skepticism," and to the idea that "truth can never be attained" (pp. 27-28). He goes on in this very book to demonstrate a considerable modification or rejection of some of the tenets of the philosophy on the basis of his Calvinistic theological stance. For a rather conventional discussion of the role of Common Sense Realism in Machen's thought but with somewhat more positive conclusions, see Darryl G. Hart, "The Princeton Mind in the Modern World and the Common Sense of J. Gresham Machen," *Westminster Theological Journal* 46 (1984): 1-25.

As an example of the danger of predicating of Machen a thoroughgoing commitment to Common Sense Realism and then extrapolating further conclusions therefrom, note Longfield's claim that Machen's adherence to this philosophy rendered him incapable of understanding perspectives other than his own (*The Presbyterian Controversy*, p. 173). To anyone familiar with Machen's scholarly writings, in which he dealt continually with alternative perspectives and interpretations, such an assertion will appear ludicrous.

[6] Machen's emphases on the functional purpose of inspiration and the accommodation of divine revelation contradict the characterization of the Princeton view of scripture set forth by Jack B. Rogers and Donald K. McKim, *The Authority and Interpretation of the Bible: An Historical Approach* (San Francisco: Harper & Row, 1979), pp. 323-79.

[7] See Massa, *Charles Augustus Briggs*, pp. 149-56.

[8] For the offer of the college presidency to Machen, and his response, see Stonehouse, pp. 425-29; Hart, *Defending the Faith*, pp. 105-06; Hart and Muether, *Fighting the Good Fight*, pp. 12-14. The understanding of Machen's theological development presented here is in accord with that of W. Stanford Reid in "J. Gresham Machen," in *Reformed Theology in America*, ed. David F. Wells (Grand Rapids: Wm. B. Eerdmans Publishing Co., 1985), p. 106.

[9] Citations from Machen, *What Is Faith?*, p. 87; Harrisville and Sundberg, *The Bible in Modern Culture*, p. 270.

[10] Citations from Marsden, "J. Gresham Machen, History, and Truth," p.168; Machen, *What Is Faith?*, p. 241.

[11] C. Stephen Evans, *The Historical Christ and the Jesus of Faith: The Incarnational Narrative as History* (Oxford: Oxford University Press, 1996), p. 20; Evans' entire paragraph on pp. 20-21 is worthy of attention. Note also Henry Warner Bowden's comment in his review of Wacker, *Augustus H. Strong*: Wacker "does not . . . give sufficient weight to the naturalism endemic to modern science, in history or in the laboratory. The issue was not critical method per se . . . ." *Church History* 55 (1986): 391.

[12] See William E. Leuchtenburg, *The Perils of Prosperity, 1914-32* (Chicago: University of Chicago Press, 1958), pp. 204-224; Ernest R. Sandeen, *The Roots of Fundamentalism*; George M. Marsden, *Fundamentalism and American Culture*; R. Laurence Moore, *Religious Outsiders and the Making of Americans* (New York: Oxford University Press, 1986), pp. 150-72, citation from p. 153.

[13] This is not to deny that there were common features appearing in both Machen's stance and the anti-evolution crusade (though Machen declined to become involved in the latter). Both were concerned to uphold the truthfulness of the Bible and both were opposed to the viewpoint which saw only natural developmental processes at the basis of history.

Neither is this to deny the social nature of the fundamentalist movement, but, at least in the case of Machen and likeminded conservatives, the present interpretation does minimize its social basis. Machen and other conservatives desired, of course, to influence American society and culture in behalf of evangelical Christianity, and variously organized their efforts to do so. But socially, Machen had little in common with self-styled fundamentalists.

[14] Historians acknowledge that Machen provides a major exception to most generalizations about the fundamentalist movement; see, for example, Marsden, *Fundamentalism and American Culture*, pp. 174, 217, 287 note 10; Russell, *Voices of American Fundamentalism*, pp. 13, 135, 139, 142, 143, 146, 214; Hart, *Defending the Faith*, pp. 63-65, 68-69, 106. This piling up of exceptions leads naturally to the question, If Machen was unlike the fundamentalists culturally, theologically, socially, politically, and intellectually, what remains of fundamentalism that is applicable to him? Marsden's response is that Machen was militantly opposed to theological modernism (a criterion addressed below) and that he adhered to the view of science, philosophy and facts held in common by almost all fundamentalists, i.e., that of Common Sense Realism (*Fundamentalism and American Culture*, pp. 4, 217). The present study suggests that Machen's commitment to Common Sense Realism was sufficiently qualified by his Calvinistic theological perspective that use of the former as a criterion for counting him among the fundamentalists must be called into question. Marsden acknowledges that Machen represented Old School Presbyterianism and that the New School exhibited affinities with fundamentalism (*The Evangelical Mind*, pp. 245-46); Hart points out that the theology which Machen defended was "seventeenth-century British Calvinism" (*Defending the Faith*, p. 93).

George Dollar offers the solution of labeling Machen an "orthodox ally" of the fundamentalists; see Dollar, *A History of Fundamentalism in America*, Chapter 10. Dollar suggests several ways in which Machen and his Presbyterian colleagues differed from those whom Dollar considers fundamentalists, pp. 181-83. Stonehouse also denies that Machen was a fundamentalist, pp. 336-37. See as well Hart and Muether, *Fighting the Good*

Fight, pp. 12-14, 42-43, who argue in the latter passage that opposition to modernist theology is an inadequate category for defining fundamentalism, for it is too broad. That movement exhibited distinctive characteristics including "dispensationalist theology, revivalistic techniques of soul-winning, stern prohibitions against worldly entertainments, and a low view of the institutional church" which did not apply to Machen.

On Lewis, see *The New International Dictionary of the Christian Church*, s.v. "Lewis, C(live) S(taples)," by Joan Ostling; and *Evangelical Dictionary of Theology*, s.v. "Lewis, Clive Staples," by R. N. Hein.

[15] Grant Wacker, "The Demise of Biblical Civilization," in *The Bible in America*, first citation from pp. 126-27, latter two from p. 127; see also Marsden, *Fundamentalism and American Culture*, pp. 62-66, although Marsden's emphasis is more on the premillennial view of history, which Machen did not share.

[16] The Machen citation is from his review of *Interpretation of the Bible: A Short History*, by George Holley Gilbert, in *PTR* 7 (1909):349; Winthrop S. Hudson, *American Protestantism* (Chicago: University of Chicago Press, 1961), pp. 128-76, citation from pp. 152-53. For recent trends in Protestantism, see Dean M. Kelley, *Why Conservative Churches Are Growing: A Study in Sociology of Religion* (New York: Harper & Row, 1972), especially pp. 1-16; "From 'Mainline' to Sideline," *Newsweek*, December 22, 1986, pp. 54-56. Support for this conclusion is offered by Longfield, *The Presbyterian Controversy*, pp. 229-35; Calhoun, *Princeton Seminary*, 2:398.

[17] The relativism fostered by historicism has been embodied in a distinct cultural outlook known as postmodernism. It was precisely this collapse into complete relativism that historians have treated as the "crisis of historicism" and which some historicists sought to overcome; see Baumer, *Modern European Thought*, p. 410, 494-513; James C. Livingston, *Modern Christian Thought: From the Enlightenment to Vatican II* (New York: Macmillan Publishing Co., 1971), pp. 305-307; Breisach, *Historiography*, pp. 280-84; Iggers, "The Dissolution of German Historism," especially pp. 308-309. On Machen's relationship to this relativistic environment, see Terry A. Chrisope, "J. Gresham Machen and the Modern Intellectual Crisis," *Presbyterion: Covenant Seminary Review* 24/2 (Fall 1998): 92-109.

Richard Tarnas observes that applying the method of historicism to itself results in seeing that outlook as merely the temporal expression of a particular historical environment:

> On its own terms, the assertion of the historical relativity and cultural-linguistic bondage of all truth and knowledge must itself be regarded as reflecting but one more local and temporal perspective having no necessarily universal, extrahistoricalvalue. Everything could change tomorrow. Implicitly, the one postmodern absolute is critical

consciousness, which, by deconstructing all, seems compelled by its own logic to do so to itself as well. This is the unstable paradox that permeates the postmodern mind.

Thus it is possible to relativize the relativizers, using their own method.
Richard Tarnas, *The Passion of the Western Mind: Understanding the Ideas That Have Shaped Our World View* (New York: Harmony Books, 1991), p. 402.

[18] Henry Steele Commager, *The American Mind: An Interpretation of American Thought and Character Since the 1880's* (New Haven: Yale University Press, 1950), pp. 407-408, citations from p. 407.

Persons Index

Abbott, Lyman 43
Adams, Henry 34
Ahlstrom, Sydney 25, 33, 34, 46, 47, 133, 173
Alexander, Archibald 63, 64
Aristides 122
Armstrong, William Park 43, 66-7, 69, 81, 82, 83, 86, 87, 101, 106, 148
Bacon, Benjamin W. 108-9, 113
Baumer, Franklin 34
Baur, Ferdinand Christian 33, 34-5, 37, 127, 140-1, 162
Baur, Walter 78
Beard, Charles A. 29, 30
Beattie, James 63
Bird, Mrs Sarah Edgeworth 58
Bonwetsch, N. 83
Bousset, Wilhelm 34, 38, 83-6, 87, 93, 160, 162, 171
Breisach, Ernst 179
Briggs, Charles A. 27, 41-2, 48, 50-1, 63, 140, 190
Brown, James B. 67
Browning, Robert 60
Bruce, F.F. 33
Bultmann, Rudolf 38-9
Butterfield, Herbert 32
Calhoun, David B. 20
Campbell, George 63
Carpocrates 122
Case, Shirley Jackson 48, 121
Celsus 122
Cerinthus 122
Clarke, William Newton 48, 51-3
Clement of Alexandria 122
Commager, Henry Steele 197
Comte, Auguste 29
Curtiss, Samuel I. 41
Darwin, Charles 28, 29
Davis, John D. 43, 106

Dennison, Charles G. 92
Dewey, John 29, 31
Dilthey, Wilhelm 27
Dollar, George W. 20
Driver, Samuel R. 40, 43
Durand, Alfred 110
Epiphanius 123
Evans, C. Stephen 192
Gerard, Alexander 63
Gilbert, George Holley 103-4, 105, 113
Gildersleeve, Basil L. 58, 60, 61
Gilman, Daniel Coit 58, 61
Gladden, Washington 43
Goodspeed, Edgar J. 142
Gould, Ezra P. 42
Griesbach, Johann Jakob 33
Hamilton, William 63
Harnack, Adolf 34, 36, 116-7, 118-9, 121, 123, 127, 132, 160
Harper, William Rainey 42-3
Harrisville, Roy A. 20, 191
Hart, D.G. 11, 20
Hegel, Georg Wilhelm Friedrich 28-9, 34
Heidegger, Martin 38
Heitmüller, Wilhelm 37, 83, 85-6, 93, 174
Hermann, Wilhelm 36, 78-81, 87, 92, 93, 149
Hitchcock, F.R. Montgomery 111
Hodge, Archibald Alexander 43, 48-50, 51, 63
Hodge, Charles 40, 43, 62, 65
Holmes, Oliver Wendell Jnr. 29
Holtzman, H.J. 128
Hudson, Winthrop 62, 196
Hume, David 28, 63
Hutchison, William 43, 46-7, 133
Hutton, John B. 177
Ignatius 122

234

Irenaeus 107, 122
Jerome 123
Jülicher, Adolf 78, 85, 87
Justin Martyr 122, 123
Kabisch, Richard 39
Kattenbusch, Ferdinand 83
Kirk, Harris E. 65
Knopf, Rudolf 78
Kümmel, Werner G. 32-3, 140-1
Lake, Kirsopp 38
Lang, August 101
Lanier, Sydney 58
Leuchtenburg, William E. 193
Lewis, C.S. 195
Lewis, Frank Grant 107
Lightfoot, Joseph Barber 35
Loetscher, Lefferts 41-2
Longfield, Bradley 20
Luther, Martin 103
McGiffert, Arthur C. 42, 121
Machen, Arthur Jnr. 60, 80, 82, 83, 86
Machen, Arthur W. 58, 59
Machen, May (Minnie) 58, 59-60, 88-90
Marcion 122
Maring, Norman 42
Marsden, George 20, 25, 191-2, 193-4, 195
Marx, Karl 29, 34
Massa, Mark 27, 195
Mathews, Shailer 48
May, Henry F. 30, 115
Meyer, Konrad 102
Michaelis, J.D. 32, 140-1
Milligan, George, 105, 110
Mitchell, Hinckley G. 42
Montesquieu 28
Moore, R. Laurence 193
Muether, John 20
Neill, Stephen 35, 37
Noll, Mark 40, 44-5, 46, 64, 188
Origen 123

Ormond, A.T. 67
Orr, James 102-3, 113
Patton, Francis L. 43, 65-6, 68, 100, 106, 126, 148
Pfleiderer, Otto 37
Polycarp 107
Purves, G.T. 67
Rauschenbusch, Walter 47, 48
Reid, Thomas 63
Reid, W. Stanford 21
Reitzenstein, Richard 37-8, 162
Ritschl, Albrecht 35-6, 127
Robertson, A.T. 104
Robinson, James Harvey 29
Royce, Josiah 47
Russell, C. Allyn 20
Sandeen, Ernest 193
Santayana, George 31
Schmidtke, Alfred 123
Schmiedel, Paul N. 105
Schürer, Emil 36, 83, 85, 87
Schweitzer, Albert 39
Scopes, John T. 178
Scott, Robert 107, 113
Semler, Johann 32-3
Shorey, Prof Paul 68
Smith, Gerald Birney 121
Smith, Henry Preserved 41, 42
Smith, Robertson W. 40
Smyth, E.C. 42
Smyth, Newman 47
Spencer, Herbert 29, 34, 52
Spitta, Friedrich 116, 118
Stanford, Michael 27
Steinman, Alphons 107
Stephanus (Robert Estienne) 123
Stewart, Dugald 63
Stewart, Lyman & Milton 45
Stockhardt, George 108
Stonehouse, Ned B. 20, 57, 65, 67, 77, 79, 82-3, 86, 88, 89, 94, 99, 100, 101, 105-6, 114, 126, 130, 132, 147, 149, 177

Strauss, David Friedrich 33
Sumner, William Graham 34
Sundberg, Walter 20, 191
Sweet, Louis Matthews 101-2, 113
Swing, David 66
Taft, William Howard 125
Theodore of Mopsuestia 103
Toy, Crawford H. 42
Trypho 122
Vatke, Wilhelm 33
Veblen, Thorstein 29
Vico 28
Voltaire 28
Von Herder, Johann Gottfried 28
Von Ranke, Leopold 29
Vos, Geerhardus 43
Wacker, Grant 12, 25, 26, 31, 151, 168, 195

Wallis, Louis 30
Warfield, BenjaminB. 43, 45, 48, 50, 51, 62, 63, 64, 66, 194
Warfield, Ethelbert D. 87
Weber, Max 31
Weiss, Bernhard 78
Weis, Johannes 36, 39, 78
Wellhausen, Julius 33
White, Edward D. 125
White, Morton G. 29, 30, 115
Wiebe, Robert 32
Wieman, Henry Nelson 47
Wilson, Robert Dick 43
Wilson, Woodrow 67-8
Witherspoon, John 64
Wrede, Wilhelm 126, 160, 161
Zahn, Theodor 86
Zimmerman 116

Subject Index

American Journal of Philology 61
(American) South (erner) 20, 57, 58, 61, 65, 67, 68
Andover Seminary 42
Anglican(s) 40, 45
anti-intellectualism 11, 133, 144-5, 177, 196
Baptist(s) 42, 45, 47, 48, 51, 62
Benham Club 67
Berlin, Univ. of 41
Bible 13, 14, 15, 16, 17, 18, 19, 21, 25, 27, 31, 32, 35, 39, 40, 4142, 43, 44, 45, 46, 48, 50, 51, 52, 53, 57, 59, 60, 62, 63, 66, 70, 73, 75, 80, 86, 92, 93, 94, 95, 100, 103-4, 105, 113, 124, 137, 139, 143, 144, 145, 149, 151, 152, 153, 166, 167, 168, 169, 174, 175, 176, 178, 185, 186, 187, 189, 190, 192, 196, 197
biblical authority 13, 14, 15, 19, 25, 40, 41, 49, 51, 52, 53, 62, 87, 139-40, 141, 142, 143, 151-2, 163, 168-9, 175-6, 189, 197
biblical criticism 14-16, 17, 18, 21, 33, 34, 40, 41, 42, 43, 45, 46, 48, 49, 50, 51, 53, 62, 86, 93, 94, 107, 110, 115, 152, 157, 174, 182, 185, 187, 188, 190, 191, 192
biblical documents/literature 12, 14, 15, 18, 19, 33, 35, 41, 49, 75, 105, 109, 112, 113, 120, 122, 142, 175, 179, 182, 190

biblical /NT scholarship 25, 33, 38, 39, 43, 45, 67, 68, 104, 110, 121, 135, 153, 191, 193
biblical studies 12, 26, 44, 48, 65, 86, 121
Bryan Memorial University 191
Calvinism(ist) 61, 62, 66, 92, 102, 125, 126, 132, 181, 190-1, 194
canon(icity) 32, 49, 51, 140-1
Chicago, Univ. of 42-3, 48, 65, 68, 142
civilisation 31
Colgate Seminary 53
Columbia Theological Seminary 163
Common Sense Realism 20, 63, 64, (71,)134, 180, 181, 183, 189
Congregational(ist) 42, 45, 47, 62
conservative 13, 15, 25, 36, 41, 42, 43, 44, 45, 46, 48, 51, 70, 71, 78, 83, 86, 91, 92, 103, 105, 112, 113, 119, 131, 138, 141, 142, 146, 171, 172, 178, 185, 186, 188, 195, 196, 197
cultural forms/phenomena 26, 27, 28, 29, 32
culture 12, 13, 15, 17, 25, 28, 29, 30, 47, 51, 62, 92, 100, 115, 132-5, 144, 159, 182, 185, 187, 188, 190-1, 193, 196, 197
determinism 34
development 25, 28, 29, 30, 31, 33, 34, 38, 47, 52, 151, 159, 173
development (evolutionary) 31, 42, 44, 49, 52, 129, 130
developmental 25, 26, 28, 29, 151, 159, 172, 173
directional 28, 29, 31, 151
Disciples (Churches) 47, 62
divine providence/action 33, 39, 95, 121, 125, 159, 166, 168, 172-3, 178, 186, 195
Doctrine of Scripture 113, 170, 189-90
Enlightenment 14, 17, 26, 28, 63, 83, 188
(post)Enlightenment 16, 18
Episcopal 47, 62
epistemology(logical) 26, 27, 31, 64, 115, 172, 176, 180, 182, 183, 197
ethic(s) 27, 36, 47, 72, 149, 168
evangelical 19, 44-5, 46, 47-8, 61, 62, 65, 66, 78, 85, 95, 108, 117, 121, 176, 178, 188, 194, 196
evangelical liberals 47-8
existentialism 38
faith 15, 17, 18, 19, 35, 37, 39, 40, 43, 44, 50, 51, 53, 57, 58, 81, 83, 84, 85, 87, 88, 89, 91, 92, 93, 94, 101, 110, 111, 129, 130, 131, 134, 143, 147, 148-53, 160, 167, 169, 175, 177-83, 187, 188, 189, 191, 197
form criticism 38
fundamentalism/ist 11, 17, 20, 21, 25, 153, 178, 179, 193-5, 196
Göttingen, Univ. of 32, 33, 35, 37, 38, 69, 83-7
Grove City Bible School 177

Harvard 38, 58

Hellenistic 34, 36, 37, 38, 105, 160, 161, 162

historic christianity 14, 18, 19, 27, 57, 84, 129, 152, 178, 182, 193, 196, 197

historical biblical criticism 13, 14, 15, 16

historical conditioning 27

historical consciousness 12, 13, 25-53, 62, 130, 144, 192

historical criticism 13, 16, 37, 43, 50, 51, 53, 86, 108, 111, 140, 141, 168, 169, 186

historical method 18, 32, 38-9, 124, 125, 131, 139, 179, 186

historical scholarship 13-14, 25, 32, 33, 36, 39, 40, 44, 53, 71, 89, 108, 111, 112, 130, 131, 141, 152, 185, 189

historical studies 13, 19, 32, 33, 39, 40, 61, 93, 104, 124, 139, 146, 171, 172, 186, 192

historical theology 33

historicism(ist) 12, 13, 16, 18, 19, 21, 25-6, 27, 29, 30, 31, 34, 37, 38, 46, 48, 75, 83, 115, 121, 124, 130, 133, 134, 135, 139, 144, 145, 146, 149, 150, 151, 157, 159, 166, 168, 169, 171, 172, 173, 178, 181, 182, 183, 185, 186, 187, 191, 192, 193, 194, 195, 196, 197

historicity 14, 15, 16, 18, 19, 29, 34, 70, 101, 110, 111-2, 113, 114, 119, 120, 170, 191

history 19, 25, 27, 28, 29, 30, 31, 39, 49, 50, 53, 61, 67, 83, 84, 85, 95, 103, 104, 109, 128, 129, 137, 138, 139, 143, 148-53, 159, 162, 165, 167, 168, 169, 170, 171, 172, 173, 174, 176, 179, 186, 187, 188, 189, 190, 191, 195, 196, 197

history of religions school 34, 36, 37, 38, 39, 83, 95, 161-2

idealism 30

immanence (of God) 47, 173

incarnation 47, 72, 85, 103, 112, 113, 153, 166, 167, 187

inerrancy 40, 41, 42, 50, 52, 63, 73

inspiration (biblical) 19, 25, 40, 41, 48-9, 50, 52, 53, 62, 63, 73, 75, 103, 104, 105, 113, 114, 139, 140, 146, 151, 175, 189-90

interpretation 13, 33, 34, 35, 36, 38, 39, 103, 104, 109, 118, 127, 130, 133, 186, 193

John Hopkins University 58, 60, 61, 68, 92

Journal of Biblical Literature 45

Lafayette College 87

liberal(ism) 12, 35, 36, 39, 43, 44, 46, 47, 48, 51, 53, 62, 78, 79, 80, 84, 85, 87, 93, 121, 126-7, 131, 133, 134, 145, 149, 150, 157, 160, 161, 169, 171-177, 179, 186, 187, 188, 191, 194, 195, 196

liberal theology 43, 46, 78, 85, 93, 110, 114, 173, 185, 187, 196

literary criticism 33, 102, 140

Lutheran(s) 37, 40, 45

Marburg, Univ. of 39, 77-83

Methodist(s) 42, 47, 62

ministry 65, 68, 77, 81-2, 87-8, 93, 94, 99, 106, 114, 137, 147, 148, 177, 186

modern criticism 15, 111, 128

modernism 46, 47, 48, 157, 173, 177, 193

modernist 46, 48, 157, 173, 187

modernist-fundamentalist 11, 25, 178

natural forces/causes 12, 14, 37, 159, 171, 173, 186

naturalism 9, 16, 151, 157, 172, 178

naturalistic 16, 18, 19, 27, 33, 43, 49, 109, 110, 128, 130, 135, 139, 146, 151, 152, 166, 167, 169, 172, 178, 181, 182, 186, 191, 192, 194, 195

Ohio State University 31

orthodox(y) 18, 20, 41, 46, 50, 57, 72, 81, 85, 90, 93, 102, 105, 108, 111, 122, 123, 142, 178, 187, 197

Orthodox Presbyterian Church 11, 20, 92, 172

Paul (relation to Jesus) 12, 30, 34, 37, 100, 109, 115, 125-31, 157-159, 160-2, 188

philosophical/philosophy 16, 18, 26, 27, 28, 47, 49, 50, 61, 63, 64, 65, 66, 67, 71, 72, 95, 102, 113, 123, 124, 134, 151, 159, 162, 164, 169, 170, 171, 172, 178, 180, 181, 186, 187, 188, 189, 192, 197

philosophers 26, 28, 30, 31, 38, 47, 192

positivism (Anglo-French) 29

Presbyterian(Church etc) 11, 40, 41, 42, 45, 47, 48, 50, 57, 58, 59, 62, 63, 65, 66, 68, 79, 80, 92, 93, 94, 95, 99, 100, 125, 137, 142, 147, 148, 157, 171, 172, 177, 194

presupposition 14, 16, 18, 39, 70, 71, 73, 102, 103, 113, 114, 120, 123, 124, 134, 166, 168, 169-70, 171, 180, 181, 182, 189, 190, 192

Princeton Theological Review 30, 45, 69-70, 100, 110, 112, 114, 115, 116, 122

Princeton Theological Seminary 11, 20, 30, 41, 43, 44, 45, 50-1, 61-5, 65-75, 77, 82, 83, 86, 87-91, 92, 93, 94, 99, 100, 101, 105-6, 112, 114, 115, 125, 126, 132, 137, 140, 148, 153, 157, 158, 171, 175, 183, 186, 193, 194

Reformation 3, 131-2, 197

Reformed 40, 61, 62, 64, 87, 181, 186, 190-1

relativism(istic) 12, 26, 27, 30, 31, 36, 115, 133, 167, 180, 182, 197

religion 12, 27, 30, 32, 33, 37, 38, 47, 52, 53, 57, 62, 79, 83-4, 85, 90, 94, 103, 104, 109, 127, 131, 134-5, 149, 150, 158, 159, 160, 161, 162, 163, 168, 169, 172, 174, 176, 178, 183, 188, 196

revelation 27, 32, 43, 47, 73, 74, 103, 173, 174, 190, 195

Ritschlian school 34, 35, 39, 78, 79, 80, 93

romantic idealism 28

social thinkers/theorists 29, 30, 31

supernatural(ism) 12, 14, 19, 27, 30, 39, 43, 49, 57, 64, 72, 73, 78, 104, 109, 110, 111, 112, 113, 114, 115, 119, 120, 125, 126, 127, 128, 129, 130, 131, 132, 133, 139, 143, 147, 149-50, 151, 158, 159, 160, 161, 163, 166, 167, 170, 178, 182, 186, 187, 189, 190, 191, 197

synthesis of truth/knowledge 168, 192

The British Weekly 177-8

theological liberalism 12, 17, 25, 46, 62, 93, 133, 135, 138, 144-5, 149, 150, 157, 168, 169, 171, 172, 191, 192, 193, 194

theology 11, 33, 34, 35, 36, 37, 41, 50, 52, 57, 62, 64, 65, 66, 78, 80, 83, 84, 85, 93, 101, 102, 103, 105, 112, 127, 130, 138, 142, 144, 145, 160, 162, 173, 178, 179, 181, 182, 183, 187, 189, 196

transcendent 27, 28, 39, 160

truth(fulness) 12, 15, 18, 19, 26, 27, 28, 34, 36, 49, 51, 64, 71, 72, 80, 84, 85, 86, 92, 93, 94, 99, 111, 113, 119, 129, 131, 134, 144, 151, 152, 162, 167, 170, 175, 176, 179, 180, 181, 182-3, 186, 188, 189, 190, 191, 193, 196

truth (unity of) 31, 134, 167, 168, 169, 192

Tübingen (school) 34, 35, 109

Union Theological Seminary 41, 158

Unitarianism 46-7, 62

virgin birth 12, 30, 69, 70, 72, 78, 100, 102, 103, 110, 112, 113, 114, 115, 116-25, 157, 163-70, 188, 189, 190, 195-6

Virginia, Univ. of 61

Wesleyan College 58

Western Seminary 66

Westminster Shorter Catechism 59, 60, 142-3, 147, 181, 187, 191

Westminster Standards 50, 62, 94, 142-3, 146, 147

Westminster Theological Seminary 11, 171

Yale 108